Severed Trust

Severed Trust

Why American Medicine
Hasn't Been Fixed

George D. Lundberg, M.D.

with James Stacey

BASIC
BOOKS

A Member of the Perseus Books Group

Library of Congress Cataloging-in-Publication Data
Lundberg, George D.
  Severed trust : why American medicine hasn't been fixed /
George D. Lundberg, with James Stacey.
     p.   cm.
  Includes index.
  ISBN: 0–465–04292–9 (pbk)
   1. Medical care—United States.   2. Public Health—United States.
3. Social medicine—United States.   4. Medical policy—United States.
5. Medical care, Cost of—United States.   I. Stacey, James.   II. Title.

RA395.A3 L86   2001
362.1'0973—dc21

                                                                        00-049814

FIRST EDITION

02 03 04 05/ 10 9 8 7 6 5 4 3 2 1

To Patti always

and to James Simon Peter in 1952

and another Peter in 2000 and

all those dedicated people in between

who have endeavored to teach me

Contents

Prologue

IN OCTOBER 1998, I WAS in Hong Kong as an invited speaker at an international medical congress. Several hundred researchers were there, representing many countries, languages, cultures, and institutions. As the editor of the *Journal of the American Medical Association,* I was assigned to a panel on medical ethics, specifically the ethics of medical journals.

The topic was close to my heart. During my seventeen years as editor of *JAMA,* many of the articles and studies that I published on health and social issues also had ethical overtones. These included calls for gun controls, seat belt and motorcycle helmet legislation, curbs on drunken driving, a total ban on boxing, and challenges to the process of how medical journals work. Some of my positions on these and other issues took me outside the mainstream medical establishment, but all were mediated by ethical considerations.

At the Hong Kong conference, a fellow panelist was Poul Riis, a former editor of the *Danish Medical Journal* who had retired after twenty-five years of service. Poul also happened to be a member of the *JAMA* editorial board. During a panel break, he asked me how things were going with the American Medical Association. "Not well," I had to confess. An outcry over an agreement to endorse commercial products manufactured by the Sunbeam Corporation had led to top management turnovers. The problem with Sunbeam had been solved when the AMA backed away from the deal, but as might be expected, the resulting mood was uneasy. My relationship with senior management was affected, I told Poul, for several reasons, including my recent appearance on *60 Minutes,* where I spoke out about the need for hospitals to perform more autopsies.

Poul furrowed his brow and then asked how many changes of administration had occurred during my seventeen-year tenure. "About five," I said, and explained that most had worked out well for me. He remarked that he had run into problems with approximately every fifth new administration during his twenty-five-year tenure in Denmark. Maybe, I thought, one out of five collaborations of this sort just doesn't work, given the different roles medical journal editors are expected to play, and the many publics they serve.

I thought about that on my way back from Hong Kong, remembering my interview with Mike Wallace on *60 Minutes.* Had I gone too far, agreeing that doctors were burying their mistakes? Had I been too insistent on the need to dramatically increase autopsy rates? Had I made too much of the fact that there was so much discordance between the diagnoses doctors make and those revealed by autopsies? I thought about these questions again in the summer of 2000 when *60 Minutes* rebroadcast the segment.

Controversy is in the nature of medical journal publishing, and I had been embroiled in many disagreements and highly visible debates. In the spring of 1982, in the course of putting together profiles of my thirteen predecessors as part of the centennial celebration of the journal, I discovered that the tenures of previous editors had run from forty-eight days to twenty-five years. All but one were fired, forced to resign, or retired under pressure.

I assumed early on that something like that would happen to me, and had often said so. The only thing I couldn't be sure of was when or why. I couldn't know which day or which issue would take me out, but clearly my end was not unforeseen, and perhaps not even unjustified. What I didn't know on the flight back from Hong Kong was that the end of my tenure at *JAMA* was only weeks away.

It was a public event, intensely covered by the media at a press conference called by the AMA on Friday, January 15, 1999. The headlines told the story: "Editor Fired for Article on Definition of Sex"; "Science, Sex, and Semantics: The Firing of George Lundberg"; and "AMA Firing Impolitic—Or Just Politics?"

The event that precipitated my parting of the ways with the AMA was related to my decision to publish an unsolicited, peer-reviewed study by researchers at the Kinsey Institute at Indiana University who surveyed college student attitudes about sex. Fifty-nine percent said that they did not consider having oral sex as having "had sex." The article appeared in *JAMA* during the Senate impeachment trial of President Clinton. It was said that I had inappropriately and inexcusably interjected *JAMA* into the middle of a debate that had nothing to do with science or medicine. Not surprisingly, editors and journalists expressed alarm about what they saw as a challenge to editorial independence.

Now, two years later, I have discovered that, like most experiences in my life, including my eleven-year experience with the army, the end signaled a new beginning—in this case, for me and the AMA. The association not only fixed its Sunbeam problem; it also fixed its *JAMA* editor problem. The AMA appointed an excellent new editor and installed a much-improved reporting process. Now the editor reports to an oversight board made up of high-level academic physicians to ensure editorial integrity and independence. *JAMA* was strengthened and enhanced thereby.

Exactly one month after my public firing, on February 15, 1999, I joined the New York electronic health information company Medscape. Since then, Medscape has flourished by growth, by acquisitions, and by mergers. The number of employees has grown from 70 to 1,300 in less than two years, and I am now editor-in-chief, executive vice president, and a member of the board of directors. I was pleased when the *Industry Standard* named me "the health care Internet's medicine man" in the year 2000.

Although the AMA and I went our separate ways in a public fashion, and the parting was controversial, serious and reasonable people can still disagree about what should or should not have taken place. However, this is not a book about the AMA. Rather, I have included my experience with the AMA, and its policies and history, to help formulate my arguments for a new approach to medical care delivery. My goal in this book is to present these arguments in the most persuasive and informed manner.

During my lifetime in medicine, I have witnessed a disastrous severance of trust, one that has led to runaway costs, constrained access, skewed coverage, and diminished quality. We cannot fix the American health care delivery system until we restore trust in medicine. Proper disclosure, assurance of access to scientifically proven therapies and preventive services, and complete patient and family participation in decisions about patient care are among the critical changes that must be made to mend our broken system.

I can't close this prologue without commenting on the irony of my public departure from the American Medical Association: the Monica Lewinsky affair resulted in the loss of my job, but not Bill Clinton's.

Introduction

A Medical Memoir

S HORTLY AFTER I LEFT THE American Medical Association on January 15, 1999, I traveled to a mountain retreat in the Sierras above Lake Tahoe. Surrounded by snow-heavy pines and snow-topped mountains, I contemplated my next professional moves. When Morris Fishbein, the legendary editor of *JAMA,* was fired in 1949, he moved right ahead, writing a book and becoming an advisory editor for other medical publications. His indefatigable energy kept him going for several more decades, up to his death in the mid 1970s at age eighty-eight. There was a worthy model, I thought, and I sat down to begin writing this book.

This is a medical memoir, not the story of what happened to me in medicine. Rather, it is the story of what has happened to medicine during the last fifty years. When I first entered a hospital as a teenage worker mopping floors in the early 1950s, I was eager to learn everything I could about medicine and was looking forward to becoming a physician one day. My inspiration was Henry C. Jordan, a country doctor in Lower Alabama who had taken care of me during some childhood bouts of illness. He was the ideal of the friendly, caring family doctor—approachable, sympathetic, and professionally competent.

Medicine was a caring profession in those days. Medical technology was relatively primitive and inexpensive. Cures were elusive, but the need for care was pervasive, so the money available for health care services was essentially directed toward compassionate care for people in need. Comfort, attention, and reassurance when possible were the keynotes of care.

That system stands in stark contrast to the one that exists to-day. Medical technology has become enormously complex and expensive. The system is set up to jump into interventions, some entailing considerable risks, while it largely neglects giving attention, comfort, and reassurance to patients. In fact, the less said, the better, often seems to be the policy followed by medicine's technical wizards. Billions of dollars are spent on heroic efforts to "save" lives, but very little money is allocated for the kind of compassionate patient care that was the traditional hallmark of the profession.

This is the crisis of contemporary medicine: billions for cures, and peanuts for care. No wonder people are frustrated. No wonder we see daily news stories about some new disaster connected with medical care—too many errors, too many denials of care, and too little concern for patients, who are mere numbers to be counted, checked off, and disposed of. But guess what: cures are still elusive, and the need for care is still pervasive.

What a ghastly paradox. Physicians have the means to perform almost any expensive technical procedure, and yet they all too often fail to perform the service that medicine was created for. We doctors do not care for our patients as we ought to. In the early 1970s, Archie Cochrane, a renowned British physician and epidemiologist, made the point that cures in medicine were rare, but the need for care was widespread. He added that he feared that the heroic pursuit of cure at all costs would restrict the supply of care available for patients. That is exactly what has happened.

In our quest to find multimillion-dollar cures, we physicians have neglected to provide reasonable care for our patients. We whip them in and out of hospitals and almost ignore them during hospital stays. All too often, we don't know who they are or what they need. We see only a case, a problem, a riddle to be solved. When patients near death, we often disregard their express wishes, as recorded in living wills, instead pummeling, prodding, infusing, and respirating them until what remains no longer resembles the parent, spouse, or sibling the family once knew.

This is not the way it was fifty years ago. Patients knew their doctors then. Physicians talked to them, and they tried to follow the doctor's advice. When patients had to enter hospitals, they knew they would be cared for by Sisters of Mercy, Sisters of Charity, or other nurses and hospital staff who were attentive and responded quickly to calls for help. They also knew that they would not be released from the hospital until the doctor thought they were ready to return home. Sometimes a stay would be lengthened solely to accommodate family members who needed an extra day or two to prepare the house. Compassion was an integral part of therapy.

That was true patient care, and at a fraction of the cost of what passes for care today. Why are patients spending so much—whether they pay for medical treatment directly or through third-party insurers—and getting so little of the care they need and desire?

Another medical paradox relates to health itself. Today Americans are remarkably healthy people. Life expectancy approaches eighty years. Disorders such as cataract formation can be corrected in a thirty-minute operation by a skilled surgeon. Hips can be replaced and clinical depression controlled, offering a quality of life unimagined when I entered medicine. The story goes that in the United Kingdom death is imminent, in Canada death is inevitable, and in California death is optional. Yet our extraordinary health care system is sick, and our society is almost morbidly obsessed with health. The only news stories that compete with health care horror stories are those that offer advice on limiting cholesterol intake, controlling hypertension (high blood pressure), and mitigating other risk factors associated with death by heart disease, cancer, or stroke.

Looking back, we can clearly see that we have made remarkable progress during the past half century. Polio was a scourge when I entered medicine. Now it's a distant memory because of vaccines. Smallpox has been eliminated from the world, and lining up for inoculations against it at school has long since been abandoned. Vaccines have been developed for measles, tetanus, diphtheria, whooping cough, and hepatitis, diseases that once threatened life and daily occupied the attention of physicians.

Early detection has led to cures for once deadly cancers, such as Hodgkin's disease, testicular cancer, and cervical cancer. Diagnostic technologies such as computed tomography (CT) scans, magnetic resonance imaging (MRI), and positron emission tomography (PET) scans have detected cancers that can be controlled by new drugs, surgery, and radiotherapy.

The incidence of death from heart disease has diminished as a result of new technologies, including coronary artery bypass surgery, angioplasty, stenting, and clot-dissolving drugs. Today patients can return home a few days after a heart attack, whereas heart attack patients used to be hospitalized for six weeks when standard treatment consisted of bed rest and oxygen therapy.

Perhaps the greatest advance has come from the development of antibiotics. Bacterial infections that once were lethal now can be tamed, and the expectant, hopeful waiting that characterized medical care for centuries is truly a thing of the past. All that a doctor could do for someone suffering from pneumonia a few years before I entered medicine was offer a diagnosis and help the patient and family through the so-called crisis, as the patient's immune system either mounted a successful attack against the infection or succumbed to it. Now the crisis is over as soon as the diagnosis is made and antibiotic therapy applied.

Yet for all our progress, cures remain elusive for a wide range of chronic disorders and life-threatening diseases. At the moment, there is no cure for diabetes, Parkinson's disease, multiple sclerosis, arthritis, or Alzheimer's, among many other illnesses. Despite decades of intense research, the dynamics of cancer are still not understood, and cures are all too uncommonly achieved for the major cancer killers, colon, lung, and breast cancer. In some ways, we haven't advanced from Cochrane's thirty-year-old observation that cures are rare and the need for care widespread.

But in an important, almost devastating way we have moved forward. The costs of care have skyrocketed. In 1950, the total costs were $12.7 billion, representing 4.4 percent of gross domestic product (GDP). Today the costs are more than $1 trillion and represent more than 14 percent of GDP. The United States spends more per capita, and as a percentage of GDP, than any other developed nation in the world, yet we exclude close to 20 percent of our population from insurance coverage, and our medical outcomes are not discernibly better than those achieved in other developed countries.

Where does all the money go? People will point to an overbuilt system, to an oversupply of physicians, to an overuse of therapies and pharmaceuticals, but I would suggest that we are putting too many resources into a heroic, almost irrational chase for impossible cures. We never will "cure" death, after all, and in the process of trying to cure it we're not practicing evidence-based medicine. We're too often investing in hopes, dreams, and illusions instead of therapies that have been proven effective. We're forgetting about our traditional obligations to care for the sick and disabled, to reach out to the poor, and to humanely attend to the distressed.

The profession of medicine has been bought out by business, and unless physicians take it back, it will devolve into a business technology in which faceless patients will be treated by faceless technicians. That is the theme of this book. I will explore the process that has led to this crisis. There are no clear-cut villains in this drama. Doctors and patients, hospital administrators and health insurers, employers and government officials all played equally malign and benign roles characterized, paradoxically, by good intentions. Everyone wanted the best, but unhappily everyone's self-interest led them on to the worst.

There is simply too much money pouring into medicine for what we've gotten out of it. It's not good for our health care delivery system, and it's not good for our health. We cannot buy eternal youth, nor can we buy perfect bodies, despite the billions of dollars put into the effort every year. The knowledge to control infectious diseases that have plagued humankind from the dawn of history cannot be applied to control life itself. Too often that is the delusion driving intensive medical interventions. This is not to say that we shouldn't go on seeking cures, but neither should we indiscriminately fund and promote unproven new "cures" on demand. Evidence of efficacy is crucial.

In the first three chapters I discuss the major problems affecting medicine today: high costs, limited access, and spotty coverage. Everyone knows about million-dollar neonatal infants, $200,000 bone marrow transplant procedures, and $40,000 coronary artery bypass operations, but I will add an inside perspective on costs generated by health care providers, including physicians, hospitals, medical device suppliers, and pharmaceutical manufacturers.

Then I will argue that access to health care should be limited. My point is that unless we want to put all our resources into all our medical hopes, we must ration care. The United States could pour its entire GDP into health care in pursuit of perfect outcomes. With enough money and effort, we possibly could get to the bottom of low back pain and even find a cure for the common cold, but the results might not be worth the effort and resources expended. We have to ration care, but we should ration it rationally. We should make sure that beneficial therapies are available to people who need them. We should also make sure that people who are willing to pay for whatever they think they may need retain the freedom to buy it, as long as there is a plentiful supply and as long as harm is unlikely to come from such interventions.

Many of the distortions in our health care delivery system derive from our contorted insurance system. Nothing is standardized: not coverages or premiums, or even the claims forms. This confusion and complexity goes to the heart of the health care system today. Whose needs are we trying to satisfy? Are they the needs of the health insurance companies, the hospitals, the employers, the state or federal regulators, the physicians, the patients' families, or the patients themselves? In our current system, the only answer is, All of the above.

That can't be right. Surely, the consumer of health care services matters most. But who is that consumer? Most often we think of the consumer as the one who pays the bill, but in the United States the payer of medical bills typically is an insurance company or the government. So in health care should we consider the consumer to be the person who purchases the health insurance? For 45 percent of the population, the purchaser is the employer. Does that make the employer the consumer? Some 70 million Americans are covered by Medicare or Medicaid, which are paid for by federal, state, and local governments. Does that make government the consumer? Are the only genuine consumers the patients without insurance, who pay their medical bills out of pocket?

Where does the buck stop, or in this case, where does it begin? The difficulty of identifying the true consumer of health care in the United States exposes the fundamental flaw of the so-called system. Without question, the patient is the only real consumer, no matter who nominally pays the bill. (The real money comes from the value of wages applied to insurance premiums and from taxes.) We have to puncture the hypocrisy that envelops our health insurance system and honestly acknowledge the disparities of coverage that exist today. Powerful unions have won high-end coverage for their workers. High-level executives universally enjoy better benefits than lower-level staffs. In fact, we have a three-tiered system, which includes minimal coverage adequate for little more than emergencies, mid-range coverage such as most businesses offer to full-time employees, and superb coverage of almost any medical expense imaginable. These are what Uwe Reinhardt has called "basic," "business," and "boutique" coverage. Why not just accept this reality, but make sure that basic insurance covers preventive medicine and scientifically proven care for all of our people?

What I am arguing for, in fact, is a return to professional autonomy and responsibility. From the time of Hippocrates, medicine has been guided by clear rules. Physicians were obliged to teach others the art of healing. They were to respect their patients and protect their privacy. As members of a learned profession, they were expected to provide services to the poor without charge. They were also obliged not to solicit patients by making claims or offering testimonials about the effectiveness of their therapies. As a result of their service to patients, physicians were accorded a respected place in society.

If the profession does not recapture medicine from commerce, it will lose the respect it has traditionally earned. Already there is an erosion of respect, as people read news accounts of physicians who tout new therapies in which they have a financial interest or who earn scandalously high incomes. In the past, society accepted the fact that doctors could expect to make more money than average as a reasonable reward for the crucial services they offered. But when people hear of multimillion-dollar incomes, they not only lose respect for a profession committed to the healing arts; they also lose trust in its practitioners.

The quickest way to restore trust is to assure quality of care. That sounds simple, but quality is difficult to define. It tends to be a matter of personal judgment. The American Society of Quality Control defines quality as "the totality of features and characteristics of a product or service that bears on its ability to satisfy given needs." By that definition, an assurance of quality is a promise to satisfy needs, and nothing more.

That won't do for medicine today. We need something better; we need to assure the public that we are providing the right medical care. Medical interventions have to be based on better science, and in medicine that means investigating when something goes wrong. The place to begin is the autopsy. As a pathologist, I was trained to understand the unique contributions to science made by autopsies. As a medical editor, I reviewed countless studies that underscored the autopsy's value. Doctors *do* bury their mistakes, not deliberately or maliciously, but because their mistakes go unrecognized. Studies from autopsies even in the 1990s have shown that a remarkably high percentage of causes of death entered by attending physicians are incorrect.

What has happened to the autopsy is analogous to what has happened to the health care system itself. Medicare provided funding to cover the cost of autopsies, but that money has been diverted to cover any and all other hospital costs at the discretion of hospital administrators. Typically, administrators siphon funds to those services that make big money for their hospitals. This is a completely wrongheaded use of resources. Many diagnostic tests, a historically lucrative source of hospital income, are blind probes for information. By contrast, autopsies frequently provide information that can guide and focus diagnostic testing. Here is an example in which the self-interest of the providers, hospitals, and physicians takes precedence over the interests of science and patient care.

A similar problem relates to all discussions concerning quality in medicine. When the American Medical Association talks about quality, what it really means is letting doctors do and order whatever they wish, and thereby letting them make as much money as they can. When patients talk about quality, what they mean is getting whatever they think they need and sparing no cost to get it, as long as the insurance company pays for it. When members of Congress talk about quality, what they mean is pouring billions of dollars into research aimed at curing all the ills that make their constituents (and themselves) unhappy. Every year, Congress appropriates billions of dollars for the National Institutes of Health but grudgingly offers only millions to the Agency for Healthcare Research and Quality (AHRQ). Once again, the search for farfetched cures is hugely funded, while the search for scientific standards and guidelines, the work that AHRQ undertakes, goes begging for dollars.

Quality medicine is not as elusive as it may seem. It comes from two sources: accurate diagnosis of an illness and correct application of scientifically proven therapies. It sounds simple, but it isn't. A surprising number of doctors can't accurately diagnose a patient's symptoms, and therefore they initiate an entirely inappropriate course of treatment. These incompetent physicians ought to be confronted by their peers. The second principle of the

AMA's Code of Ethics states that "a physician shall deal honestly with patients and colleagues, and strive to expose those physicians deficient in character or competence, or who engage in fraud or deception." But often they are not, either for legal reasons or because they hide themselves in private office practice, away from virtually all supervision.

Many incompetent (and many competent) physicians are sued for malpractice. The National Practitioner Data Bank, which keeps track of malpractice actions and charges, was created to make sure that doctors who lose their license to practice medicine in one state cannot cross into another and pick up a license there. Licensing boards in all states can tap into the data bank for information on doctors, as can hospitals reviewing physicians' applications for privileges. Information in the data bank includes license revocations and suspensions as well as malpractice awards and settlements registered against physicians. Public officials have access to all that information, but the public does not.

Year after year, the AMA fights to keep the lid on the data bank. It contends that trial lawyers will use the data to go on fishing expeditions, or that patients will incorrectly assume that physicians named in the data banks' records must not be "good doctors." These are bogus arguments. It's common knowledge that physicians, good and bad, are often sued. Obstetricians pay horrendous malpractice premiums, and probably perform more cesarean sections than they should, partly because jury awards for injuries to babies in the course of labor and natural childbirth, no matter what the cause, are exceptionally high. Neurosurgeons, who are no less competent than other doctors, are frequent targets of malpractice suits because they perform extremely high-risk surgery. Removing life-threatening tumors intricately entangled in brain tissue may save a person's life at the cost of causing some unforeseen disability, and a successful operation may be portrayed in a lawyer's brief as a rank failure. Some doctors who are often sued, though, really are incompetent. One complaint against them follows another, and a pattern emerges. These doctors should be drummed out of practice. But if the court records are sealed—a common condition of financial settlements—the evidence that proves their malpractice cannot be examined. The public should be warned about them, and public access to the data bank would help. Explanatory information, such as that offered in Massachusetts, which opened the data bank with the cooperation of the Massachusetts Medical Society, helps patients understand the meaning of listings. The Massachusetts experiment has demonstrated that good doctors survive the scrutiny, and that their good reputations prevail in their communities even when they practice in high-risk specialties.

Correct application of scientifically proven therapies is the second hallmark of quality. Use of antibiotics to treat strep throat, pneumonia, gonorrhea, or other bacterial infections is quality care. Other practices are less clear-cut. Although the coronary artery bypass graft is now the nation's most common surgical procedure, it enjoyed widespread application before undergoing a true clinical trial, and indications for its use are still not as clearly defined as they should be. The second most common procedure, hysterectomy, owes its frequency more to established practice patterns in various communities than it does to scientifically validated clinical guidelines. That is, doctors practicing in a city where for many ills hysterectomy has long been the favored treatment tend to continue to recommend hysterectomy over less drastic treatments, even though solid studies of patient outcomes have been inconclusive. Bone marrow transplantation became a standard treatment for stage 4 breast cancer while it was still an experimental procedure, more than a decade before studies showed that it is no more helpful than chemotherapy. No matter how great the talent, expertise, and daring behind innovative, high-tech interventions, they do not constitute quality medicine. The quality of the procedure is defined by its scientific efficacy. Difficult as this may be for patients, physicians, and hospitals to accept, we need to base medicine on science, not on hopes and dreams of cures and profits. This theme will be sounded in several chapters, but especially in the chapters on insurance coverage, alternative medicine, and quality care.

A particularly onerous deviation from quality standards is so-called futile care, the practice of subjecting terminally ill patients to painful, costly, debilitating treatments that offer little or no hope of any meaningful recovery. No accurate assessments of the dollar cost of futile care are available, but it surely adds up to many billions, raked in by hospitals and physicians. The emotional cost of futile care has been felt by millions of patients and families. Time and again, people say they do not want to end their lives hooked up to respirators, IVs, and monitoring devices, but when in the final stages of a terminal illness they are admitted to a sophisticated medical center, that is precisely how they end their lives. Futile care, a contradiction in terms, is the most distressing example of the search for cure taking precedence over the need for true care.

In some situations, cure is simply out of the question. Patients in their nineties who display symptoms of multiple organ system failure do not need to have another operation, or to undergo another round of chemotherapy, or to be tethered every other day to a hemodialysis machine. What they need is more attentive care. They need physicians who will listen to them and their families, and who will talk about the nature of their terminal illnesses. In some clearly defined situations, they need doctors who will help them die. Polls consistently report that a majority of U.S. physicians say they have been inadequately prepared to deal with dying patients. Issues concerning the traditional value of medicine come together in the chapter on futile care.

Finally, we need to devise a new system for the delivery of health services in the United States. It will be difficult to do, not only because of powerful stakeholders—doctors, hospitals, insurers, politicians, and employers—but also because of the unique traditions, aspirations, and expectations that Americans of different regions and cultures, different religions and ethnicities, bring to health care issues.

The first step is to rein in the business of medicine, something the AMA failed to address during the period of the profession's worst excesses. Too many entrepreneurs are operating too many diagnostic and therapeutic facilities. We have to get back to basics. Physicians must be rewarded for their scientific and clinical expertise, not for their investments in high-tech devices and peripheral services. They should not run a medical practice like a retail store, marking up lab tests and diagnostic procedures to pad their already substantial incomes. People come to physicians for counsel, advice, and direction. That is what we value most from caregivers. Every day, we see people reach into their pockets and pay hard cash for care from alternative practitioners, such as homeopaths and acupuncturists, when their insurance won't cover nontraditional or non-Western therapies. Those practitioners have earned a degree of trust by seeming more interested in their patients than they are in high incomes.

A lifelong member of the AMA once asked me why the association never took a stand against excessive physician incomes. Why didn't AMA officials speak out and castigate the money-grubbers? Why didn't they remind physicians of their traditional obligation to serve? Why didn't they insist that efficiencies and economies should result in reduced fees for services instead of increased revenues for the service providers?

I had no answer. The AMA has been driven by its responsibilities to maintain high academic standards in medical schools and residency programs, as well as high scientific standards in its publications, and by its desire to please members who are concerned about their economic well-being. When the association sticks to science, it enjoys enormous public goodwill. But when it talks about Medicare or other organizations or agencies, it arouses skepticism and suspicion.

If the AMA does not take back responsibility for professional standards, other agencies will gladly fill the void. Some administrator will step in and say: We cannot open another transplant center. We cannot allow proliferation of physician laboratory services and diagnostic facilities. We need to rationalize facilities within communities, and to oppose those within the medical profession who would encourage wasteful duplication of services. We need to manage and restrain the supply of physicians, and we need to let failing hospitals close their doors. With or without the AMA's help, the profession has to reconstitute itself and make professional service its top priority.

The next thing we have to do is to reform the health insurance industry. Allowing for-profit companies to take medicine over was a colossal mistake, but for the moment the for-profits are here to stay. If we can't make them go away, however, we can make them perform and pay for services that really work. We can also make them participate in clinical trials to determine the efficacy of new therapies, and they will soon learn that covering science-based medicine is cost effective. They must play by a standard set of rules designed to benefit patients rather than insurers, employers, hospitals, or physicians.

Whether or not we stick with an employment-based health insurance system is problematic. We have a lot invested in it. Workers have won benefit rights at the bargaining table. The public prefers a private rather than a public health insurance system, with the exception of those who depend on Medicare. We have to take into account the $100 billion a year contributed to employment-based insurance by the federal government. That is the amount of tax dollars foregone as a result of treating health benefits as a cost of doing business for employers.

That government subsidy should be cross-subsidized to cover the insurance cost for those without employment-based insurance. One argument holds that a government program would siphon off employment-based insurance. If employees are willing to let that happen, why shouldn't it happen? Of course, employees would be more likely to fight for their health benefits if they had an opportunity to choose their own insurers and providers. That raises the question of whether health insurance prices should be based on individual risks of getting or being sick (risk rating) or whether they should cover large groups of patients as a community (community rating) in order to spread the risk across many insured persons, evening out prices. The issue of adverse selection comes up as well.

How do we cost out individual policies? How do we encourage more insurers to design policies for people with chronic health problems or serious illnesses? These are problems that the insurance industry can solve, if it is motivated. Certainly, the threat of a single-payer, government-sponsored insurance system should provide some motivation, but all incentives will be lost if insurance packages are not standardized.

Finally, room must be made for individuals who are willing to spend their own money to get whatever medical services they want. That is the only system that will survive a public test. For all our devotion to egalitarianism, most of us do not mind differentiation based on wealth and ability to pay. Where one lives, what one eats, or how one dresses is left to individual discretion, even though Americans do support programs to provide basic shelter, food, and clothing. Still, there is a belief that a democratic society should assure access to education and health care, and under our fractured current systems such access is somehow universally provided, although hardly in an egalitarian fashion.

While it may be difficult to fashion a program that will serve the genuine health needs of all Americans, it is doable. We may have to think in expansive new ways. For example, we may need to pass a constitutional amendment entitling everyone to proven health care services. We may then need the equivalent of a Securities and Exchange Commission or Federal Reserve Board to set the health care standards and enforce the rules. Or the profession itself may need to organize a system that assures access to care that works. In any event, the result would be a system that serves patients, that addresses their concerns, that accurately diagnoses their problems, and that correctly treats their disorders. If we do this right, and I'm convinced we can, we will have a system that prudently and effectively uses high-tech medicine that truly benefits patients at reasonable rather than runaway costs.

1

The Enemy Is Us

*Why Medical Care Costs So Much
and What We Can Do About It*

SOME TIME AGO A COLLEAGUE and I chatted about the high costs of medical care. Now retired from active practice, my friend recalled how remarkably inexpensive things were when he was young. He told of a childhood friend's appendectomy in the late 1930s. The boy presented his symptoms—nausea, vomiting, and abdominal pain—to the town's lone general practitioner. After taking the history and conducting a physical examination, the doctor admitted the patient to the town's small community hospital and prepared to operate.

He was assisted by two nurses, one of whom handled the ether mask; the doctor opened the boy's abdomen, resected the infected appendix, and closed. Sulfa drugs were used to fight infection, and the boy was moved to a hospital bed, where he was infused with intravenous fluids for one day. He remained in the hospital for another five days before being released. The hospital charges were less than $10 per day, and the total cost of the operation probably was something like $100, including hospitalization and the physician's fee.

Today an appendectomy would cost more than $9,000. Of course, the operation is now safer, but factors other than increased safety and inflation account for the fantastic increase in cost—a little bit of greed, expertise overload, and lots of unneeded administrative costs.

To control runaway medical costs, I would begin by banning all direct-to-consumer medical advertising. Advertising clearly wastes precious health care dollars and, in some cases, such as in drug advertising, inappropriately pushes for utilization that promotes commerce while undermining professionalism. It also pumps up costs. In 1990, before drug ads to consumers began appearing, drug costs accounted for about 6 percent of total health care costs in the United States. Ten years later they accounted for 11 percent. Without intervention, this percentage will soon skyrocket.

Then I would attack overpriced diagnostic tests and medical equipment charges. About 80 percent of lab tests now ordered are not needed by anyone other than laboratory directors, hospital administrators, and often physicians, and many are priced at scandalously high levels. These are the scattershot tests encouraged by lab ordering forms and by physicians accustomed to asking for any and all test results. I also would insist that charges moderate for new technologies as they become commonplace and less costly to deliver. The savings should diminish consumer costs rather than fatten provider wallets.

But there's a lot of work to be done if we wish to contain the monstrous costs of medical care in this country, now totaling some $1.2 trillion per year. That figure would have been unimaginable when I was working as a hospital orderly in Mobile, Alabama, in the early 1950s. Care cost about $12 billion per year in those days. How did we get from there to here?

There are potential villains everywhere in this macabre story, including greedy doctors, self-indulgent and demanding patients, self-centered hospital administrators, uncaring third-party payers, and self-absorbed employers. Each group not only contributed to this wild skyrocket ride but often did so with the best intentions.

Everyone involved played a role in creating incentives that were bound to drive costs upward and out of control. The bottom line is that no one has been accountable for managing the costs of care. Physicians were encouraged to try new therapies, order more tests, and offer more services, always without regard to cost. Patients, who wanted free care, were the first to press for "first dollar" insurance coverage—that is, total insurance coverage from the first office visit to the most expensive procedure, a system that removes any barrier to immediate care on demand. Through support for capital expenditures, hospitals were rewarded for adding new wings, buying expensive new equipment, and developing new programs. Third-party payers were appreciated for shuffling papers, paying bills without question, and generally staying out of the way, while employers paid for it all with tax-exempt dollars, writing off health benefit premiums as a cost of doing business. It's a wonder we kept it down to $1.2 trillion.

The United States began measuring the costs of health care in 1929; from that year until 1955 there was little real change. As a percentage of gross domestic product, costs barely inched up and stayed confined to a range of 3.5 to 4.5 percent during that twenty-six-year period before shooting up to today's 14 percent of GDP. Yet even in the 1930s, when costs were low, national commissions were created to study the excess costs of medical care. People were tearing out their hair because health care was so expensive. Looking back, it's clear that they were reacting to a change in the environment of medical care: a charitable activity had been transformed into a professional activity.

I was reminded of this a few years ago when I gave a presentation at Harvard on the escalation of health care costs. Conventional wisdom has blamed Medicare, with its generous coverage of elderly patients, for the dramatic increase in the costs of care. I said that Medicare was one culprit but pointed out that, though I didn't understand why, the real increases began in 1955, ten years before the enactment of Medicare. Then I heard from a gentleman in the back of the room, John Dunlop, who was a Harvard professor of economics.

He explained that until 1955 the medical workforce was woefully underpaid because health care was seen as a charitable effort. The Sisters of Mercy or the Sisters of Charity staffed many hospitals. They expected to have a decent place to live, but they did not expect much in the way of salary. That expectation about the delivery of health care changed in the mid-1950s, Dunlop said, as a result of federal law that required better standards of pay for hospital workers.

That was too late for me at my first hospital job in 1951, when I earned about $100 per month, roughly half of the minimum wage at that time. I went to work for the City Hospital of Mobile, a racially segregated (by law) charity hospital owned by the city and run by the Sisters of Charity. I was hired to mop the floors of operating rooms between operations and to clean everything up before the next patient was wheeled in. By then I was in my third year of premed studies and terribly excited about medicine, eager to learn every aspect of it. Mopping up floors was just fine for a start.

After a few weeks pushing a mop, I was asked by one of the nuns whether I would like to be promoted to orderly. Of course, I agreed, and soon I was out on the wards, working with nurses, student nurses, and nurses' aides and doing a lot of the tasks they performed for patients. I also worked with interns—the medical school graduates completing their first year of postgraduate training. (One of them was James H. Sammons, later to become the executive vice president of the AMA.) They received room, board, uniforms, and a few dollars per month. This was a care-intensive but inexpensive system of health care delivery.

All this began to change in the mid-1950s as the value of medical services became more apparent. Not only were health care workers paid a little more, but hospital services became more sophisticated and expensive. More and more laboratory tests were performed, more X rays taken, and more services added. So began the steep climb in health care costs.

When we look at the total, a 100 percent increase, we have to acknowledge that 40 percent of it is accounted for by general inflation. That is, if health care expenses increased 6 percent in any given year, 2.4 percent of that increase is accounted for by across-the-board inflation.

That leaves 60 percent of the increase unaccounted for. About 10 percent of the increase is related to the increased number of elderly in our population. We've been very successful at extending our lives. In fact, demographically those over the age of one hundred constitute the most rapidly expanding segment of our population. This wonderful development is expensive, but nowhere near as costly as some critics complain. Care for the elderly amounts to only 10 percent of the total cost inflation. That figure is not all that great, but it certainly is not all that bad either. I'll talk more about the downside of costs for terminal illness in chapter 8.

A more serious cost problem is the 16 percent economic inflation on health-related goods: ambulances, hospital mattresses, and the pharmaceutical products, surgical knives, bandages, and other supplies bought by hospitals. The markups are outrageous. Why is a hospital mattress different from any other? What is so special about the truck base of an ambulance? Why do they all cost so much more than comparable products sold outside of hospitals? There is only one reason: the manufacturers have charged more because they can get away with it. In the cost-plus environment created by Medicare and Blue Cross, third-party payers promptly paid for whatever the provider billed. There were no negotiations. A bandage for $16? Why not—the insurer will pay. With patients as a captive market, pharmacies have also been able to charge whatever they want. Physicians prescribe heavily marketed drugs even when less expensive drugs that work as well are readily available. Again, insurance will cover the cost, so why be concerned?

Unlike the 40 percent representing general inflation or the 10 percent reflecting the increase in the number of elderly, the 16 percent inflation for health-related goods offers a promising area for cost containment. We can start by refusing to pay those exorbitant prices and making suppliers bid for our business. Then we need to establish hospital formularies—centralized drug-purchasing and -dispensing departments that would provide cheaper drugs. Managed care has already instituted some of these controls.

The remaining 34 percent of health care inflation is accounted for by the volume and intensity of services offered by providers responding to everything from the AIDS epidemic and gunshot wounds to open-heart surgery and organ transplantation. One liver transplant, for example, requires that one hundred transfusion units be available. These procedures are expensive, and they need to be addressed in turn. Indeed, an important goal of this book is to examine the problems associated with this area of inflated health care costs.

Let's start with laboratory tests, something with which I'm familiar as a pathologist. Studies and observations demonstrate that more than half of all lab tests done and paid for by Medicare are unnecessary. In fact, I would say that about 80 percent of the tests carried out in the laboratories I oversaw in academic medical centers did not need to be done. Moreover, because they are keyed to whatever the market will bear, lab tests often are overpriced. A famous pathologist in Sacramento, California, used to call test charges "excess profit for a good cause."

I well remember setting up a chemistry lab at the Druid City Hospital, a brand-new, federally financed Hill-Burton facility, in Tuscaloosa, Alabama, shortly before entering medical school in 1953. I had just completed biochemistry studies in graduate school and felt privileged to be the first chemistry technician in that laboratory. A lot of the work then was manual, and there were no automated instruments at first; in my job I would introduce the first Flame photometer in the western part of Alabama. By allowing us to analyze for serum potassium, sodium, and serum chloride, this instrument offered a huge advance in the care of diabetics in coma. Until then coma and other electrolyte problems had been extremely difficult to handle, and the new lab tests represented true lifesaving technology.

But this technology was labor-intensive. I had to do one test at a time by hand, and the cost was passed on at a fairly high rate for those days. The hospital charged five dollars for one blood sugar analysis. Then automation entered the laboratories in the late 1950s and early 1960s. The first major instrument was the Autoanalyzer, produced by Technicon, a firm then located in Tarrytown, New York. This instrument revolutionized the chemical lab business by making it possible to load multiple serum samples from patients into the machine and to run through one after another without any handling by humans. So what happened to the price? It stayed the same. The hospital continued to charge five dollars per test even though one person, running the machine, could do fifty in the time it used to take to do one. Why did the hospital continue to charge five dollars? Because it could get it.

Standard practice now may require blood sample analysis every hour, and sometimes instantaneously. I knew many pathologists who received a percentage of all the income coming into hospital labs. This percentage contract model (I never had one) was initiated by Catholic hospitals as a way to generate income to build modern labs. With the hospitals and the pathologists splitting the profits, the latter had an incentive to develop labs in which multiple tests could be conducted. The clinical laboratory thus became a major profit center for hospitals.

Many other medical procedures have a similar pricing history. Charges are initially high because of the labor-intensive nature of developing new procedures. The coronary artery bypass operation provides a perfect example. The surgeons who pioneered the procedure spent a lot of time and money on research and development. They spent many hours in laboratories, working with animal models, to perfect the technique. The time they spent with their first patients also was intensive. Everything was new, and it all required close monitoring and attention. The total cost for the new procedure exceeded $60,000—a reasonable price considering the investment that had gone into it.

But then more and more surgeons learned the procedure, often in the course of their regular residency training. They had no research and development costs, and their patients did not need to be so intensively monitored. In fact, the bypass operation now is the most common in hospitals, but the charges haven't moderated in many places. Most hospitals still charge in the $50,000 to $60,000 range. Some hospitals, like the Cleveland Clinic, have been able to offer lower prices, around $30,000, in part because of the large volume of operations they perform.

Over and over again in the medical marketplace, a new commodity is introduced, high prices are charged because the commodity is rare, but the high prices are maintained even when the commodity becomes commonplace. Why does this happen? Because the patients do not know any better, the insurance companies let it happen, and the purchasers do not care or are hoodwinked. That is how the costs of care in this country have gotten out of control.

Insurance is the key. It provides funny money. We have never had anything approaching real Adam Smith economics in the United States when it comes to health care. Even in the turbulent managed care arena of today the purchasers and providers have never played real economic hardball in a marketplace of oversupply.

The Insurance Scam, or How Providers Rigged the Market

First it should be noted that "health" insurance is a misnomer. What we call health insurance is really "sickness" insurance, but with such a label it couldn't be sold on the open market. Healthy people have little incentive to buy sickness insurance. The only ones interested are those who are either sick or concerned enough about their health to make periodic visits to physicians. In insurance terms, that defines "adverse risk."

What we now call health insurance began in 1929 when the Baylor University Hospital offered hospital insurance to teachers in Dallas, Texas. For six dollars per year, the teachers would be insured for up to twenty-one days of inpatient care at Baylor, and soon 1,356 subscribers had signed on. The American Hospital Association immediately noticed the program and showed interest. Like Baylor, other hospitals across the country were having financial difficulties, and prepaid insurance, which would provide a steady stream of income, offered a solution. So began the Blue Cross plans.

These insurance plans were not begun as commercial ventures. Rather, the plans were seen as part of a social movement, and many

s if politi-
n in 1955,
physicians
ds in offices
k bag. Most
organizations
octors opened
d. Political de-
d the wild up-

n 1945 when he
adequate medical
MA, the legendary
1924 to 1949 Fish-
Dr. Medicine" in the
iously energetic man,
lumns, magazine arti-
ularly scheduled radio
of the sanctity of the
ant foe of anything that
ond. To Fishbein, group
medicine, prepaid hospi-
n, and even fee-for-service
third party into the sacred
ed all of it.
nal health insurance as early
alled the report of the Com-
an incitement to revolution,
rdly that. The chairman of the
a past president of the AMA, a
rsity, and clearly not a revolu-
tions included a call for group
rance programs.
t, although a subsequent attack—
om the Committee of 430 Physi-

of the early plans, as Emily Friedman observed in a 1998 *JAMA* article on Blue Cross, were chartered as hospital service organizations or charities and given tax-exempt status. Their mission was to prepay for hospital services rather than to provide cash benefits for subscribers. Although the plans benefited patients who needed hospitalization, they were created to keep hospitals solvent with a steady income.

Blue Cross plans opened throughout the country in the 1930s as agents sold insurance to employer groups. Family coverage sold for about $1.30 per month, paid for by employees with after-tax dollars but usually deducted from their paychecks by employers. Most workers saw such insurance as a good deal. It didn't cost much, and if serious illness struck, they wouldn't have to worry about hospital bills.

The system began to change as a result of the crisis created by World War II. High on the list of government concerns was inflation. Officials worried that a wartime shortage of consumer goods, plus a shortage in the labor supply, with so many workers now in uniform, could send prices spiraling skyward. So they came up with price and wage controls, set by the Office of Price Administration. Labor union leaders, who were particularly frustrated by wage freezes, petitioned government for a ruling that would exempt fringe benefits from controls. In 1942 labor won when the government ruled that benefit increases up to 5 percent would not be considered inflationary.

The new rule had an immediate and long-lasting impact on the costs of health care. First, it transferred premium payment responsibility from workers to employers. Second, it provided a government subsidy to health care insurance: employer payments were exempt from taxation because they were considered a cost of doing business. As a result, neither workers nor employers had to pay for health insurance with after-tax dollars. (By contrast, individuals pay for auto or home insurance out of take-home earnings.) By creating the illusion that health care services for the insured came apparently free of charge, the new arrangement changed everyone's thinking about costs. So what if costs went up? The money didn't come out of the worker's pocket, and the employer simply w. off the cost. This mentality was the genesis of funny money.

Physicians compounded the problem by enthusiastically ac cepting third-party health insurance payments when they became available, even though organized medicine—as represented by the American Medical Association and state and county medical societies—was critical of the practice. An older colleague of mine, a family physician from Oregon, has pointed out that at first physicians continued to bill patients, who then filed claims with their insurers and paid their doctors after receiving the insurance check. When it became apparent that many patients were not forwarding insurance payments but instead pocketing the checks, physicians worked out agreements with insurers for direct payment. When physicians began to bill insurance companies instead of patients, the perception was reinforced that care was free of charge.

"If physicians hadn't done that, they would have kept third-party payers out of the patient-physician relationship," my friend added, with a wry smile. But that would have been too much work, for doctors and patients alike. When physicians accepted direct payment, they were freed from the disagreeable need to dun patients, who were freed up in turn from the bother of paperwork. Physicians didn't have to worry about reimbursement anymore; it came directly from the insurer. Physicians made it even easier for patients by waiving the 20 percent co-payment that insurance policies required, a quasi-illegal practice that no one complained about. But, as my friend pointed out, every step taken intruded the third-party payer more deeply into the patient-physician relationship. Moreover, the cost of care increased, since patients had no incentive to resist higher physician charges. Patients often didn't even bother to look at the charges. Twenty-five dollars for a lab test that cost fifty cents to perform? No skin off my nose.

When, for all intents and purposes, health care services seemed to come at no cost to patients, not only were patients' anxieties relieved, but physicians were encouraged to order and perform more

cians, headed by John Peters at Yale—was less strident. The committee endorsed four principles:

1. The health of the people is a direct concern of government.
2. A national policy directed toward all groups in the population should be formulated.
3. The problems of economic need and adequate medical care are different and may require different solutions.
4. Four groups should be concerned with the provision of adequate medical care for the population—voluntary agencies and government at the local, state, and federal levels.

Fishbein's response was measured but damning. The committee was self-appointed, he charged, and its members represented special interests looking for government money for their own purposes. He warned that it would be hazardous for the federal government to control medical education, science, and medical practice. The proposed changes would enslave the medical profession, he asserted, adding that no people could endure with "a medical profession enslaved to make a politician's holiday."

This time Fishbein used less inflammatory language and took the unusual precaution of seeking approval from the AMA board of trustees before publishing his editorial. The board followed up in November 1937 with a press release in which it urged the development of a comprehensive system of medical care adapted to "the American way of living."

That was the point hammered home in 1945 by Truman in declaring a right to adequate medical care. Fishbein said the president was proposing nothing less than "socialized medicine," which would destroy good patient care. When a reporter visited Fishbein on his way to England to write about that country's new National Health Service, the reporter was urged to query doctors as to how often they asked their patients to remove their shirts. Fishbein was convinced that the new system would provide patients with assembly-line service, and that physicians would not have the time or the incentive to conduct thorough physical examinations. He became so obstreperous on the issue that a group of California physicians who didn't see anything socialistic about third-party private insurance for physician services led a revolt that finally removed Fishbein from office, after twenty-five years as editor of *JAMA*.

But he had made a point with politicians. Most would not support an overtly socialized system like England's, yet they also saw that access to good medical care was a popular issue with voters. Patients seemed to want the benefits of socialized medicine without the taint of the label. So a stealth operation of government support for medical care began in the 1940s. Politicians decided to support the health care system in a less direct and obvious way. In 1946 Congress effectively did everything Fishbein had warned against by passing the Hill-Burton Act, expanding support for the National Institutes of Health (NIH), and financing the entire Veterans Administration (VA) hospital system. By installing government oversight into hospitals, medical research, and physician training, the federal government was simply adopting an "American" rather than a "socialized" system of health care.

The Hill-Burton legislation poured billions of dollars into hospital construction and improvement over the next two decades. Similar amounts were appropriated for the NIH after the polio vaccines demonstrated the power of new medical technologies. The VA system was expanded and strengthened dramatically, and its hospitals became a major teaching venue for resident physicians.

The political thinking of the era found a representative figure in Lister Hill, co-sponsor of the Hill-Burton legislation. A conservative, all-American senator from my home state of Alabama, Hill was genuinely interested in the welfare of the people. He was a descendant of Luther Leonidas Hill, said to be the first American physician to suture the human heart. Luther L. Hill no doubt named his son after John Lister, one of the most illustrious names in the history of medicine and a giant in the area of infectious diseases at the beginning of the microbiology era. Senator Lister Hill probably dated his interest in medicine from the day of his birth, but after World War II his interest coincided with the interests of the nation. He was in the forefront of support for the NIH, the building of hospitals, and other government funding for medicine, but as a conservative senator from the South, he would no more have considered himself a socialist than his constituents would have.

More direct federal involvement came in the wake of faltering employment. The postwar expansion that had guaranteed full employment stumbled in the late 1950s, uncovering a painful reality: employment-based health insurance left many people out of the system, not the least of whom were the growing number of retirees. Elderly retirees had plenty of time to read, think, talk to one another, and stand in line at polling booths to vote. They and their adult children felt a desperate need for insurance to cover the costs of hospitalization.

Members of Congress responded in 1965 by enacting Medicare, which offered insurance to the elderly, and Medicaid, a federal, state, and local government program promising health care services to the indigent. Most observers would single out Medicare as the most powerful engine behind the cost escalation in health care. After all, the illnesses that affect the elderly are more frequent, chronic, disabling, and costly. To guarantee coverage for such a vulnerable population, the argument goes, is to guarantee significant cost escalation. As I noted earlier, however, health care costs as a percentage of GDP started to increase ten years before Medicare was enacted.

Another governmental action had a much greater impact on costs than Medicare. President Lyndon Johnson's cure for the "doctor shortage" was to double medical school enrollments through a generously funded capitation program that encouraged the development of new medical schools and the expansion of enrollments at existing schools. The thinking behind this plan to address a physician shortage had two goals: solving the distribution problem (an expanded number of physicians would force some to practice in rural areas and inner cities), and lowering physician fees when the greater supply of physicians first met and then overtook demand.

What the president and his advisers thought they were supporting was an expansion of the old system, with general practitioners making their rounds to care for patient-friends. An expansion in their numbers certainly would have produced a wider distribution and probably held down fees as general practitioners competed for patients in more desirable locations. But the politicians' thinking turned out to be misguided. First, they completely misunderstood what was happening in medicine. Second, their plan overlooked the basic market concept that consumers make informed decisions about what they choose to purchase. And no one seemed to notice that patients and physicians were both attracted to more specialized care. Nor did anyone appreciate that the hospital cost-plus reimbursement system for Medicare patients—and for many Blue Cross patients as well—though intended to expand residency programs, would greatly facilitate the move toward specialization. Science also was marching forward, with new knowledge and new technologies.

So instead of producing more general practitioners, the new federal dollars dramatically increased the number of specialists, especially those providing care for the elderly. Instead of visiting the family doctor, more and more elderly patients were consulting expert physicians they had never seen before, and these specialists were saying that they could prolong their lives by applying new, complex therapies.

Increased specialization ushered in a brave new world, or perhaps the beginning of a nightmare. In any event, it was the end of an era. Super-specialized care spelled the end of the era of general practitioners, home visits, and personal care, and the beginning of the age of subspecialization, high technology, and impersonal care.

I was part of the older system, having graduated from the Medical College of Alabama in 1957. In those days medical school graduates became interns at teaching hospitals and spent one year in a rotation program that exposed them to the major specialties, such as surgery, internal medicine, pediatrics, obstetrics and gynecology, orthopedics, anesthesiology, and emergency medicine. After completing the internship, physicians were eligible for state licensure and general practice. They also were eligible for residency training in a medical specialty. Many entered general practice. Those who entered residency training were likely to drop out after a year or two as competition for slots intensified and the need for earned income grew. It was hard to have a real life on ten dollars a month.

I completed my internship at Tripler Hospital in Hawaii, since I had joined the U.S. Army to resolve my draft status. After completing the intern year, I had two options: either to remain in the service for three years as a general medical officer or to enter a residency program and remain in the service for a longer period of time. I made a couple of discoveries during my one-year rotation. First, I learned that I was academically strong enough to do well in residency training. I also learned that internal medicine, psychiatry, and pathology were intellectually appealing, and that I could hedge a bet by starting in pathology, since training in that discipline would count for internal medicine should I choose to change after one year.

I began my residency training at Brooke General Hospital in San Antonio. Soon I discovered that anatomic and clinical pathology was completely absorbing, and by 1960 the *New England Journal of Medicine* had published the first scientific paper I ever wrote, on the lethal role of mucormycosis infection following severe burn injury. I was on my way to becoming an academic physician, and I loved it.

My experience as an academic-in-training was relatively typical, and that of a fellow Alabamian, James H. Sammons, was typical for a general practitioner. He graduated from St. Louis University School of Medicine in 1951, completed an internship at the Mobile City Hospital, and opened a general practice in Baytown, Texas, then a small city some thirty miles east of Houston. He could remember receiving payment in kind for services—many chickens, some eggs, and now and then a side of beef. He delivered babies, cared for children by setting bones and treating sore throats, and also cared for their mothers, fathers, and grandparents. He enjoyed his practice enormously, but he also discovered that he was an extremely good medical politician. He went through the various chairs in organized medicine, at the county, state, and national levels, and finally became the executive vice president of the AMA. He never lost sight, however, of what he considered his glory days in general practice.

The Role of Government-Sponsored Specialization in Jump-starting High Costs

That era ended after federal dollars rolled into medical education and residency training. To jump-start the physician-supply expansion, one-year stand-alone internship programs were abandoned and medical students went straight into residency programs at much higher salaries. (Today's annual salary is $40,000 to $50,000.) They were fully trained one year sooner but missed the benefit of exposure to a number of specialties before committing to one. Soon it didn't matter. By the time I was an academic physician at the University of Southern California and the University of California at Davis in the 1960s and 1970s, a large percentage of students knew well before matriculation exactly what they wanted: money.

It was pouring into health care by then, especially for surgery, anesthesiology, pathology, radiology, cardiology, and the new and rapidly expanding discipline of oncology. One pathologist reportedly earned $4 million a year by passing the savings derived from new laboratory technologies into his own pocket rather than into lower fees for lab services. And his laboratory was not located in Los Angeles, Chicago, or New York, as one might suppose, but in a semirural area of a mid-Atlantic state.

When the politicians enacted Medicare, Medicaid, and federal support for education and training, they had anticipated modest programs to assist the elderly and underserved. A greater supply of doctors, they thought, would help the aged as well as residents of rural areas and inner cities. No one foresaw the rapid development and diffusion of sophisticated new technologies, many of them aimed at prolonging life no matter what the cost.

The expected annual cost of Medicare and Medicaid had been $6 billion. Five years out, in 1970, it cost $10.5 billion; ten years out, it was $24.2 billion and climbing straight up. Today the annual cost of the two federal programs approaches $400 billion.

The new system, incidentally, created a crisis for the American Academy of General Practitioners. Faced with a dwindling number of members, the academy reconstituted itself by fostering new residency programs in family medicine and changing its name to the American Academy of Family Physicians. Now even our generalists had become specialists: though capable of being family doctors in the tradition of GPs, they entered practice with several more years of training and higher income expectations.

In the 1970s it was abundantly clear that costs were out of control, but it was equally clear that some of the new therapies were creating new demands for service. End-stage renal disease provides an example. Hemodialysis meant life or death for patients suffering kidney failure, but because of the costs involved, not everyone could receive the therapy. State agencies and hospital committees were forced to decide who should be treated. Decisions were based on patient age and freedom from other disease complications: patients over fifty were excluded, as were those with diabetes or coronary artery disease. Such an exclusion was a death sentence, since a patient with severe kidney failure could die within a week if untreated. Public concern forced congressional hearings, which in turn led to legislation providing Medicare benefits to all end-stage renal patients.

Initial cost estimates, based on precedent, suggested that the program expanding services to renal patients would stabilize at $250 million per year within three years. By then, however, costs had reached $500 million and were still climbing. By the 1990s costs had reached a plateau of more than $4 billion per year. What happened?

The same thing that happened with elderly patients. With various interventions, patients lived longer and became vulnerable to other expensive-to-manage complicating diseases. In addition, more and more medical students decided to go into nephrology, a largely ignored subspecialty of internal medicine before Medicare started paying for services to kidney patients. Once the money was there, the practitioners arrived in great numbers.

It should be noted that these costs were not distressing to patients or physicians. The thirst for health care seemed unquenchable. Patients with good insurance got all the care they needed, or were told they needed, and many physicians got rich. But politicians were becoming increasingly uncomfortable, caught between the hard place of keeping voters satisfied with services and the rock of keeping them happy with lower taxes.

Unfunded mandates gave them a new way to manage the problem. For example, when the public became concerned about patients being turned away from emergency rooms because of lack of insurance, Congress passed legislation requiring hospitals to accept, and admit if necessary, all emergency patients without regard to ability to pay. Since Congress chose not to appropriate funds to cover the cost of this mandate, hospitals recaptured the costs through "cross-subsidization": charging insured and self-paying patients more.

Another cost problem that Congress refused to act on was the malpractice crisis, one of the most emotional issues with which physicians must contend. Malpractice charges strike at a physician's self-image as a competent, caring, and respected medical practitioner. I remember a surgeon from North Platte, Nebraska, who delivered a thirty-minute monologue about the one time in his life he was sued for malpractice. The patient was from out of town. The surgeon didn't want to treat someone he didn't know, but he felt that as a caregiver he had to respond. He saw the patient, offered his help, and later was sued. This had taken place several years earlier, but he couldn't get over it and considered the experience a blot on his record, a stain on his career.

Although malpractice litigation is an emotional issue for most physicians, it's an economic one for society. By the mid-1970s it was apparent that jury awards for pain and suffering were approaching lottery status, with multimillion-dollar judgments. Repeated calls for legislative relief went unanswered; the costs of professional liability insurance continued to climb, and the practice of "defensive" medicine—excessive and often unnecessary documentation—became more widespread. Today liability insurance costs more than $8 billion per year, and the costs of defensive medicine are estimated by some at more than $20 billion.

No One Wants Cost Controls, Only Free Medical Care

Various methods to gain control over costs were tried in the 1970s. Most did not work out, but one had significant and long-lasting effects: legislation to foster the growth of health maintenance organizations (HMO). Prepaid plans, such as Kaiser, had been functioning cost-effectively since 1935 in President Richard Nixon's home state of California, and they became a model for a new national initiative. The legislation required employers with twenty-five employees or more to offer an HMO plan in their benefit package if a federally qualified plan was available. Congress additionally appropriated start-up funds to encourage the development of new HMOs.

Support for the legislation came from a curious alliance of liberal Democrats and AMA lobbyists. The central question was: Which services should be mandated for federal HMO certification? Liberals thought that services should be as inclusive as possible and were surprised to find that AMA lobbyists were even more generous in support of expansive services. No friend to either liberals or prepaid HMOs, the AMA was intent on pricing HMOs out of competition, since the greater the service coverage requirement, the higher the premium cost. Recalling the campaign, a now-retired AMA lobbyist couldn't help smiling. "We confounded everyone," he said.

The strategy had a short-term payoff. Certification requirements were so high that successful plans like Kaiser didn't bother to apply for federal certification, and many of the start-up HMOs that did gain certification soon failed because they could not compete successfully with fee-for-service insurance. Requirements were later modified, but the truly lasting impact of the legislation came from the mandate to include HMOs as an insurance option. The legislative language was silent on fee-for-service insurance because it was assumed that such insurance would always exist. No one foresaw the time when employers would be able to offer only an HMO option, thereby herding all their employees into lower-cost managed care plans.

Other legislative plans to control costs in the 1970s failed completely. The professional standards review organizations (PSROs) and health systems agencies (HSAs) never caught on and were resisted in various ways by the AMA, which wanted to protect physician income from government watchdogs. The programs represented attempts to ensure the medical necessity of procedures and to rationalize the diffusion of new medical technology; they failed because they gained neither professional nor public support.

No one could see the need for such assurances. Patients liked receiving valued services virtually free of out-of-pocket charges. Physicians appreciated being able to order whatever services or interventions they deemed useful without concern for costs, since the insurers would pay without question and the charges for procedures were almost like a blank check. Hospital administrators felt like community benefactors as they scrambled to create new facilities and renovate old ones, knowing that third-party payers would cover their capitalization costs. Insurers and carriers shuffled the papers while employers and governments paid the bills. No one was willing to say no because the services were much too popular with voters and workers.

Finally, a major player issued a warning shot. Near the end of the 1970s General Motors Corporation announced that BlueCross BlueShield was a more costly supplier than U.S. Steel. News reports translated this to mean that health care was more expensive for GM than steel. That wasn't quite correct, since GM had several suppliers of steel in addition to U.S. Steel, but a point had been made. Health benefits were no longer a marginal expense for employers. They had become a substantial cost of doing business.

Concerted efforts were made in the 1980s to control costs. Scores of new insurers entered the health care market and undercut traditional insurers like BlueCross BlueShield by using employer-group ratings instead of community ratings. Employers with a preponderant number of young workers represented a much less costly risk, insurance sales reps pointed out. Why pay a community rate, which included the risks associated with older workers? It wasn't fair and it wasn't sensible, the sales reps insisted.

Thus began in the 1980s the increasingly invasive practice of "cherry-picking," which would roil the health insurance market and steadily increase the number of uninsured workers and their families. What the new insurers did not tell employers was that if any of their young workers contracted a serious illness, such as breast cancer or leukemia—which can strike younger people as well as older people—the insurers would have to increase premiums dramatically, sometimes doubling them, or drop insurance coverage altogether. Some insurers would agree to continue coverage only if the seriously ill patient was dropped from the group coverage.

The Reagan administration also employed cost-control devices. It established a new system for reimbursing hospitals. Instead of cost-based reimbursement for Medicare patients, a payment system based on the average cost for handling a given diagnosis was put into effect. Called the diagnosis related group (DRG) system, it rewarded hospitals for releasing patients sooner than average and punished them for later-than-average releases. To protect themselves, hospitals increasingly stressed outpatient procedures that were not covered by DRGs, and many began to conduct major surgeries, even mastectomies, on a same-day basis. Bewildered patients were being dumped on their unprepared families, but often that was better than staying in hospitals, where compassionate care had all but disappeared. Unmerciful DRGs had modified the quality of mercy.

The Reagan administration also froze physician fees for approximately two years, then placed them under tight controls. This came as quite a surprise to doctors who thought Reagan was a true believer in free markets, and the AMA found itself in the uncomfortable position of fighting his administration. Nonetheless, the controls did not stop the upward march of physician income. Physicians as a group are smart and typically can figure out how to game almost any system devised by regulators.

Despite these market and regulatory strategies, health care costs continued to zoom upward, usually at double or triple the rate of general inflation. Indeed, the health care cost percentage increase for 1990 was a whopping 16 percent, while general inflation was held to less than 4 percent. How could that happen? Patients, physicians, and hospital administrators had developed habits that were hard to break. The same belief system with respect to new technologies prevailed: everyone wanted more, no matter what the price, especially when it was paid for by third-party insurers.

Patients with private insurance from larger employers pressed for access to new, investigational therapies, such as the bone marrow transplant procedure for stage 4 breast cancer patients. Trials were just beginning, with promising indications for certain patients, but more and more patients were petitioning for access and lawsuits had been filed. Some insurers responded by covering the hazardous, painful, and costly procedure, which can generate expenses of $200,000 per patient. By the end of the 1990s it had been found that the treatment was no better than the standard care, which was less costly and much less hazardous and painful.

In the public sector, President Reagan's response to the concerns voiced by right-to-life groups was to insist on costly medical interventions for all newborn babies. The groups alleged that some extremely low-weight, preterm infants were being allowed to die, and that infants with extreme physical or neurological deficits were not receiving appropriate care. The president responded by instituting a "Baby Doe" telephone hot line in the mid-1980s and urging all hospital personnel to use it to report any suspected instance of wrongdoing. Once again, the AMA had to resist, this time correctly complaining of government intervention in the practice of medicine.

As a result of the hot line, all end-of-life situations, involving both the very young and the very old, began to be treated with great, and highly expensive, care. The prevailing sense of being watched reinforced the costly practice of intervening, no matter what the cost. For some neonates the cost of care exceeded $1 million. It had to be paid whenever there was hope or doubt, and many parents were left with babies with lifelong impairments. In fact, the average IQ of extremely low-birthweight babies is around 80.

This pressure led to some agonizing situations for parents, who found the process of salvaging a tiny neonate no less emotionally costly than financially so. I remember an account of a couple caught in this trap on their way to a vacation retreat. The mother went into preterm labor and delivered a low-weight infant in a teaching hospital in San Francisco. The parents were advised that the baby would die without intervention. The baby was placed on a respirator, then required surgery and intensive follow-up care. Treatment went on for weeks until it was clear that the infant's physical problems had stabilized but that there would be lifetime neurological deficits. The frantic mother finally said she would have refused intervention in the first place had she known what it would lead to.

By the end of the 1980s, despite the almost heroic attempts to control costs, they had more than doubled in one decade, from approximately $300 billion to $800 billion.

*Someone Finally Says No,
and No One Really Likes It*

A dramatic change came in the early and mid-1990s. A new breed of commercial managed care insurer entered the field. These insurers promised employers that they would hold the line on premium increases, and hold the line they did. From 1993 onward, for half a dozen years, annual insurance premium costs rose by less than 4 percent, little more than general inflation.

It was a stunning, almost unbelievable achievement. How did they do it? First, they negotiated contracts with hospitals at lower-than-average rates, promising to keep their beds filled by directing patients to their doors. Then they negotiated contracts with individual physicians at lower fees, promising to supply a steady stream of patients and warning that if the physicians didn't sign up they might lose all their patients. Finally, these insurers made patients check with them before gaining access to services; the patient would then either be directed to the insurer's own physicians and hospitals or denied the request for service on the grounds that it wasn't medically necessary. At last the system had found someone who would say no.

Employers approved. Taking advantage of the legislative language that insisted they offer an HMO option without reference to any other option, employers signed up with lower-priced managed care insurers. The competition became so intense that traditional HMOs like Kaiser complained. Insurers who were offering much less comprehensive services were underbidding Kaiser's rates.

Meanwhile, patients began complaining strenuously about HMOs. Their anger about the way they were being treated, or mistreated, was palpable, and once again the politicians began to respond. Legislation banning "drive-through deliveries," which had limited hospitalization to one day for many mothers, was passed. Legislation banning same-day mastectomies was introduced, and comprehensive legislation aimed at defining patients' rights was fiercely resisted by insurers and employers. Now the AMA found itself in the curious position of supporting government intervention in the practice of medicine, to the amazement of older, more conservative physicians. Some critics contended that the AMA actually was supporting a "physicians'" rather than a "patients'" bill of rights, and there was some merit in the charge.

At the end of the decade annual insurance premium increases began to again move up toward 10 percent. The onetime savings, flowing from the switch to managed care, had been exhausted. Strangely, even in a situation of great oversupply, hospital rates and physician fees apparently could go no lower, and patients were fighting back to gain better service. The economy was in good shape, so in effect the purchasers were declining to play hardball in the oversupplied marketplace. Reviewing current trends, the Health Care Financing Administration (HCFA), which administers Medicare and Medicaid, predicted that total health care costs would reach $2.2 trillion, representing 16.2 percent of GDP, by 2008. Other developed countries are facing similar expenditure pressures but have managed to restrain their costs to the level of about 10 percent of GDP. The rate of increase in the United Kingdom is in the range of 6 to 7 percent, but the National Health Service suffers serious service problems.

Despite explanations for higher health care costs such as the ones I've given here, patients still are stunned by the costs of fairly routine surgical procedures, such as that $9,000 or more for an appendectomy. Why is that cost so high, even considering ordinary inflation, when the same procedure, or at least the same outcome, was achieved in the late 1930s for something like $100?

The medical management of appendicitis is entirely different today. The differences begin with diagnosis, made today by a specialist in internal medicine or general surgery instead of a general practitioner. The internist takes the history, conducts the physical exam, and then orders a series of laboratory and imaging tests to confirm the diagnosis.

Then the patient is referred to a surgeon, probably a subspecialist in abdominal surgery, who admits the patient to a high-tech medical center. There blood and fluids are taken and sent to the hospital laboratory for analysis under the direction of a clinical pathologist, not only to confirm the diagnosis but also to determine and document the general health of the patient. In addition, depending on the age of the patient, a cardiologist may be consulted to assess the patient's cardiovascular status.

In the operating room another physician specialist, the anesthesiologist, induces anesthesia by administering an intravenous anesthetic. She maintains anesthesia by inhalation or intravenous agents, or by a combination of both. She may also use a muscle relaxant. A number of expensive drugs are administered, possibly in conjunction with opioid analgesics and neuroleptic drugs, which, with the muscle relaxant, form the standard combination anesthesia. The effect of these drugs on the patient is monitored continuously, again with expensive equipment to monitor body temperature, blood-oxygen ratios, carbon dioxide exhalation, and heart electrical activity.

The surgeon is assisted not only by specially trained operating room nurses but also by another surgeon or resident physician and perhaps a medical student. Instead of a large incision, the surgeon may insert small instruments and complete the appendix resection by watching a television screen to manipulate his instruments. The procedure minimizes both the surgical scar and the trauma of surgery and speeds up the healing period. It also costs more than standard surgical treatment, since it is a new, and thus higher-priced, technique.

After the operation the patient is transferred to the recovery room, where costly antibiotics may be administered intravenously and recovery is monitored by another specially trained nurse. After regaining consciousness, the patient is moved to a hospital room and remains for a day or two at $1,000 per day.

Now let's look at the expertise involved. Where there was one minimally trained (by contemporary standards) general practitioner in the 1930s, now there are five extensively trained specialists involved in a routine appendectomy. All are working with expensive, state-of-the-art drugs and equipment, and all are paying hefty professional liability insurance premiums and documenting everything they do. By contrast, the general practitioner took much greater risks but was unconcerned about malpractice, a virtually nonexistent problem before the modern era, since family doctors were rarely sued.

The introduction of specialists and the growing need for liability insurance may help explain part of the cost escalation, but what about a hospital per diem of $1,000 or more? Again, the modern hospital is vastly different from the old charitable or community hospital. Now hospitals have costly, sophisticated monitoring systems, neonatal centers that resemble space stations, isolation units to guard against infection, hemodialysis centers, cardiac care facilities, rehabilitation units, oncology centers, ophthalmology programs, and various other multidisciplinary and interdisciplinary activities led by full-time physicians and supported by a vast professional and paraprofessional staff. Hospitals also have multimillion-dollar diagnostic facilities, hospital workers pressing for living wage standards, and residency and nurse training programs that are much more costly than they were in the days of charitable care.

Furthermore, the modern hospital must function on an around-the-clock basis, with all of its services available day in and day out. Patients admitted on Friday no longer can remain in the hospital over the weekend for specialized diagnostic procedures on Monday morning. Now individual patients must undergo procedures immediately, no matter what the general cost of underutilizing equipment and expertise.

New and complex billing procedures and regulatory requirements also add to the cost of hospital care. So does the cost of cross-subsidizing uncompensated care for uninsured or indigent patients. Add to that the cost of research and development. A new bone marrow treatment, for example, generated costs of $100,000 per day in experimental cancer trials. All of these costs creep into the per diem cost. Most are legitimate and necessary. Some are not, but most have been driven by well-intended political decisions and are supported by the public and quietly applauded by providers. In addition, all the new high-tech medical activities take place in a hospital that may be half-empty, and there may be another hospital just like it down the street that is also half-empty of patients but full of expensive equipment and personnel.

No one wants to go back to the good old days of less costly, charitable medical care. The risks were too great, and the benefits of high-tech medical care are too strong. The real question revolves around how extensively this good, sophisticated, and expensive medicine should be applied. How many lab and diagnostic tests are really necessary? How much should physicians be allowed to charge, especially after new techniques become standard? What kind of barriers to high-tech interventions do we need, especially with respect to futile care? How many doctors should we train since we already have so many?

Since 1965 the number of physicians has grown four times faster than the population: 160 percent for physician growth versus 36 percent for population growth. In 1960 there were 142 physicians per 100,000 population; now there are 282. Without question, we have too many doctors. U.S. medical schools have held the number of graduates at approximately 16,000 per year, but the number of residency slots at hospitals total 24,000 per year. The additional 8,000 are filled by international medical graduates (IMGs). Indeed, 23 percent of the 800,000 physicians in this country graduated from medical schools in foreign countries. This is another political football. Many of those graduates serve in inner-city residency programs. They take the tough jobs that U.S. graduates avoid; without the IMGs, city hospitals would have difficulty caring for the poor. That does not detract from the main problem. Too many doctors will do too many things to realize their income expectations. They are wily individuals and always find ways to enhance their incomes. We need to place greater controls on the growth of physician supply.

We also need to ban health care advertising. A huge amount of money is spent on marketing in medical care. It comes from premium dollars, takes away from patient care, and is a total waste of resources. The advertisers are doing nothing more than competing for market share. They're not helping patients, and they're not helping the nation as a whole. Patients may also be harmed by drug advertising's persistent push to medicate, leading to the danger of overmedication.

Administrative costs are another waste. When I worked at the Los Angeles County–USC Medical Center, the great joke was that every year the number of inpatient beds decreased while the number of lab tests and administrators increased and the number of doctors stayed the same. When the hospital inpatient beds decreased from 1,600 to 900, the number of lab tests increased tenfold. The joke was that if we got down to ten beds, we would probably be doing ten billion lab tests per year. Then there were administrators on every floor. They said that their job was to keep costs down, but the abundant number of them reflected no more than county bureaucracy at work.

The health insurance industry represents another unnecessary administrative cost. All it does is collect money, keep as much as it can, and dole out as little as possible. It doesn't add value to anything. Insurers say they're adding leverage to control costs, but purchasers could do that much more effectively if providers grouped together and took some risk. For the same number of physicians, Canada has one billing clerk while we have seventeen.

Then, even though we don't like it, we're going to have to do something about preapproval for high-tech interventions and procedures. Preapproval for liver transplants, bone marrow transplants, even coronary artery bypass surgery is perfectly acceptable. Access to high-ticket items should not be in the hands of one patient and one physician. There should be a higher level of control, no matter who is paying the bill. This is especially true for futile care. Many billions of dollars are spent on terminal care that simply does not help the patient.

What I'm talking about is the rationing of "rescue" care. We may not like the idea, but there is no way to have a sensible and truly helpful system for delivering care to patients without rationing. We already have rationing, but in an irrational form. What we need is a rational system for rationing care.

2

The Question of Queues

Why We Have to Ration Care

A MERICA NOW HAS A PUNISHING system of rationed care, but most people don't know a thing about it, even those who are systematically abused by the system. Think of a poor, uninsured woman living in the hills of eastern Kentucky. Her chances of having early sexual contact are relatively high. So are her chances of having the kind of sexually transmitted disease that could predispose her to develop cervical cancer. She is in a high-risk category and ought to have regular Pap smears. Her chances of getting them, however, are much lower than those for people who are at much lower risk, such as a middle-class woman who may have fewer risky sexual encounters and easy access to health care that provides her with a Pap smear every other year.

If every mature or sexually active woman in this country received regular Pap smears, cervical cancer could be virtually eliminated. The tests are inexpensive, have good sensitivity and specificity, and provide an excellent opportunity to detect disease early, leading to curative or preventive treatment.

So why do we ration access to this useful preventive service? Because we can get away with it. Although it should be guided by professional standards, science, and quality, rationing in the American health care system is determined instead by politics, preference, and money.

No one likes the idea of rationing care. It seems troubling, vaguely undemocratic, even un-American. But in fact, not everything can be done for everyone. The need to ration will become even more critical as our medical technological capabilities continue to expand and our global population continues to grow at historic rates. Even a rich country like the United States cannot provide the same care for everyone all of the time. So we ration care every day, but we do it in an entirely irrational fashion.

We use many rationing methods, including:

- Controls placed on access by pricing
- Differing and arbitrary payment methods
- Variations in practice patterns
- Insufficient emphasis on disease prevention
- Language and cultural barriers
- Insufficient numbers of minority health professionals
- Lack of information about available services
- Social class membership as a deterrent
- Limited organ supply for transplantation

Of that long list of rationing methods, organ supply resonates most deeply. Everyone knows that not enough organs are available for the number of patients who need transplants. About 65,000 Americans in any recent given year are on a waiting list for an organ that could save, or prolong, their life. Each year about 4,000 die while waiting. But even with organ supply there are deceptive wheels within wheels that deny organs to some while offering organs to others.

In 1984 organ allocation was by law ceded to the United Network for Organ Sharing (UNOS), a nonprofit agency under contract with the federal government. The agency divided the country into sixty-two local areas, ranging in size from a few counties to several states, with population variations running from one million to twelve million. Donated organs were first to be offered within the region of origin. If a matching patient was not found, the organ could be offered to another region. The idea was to localize the system and have recipients gain organs from those close to home. Obviously, if a patient lived in a region with a relatively abundant supply of donor organs, that patient had a better chance of receiving a transplant.

When the Clinton administration tried to change this system in 1998 to ensure greater fairness, it encountered a political minefield. The government wanted to rationalize the rationing system by making the waiting times throughout the country more consistent and ensuring that the first choices for transplantation were the sickest patients who would benefit from the procedure. The Institute of Medicine (IOM) of the National Academy of Sciences followed up with a recommendation that the country be divided into regions of approximately nine million people per region, with organs going first to the sickest patients within each region before being offered to patients in other regions.

At the heart of the resistance to rationalization of the organ supply system was the very factor I discussed in chapter 1: money. What funding can do for organ transplantation was first demonstrated by the End-Stage Renal Disease Program enacted by Congress in 1973. The program provided Medicare coverage for anyone with kidney failure for both treatment with an artificial kidney machine and organ transplantation. The intention was to forestall certain death and thereby benefit kidney patients, but its unintended consequence was to make a lot of people wealthy.

As mentioned earlier, nephrology once was an unattractive, subspecialty of internal medicine that didn't pay very well. Suddenly it became a glamorous, high-paying subspecialty. Meanwhile, transplant surgeons, apart from some in academic centers where salaries are controlled, began earning fabulous incomes; today transplant surgeons can earn in the seven-digit range in their first year of practice after residency training. Suddenly physicians had a greater stake in the funding of transplants than in the benefits that transplants offer to patients.

Money is driving the issue of how to reorganize the transplant system. Some say the issue is keeping donated organs close to home. Others say the basic issue of fairness is at stake. Still others blame institutionalized racism for resistance to changing the system. But quality of care has little to do with the arguments over the transplant system. It's mostly about money—big money for transplant surgeons, big money for hospitals with high profit margins, and jobs for local communities.

Under a rational system we would have something like 120 transplant centers in America; instead, we have close to 300. Some might care whether an organ donated by a Wisconsin resident could save the life of someone in Georgia, or even Illinois, but the politicians hovering over the debate are more concerned about the hospital in their state that might lose a big-ticket program. They want to keep the dollars and prestige of a high-tech program within their local communities, and they want to remind voters of how they succeeded in saving St. Somewhere's transplant center at election time.

A more rational approach would take into account the benefits to patient care that come from centralized expertise. The best outcomes are derived from sending patients to centers that do large numbers of any given procedure. The doctors are better trained, the nurses more experienced, and the institution and its systems better prepared and equipped. Once we accept the concept that the sickest patient who will benefit from a transplant should be first on the waiting list, it follows that the major centers are where most transplants should take place. A regionalized system would work that way. Outcomes would improve because the major centers would do the procedures better, but they would take away a lot of business from smaller centers. That is at the heart of the battle. No one wants to lose a center. In fact, more and more smaller communities want to open their own transplant centers. Such centers waste not only dollars but lives.

One other problem associated with transplant rationing is related to the people on lists who are waiting for a second transplant. When an initial transplanted organ begins to fail, the patient understandably wants a second chance. My own belief is that they shouldn't have it, not when so many people are waiting for their first chance. When transplants work, they truly bring a person back from death's door and offer additional years, sometimes even decades, of reasonably good life. Everyone on the list should have one chance for extended life, but not two, given the shortage of donated organs. These are the kinds of tough decisions that limited resources force on the health care system.

Closing the Door by Price, Culture, and Bias

Some of the other factors affecting rationing are less ethically complex. One example is pricing, the main method for rationing care today. Access to care is impeded for people who have no health insurance at all. They don't receive timely care because they can't pay the price. They put off seeing physicians because their pockets are empty, and when the problem becomes severe, they go to emergency rooms, which by law have to take care of them.

This is overt, obvious rationing, and it goes on every day, even for people who have health insurance. Think of the people covered by managed care insurance who feel they need service. They see their physician, but their insurer says they don't need the service. Then their physician, under indirect or even direct pressure, agrees that the service isn't needed. The insurance company can put pressure on a physician by threatening to add her to its negative list, to "deselect" her, or to ensure that she earns less when she does more.

Also think of the insured person whose coverage does not include preventive services. That person may not be able to afford the full range of immunizations indicated for her child. She may also be concerned about breast cancer and want a mammogram, which also may not be covered. Her husband may want an uncovered colonoscopy. Because the family cannot afford to pay for these services out of pocket, they forgo them and hope for the best. Price rationing, even when insurance is available, remains a reality.

Cultural barriers that result in rationing may not be as deliberate as rationing by price, but they are just as real. Many Korean Americans in southern California may not receive good information about what is wrong with them because their family members intercede. The family makes the decision about what to do, not the individual patient.

Language erects another barrier, particularly in southern California, where so many have emigrated from Vietnam, Cambodia, Thailand, Korea, Taiwan, and Mexico. By law and practice, hospitals do the best they can, making sure that interpreters are available, but even with interpreters, physicians are often not quite sure they are getting the right story from their patients. That problem is compounded when the patient is an undocumented worker, with no insurance and substantial fears about detection and deportation.

The cultural bias against African Americans is particularly distressing. Studies have shown that, even when blacks have insurance under Medicare, significantly fewer procedures are performed on them. The studies document that fewer procedures, fewer diagnostic tests, and fewer therapies are performed on black Medicare beneficiaries than on white Medicare beneficiaries under exactly the same presenting circumstances, whether it be cancer, heart disease, diabetes, or stroke. This is as true in Minnesota as it is in Mississippi.

In a 1991 *JAMA* editorial I asserted that our health care system is guilty of institutionalized racism. The people involved don't even know it's going on. They don't recognize it, even in the VA system, which should have been influenced by the example of the fully integrated uniformed services. Both *JAMA* and the *New England Journal of Medicine* have published studies that show that in any part of the United States blacks receive fewer services than whites, for the same diseases. That's rationing by prejudice.

As a young man in Alabama, where segregation was the law of the state until the civil rights era, I saw white physicians use a different set of criteria for treating white and black patients. That was in the 1950s, during an entirely different cultural moment in U.S. history. I did not recognize racial bias during my years in the military, and I was astonished when I saw these studies of bias in the late 1980s and early 1990s. I thought we had moved beyond institutionalized racism, but obviously we haven't.

Rationing also results from variations in practice patterns. This was first noted by John Wennberg, the Dartmouth University physician-researcher, some twenty-five years ago in a study published in *Science*. He examined two locations, both with gold-standard teaching medical centers, one in New Haven, Connecticut, and the other in Boston, Massachusetts. He found that patients admitted with the same disease, the same symptoms, the same insurance, and the same resources available to help them were treated very differently at the two locations. It was an amazing disclosure. We had all assumed that medical care at our best institutions would be comparable. Instead, it was strikingly different. Even more astonishing now is that, after twenty-five years, these radical discrepancies haven't ended.

What this means for patients is that locale may have more to do with treatment than the nature of the illness. Whether a patient will have a hysterectomy is determined less by the indicating symptoms than by where she lives. The practice styles in Boise, Idaho, can be different from those in Casper, Wyoming, and those in Provo, Utah, differ from what a patient will find in Grand Junction, Colorado. These differences, rather than good science, can determine the nature and quality of treatment. Location also remains a problem for low-income patients. In the poor areas of East Los Angeles, for example, there is one doctor for perhaps every 3,500 residents, while in affluent Beverly Hills there is more like one doctor for every 150 residents.

A potential benefit of managed care is that practice patterns could be normalized to resolve the location problem. Using good data, managed care plans can determine what ought to be done in given situations, and then get it done. Good managed care plans, like Kaiser Permanente, Puget Sound, and Harvard Pilgrim, have done this. They have demonstrated a great ability to ration care rationally by using proper guidelines.

Another form of rationing comes from a systemic bias that favors treatment of disease rather than prevention. It's hard to show a return on investment, the thinking goes. For example, very few health plans pay for prevention of tobacco addiction for adolescents. It's a number-one strategy for preventing disease, as everyone knows, but the plans don't cover it because adolescent tobacco addiction is a pediatric disease that doesn't have an impact for thirty to forty years. Health plan administrators think, *They'll be long gone from my plan by then. Why pay for that?*

In fact, very few preventive measures save money. They are helpful when they prevent the targeted disease, but they obviously don't hold down expenses when the patient comes down with another disease. Instead, prevention measures are aimed at maintaining a good quality of life, making lives more productive, and increasing longevity. The dramatic exception is the Pap smear, which saves money and lives.

Another curious form of rationing is related to social class membership. One would think that people at the upper end of the class spectrum would never suffer rationing of care, since they have the money and status to command care. But in fact, status can work against receiving needed care. In the 1960s the U.S. Navy opened a program in Long Beach called Dry Dock Number One. It was aimed at helping drunken sailors and marines. Joe Zuska directed the program and invited me to participate. Once a month, for almost ten years, I went down to give my standard lecture on alcohol abuse and addiction, usually to fifty to one hundred inpatients undergoing intensive therapy to prevent continued drinking in a self-destructive way.

During most of my ten years the inpatients were enlisted people only. The navy insisted that officers did not have alcohol problems. Finally we began seeing officers, and at last we even had a flag officer, an admiral of the navy, who entered the same rehabilitation program with grunt marines and swabbies. He was just a human being like everyone else in the program, one who happened to have a problem with alcohol. There are executives in offices across this country who suffer untreated, addictive disease. Their positions block them from undergoing useful therapy. No one will confront them, and they fail to see their problem because they appear to be functioning normally—everyone still says yes to them. They are members of SOFA—the Society of Functioning Alcoholics.

The most commanding evidence of rationing relates to the 45 million people in the United States who are uninsured. Most receive care in hospital emergency rooms when their symptoms become severe, but they do not have access to preventive services and ordinary care, which clearly promote good health. This is unique to our country among Western industrialized states. We are the only country that has decided to exclude a substantial percentage of our people from access to standard care. Make no mistake about it—by saving money on the uninsured, we gain money for those who are insured. This is the nightmare envisioned by the British epidemiologist-physician Archie Cochrane fifty years ago. As a society, we are investing massively in the search for elusive "cures" for the few at the expense of widespread care for the many when they suffer from everyday illness and discomfort. And this is happening, as we shall see, to not only the uninsured but also insured patients in managed care and other plans.

Why the Clinton Plan Failed

In 1993 the Clinton administration tried to change the system that had excluded so many with a comprehensive proposal that was doomed from the start. Why was it doomed? First, the proposal made an assumption that was unacceptable to the American public: that all Americans should have the same health care—equal access for all, and a single level for all. That was a complete misreading of the American psyche, and it killed the Clinton plan the day it was made public.

Americans have never had a single level of health care, and given our cultural beliefs, there is no particular reason to suppose that we ever should have a single level of care. We do not have a single level of transportation, a single level of apparel, or a single level of housing. The idea that we should shoehorn everyone into exactly the same level of health care was absurd from the start. If there had been nothing else wrong with the proposal, that alone would have killed it. In the United States it is unthinkable that people cannot buy, with their own money, whatever they want.

The Clinton plan also missed the point that what the United States needed was minimum comprehensive, basic health care insurance for all. We didn't need to change the whole system. Even when polls showed that people thought the system should be changed, they also showed that most people were satisfied with their own care. Despite grumblings about managed care, most people covered by such plans found their care acceptable. Not acceptable was the idea that government would come in and change everything to take care of the needy.

Another serious problem was related to the plan's development. The entire process missed critical feedback because Hillary Rodham Clinton was in charge. She was able, smart, and committed, but she was immune to criticism at the time because she was the wife of the president of the United States. She was deprived of the earned criticism that most of us get—and even welcome, because it helps us refine our thinking. Her co-director, Ira Magaziner, was another mistake. He already was known for taking on complicated problems and coming up with very complicated solutions that were either rejected or implemented and then rejected.

Finally, the Clinton strategists didn't move fast enough. They came in with a mandate for change, a majority in Congress, a moral imperative, and substantial support in the physician community. If they had resurrected the Nixon plan of the early 1970s, which included an employer mandate, and put it on the table, it could have passed.

Some say it would cost $100 billion to cover the uninsured, but that is precisely the amount of money the government now gives away to subsidize employment-based insurance. The government's decision to treat health benefits as a tax-exempt cost of doing business opened the door to huge subsidies for people within the system but closed the door on subsidies for people outside the system. Individuals who want to purchase insurance on their own can do so, but they get no tax write-off or tax consideration at all.

The government also subsidizes care for the elderly, disabled, and indigent through Medicare and Medicaid to the tune of $400 billion. Almost half of total U.S. outlays for health care are covered by tax dollars, including federal, state, county, and local taxes. Perversely, excluding a large number of people from health insurance coverage is built into the system that should have covered everyone.

But the subsidies for medical education and physician training have had an even greater adverse impact on the delivery of health care services in the United States. Under the old voluntary system, physicians were professionally obligated not only to care for the poor but also to participate in the teaching and training of physicians. It was an obligation as old as the Hippocratic oath, and the new government programs obviated it by paying for services that used to be volunteered.

James Todd, former executive vice president of the AMA, described the change some years ago in conversation. Before Medicaid, every physician at his hospital in northern New Jersey was expected to devote a number of hours per week to service in the hospital's free clinic. After enactment of Medicaid, he noticed that no one was showing up for clinic duties, and he asked a colleague about it. "We don't have to do that anymore," the colleague said. "Medicaid takes care of it." Of course, since an increasing number of Medicaid dollars went for care of the elderly in nursing homes, little was left for ordinary care for the poor.

Teaching responsibilities also were eased as more and more full-time positions were opened at teaching hospitals, constricting voluntary participation by practicing physicians. The new system compartmentalized medicine by removing from practicing physicians their historic professional responsibilities. Furthermore, it was paying them more to devote all of their time to practice within a totally insured environment. They had neither time nor incentive to care for the poor or to participate in education.

Another systemic problem relates to the mandate that employers offer managed care insurance without also offering competing fee-for-service plans. That mandate allowed employers to herd employees into managed care, where fee constraints and other restrictions have reduced the ability of physicians and hospitals to cross-subsidize for care of the poor. They can no longer bill insured patients higher fees and rates to free up time and facilities for indigent care.

But what really drove people out of insurance coverage was the "cherry-picking" of insurers, described in chapter 1. As lower-rated small groups developed problems—that is, when one beneficiary developed a disease that was expensive to manage—they were dropped from coverage. We began to see this in 1987, when studies registered some 30 million people without insurance. Three years later the number had grown to 33 million; now it is 45 million and likely to grow more.

The AMA's Failed Battle
to Preserve Professionalism

The threat to professionalism through government controls was articulated by Edward Annis in the early 1960s. He conducted a fiery campaign, worthy of Morris Fishbein, against enactment of Medicare and Medicaid. A general practitioner from Miami, Annis was a skilled debater, having honed his talents on high school and college debating teams. He also was an effective advocate for the voluntary system and its historic sense of obligation to care for the poor without charge. The AMA appointed him to its hastily formed speakers' bureau and named him chairman of the bureau when he was scheduled to debate national health insurance for the elderly with Senator Hubert Humphrey of Minnesota on television. The NBC producers said they couldn't ask Senator Humphrey to debate a nobody, Annis recalled. Thus, he became chairman of a bureau that had never met and included only himself.

His successful debate with Humphrey led to his most famous appearance on behalf of the AMA. It followed a speech by President John Kennedy in support of what became Medicare, delivered to an audience of 20,000 senior citizens in New York's Madison Square Garden on May 20, 1962. Organized by the National Council of Senior Citizens and the AFL-CIO, the rally was supposed to garner support for Medicare and was televised by the three major networks.

The AMA arranged to rent the hall immediately after the rally and had Annis deliver a rebuttal speech to an arena empty of people but littered with abandoned banners and balloons. The speech was recorded by an AMA crew and the association paid to have it televised on NBC the following evening. Annis warned that doctors probably would earn more money, not less, under Medicare. He also asserted, "This bill would put the government smack into your hospital, defining services, setting standards, establishing committees, calling for reports, deciding who gets in and who gets out, what they get and what they don't, even getting into the teaching of medicine, and all the time imposing a federally administered financial budget on our houses of mercy and healing."

The speech had a dramatic effect. When the legislation was voted on two months later, it was defeated 52 to 48. Delegates to the AMA House of Delegates were so grateful that one month later they elected Annis president of the association in a landslide vote. This was unprecedented because that office usually is occupied by a physician who has gone through all the chairs in organized medicine, including AMA delegate and member of the board of trustees. Annis had done none of that, and he was at least twenty years younger than the typical AMA president. He remains a controversial figure who is either blamed for or credited with delaying Medicare enactment for three years.

But the campaign against Medicare was a disaster for the AMA. It alienated the public, the academic medical community, and many practicing physicians. Although the association made a strong point about the runaway costs that would result from the entitlement to care, the point was lost in the perception that the AMA was pursuing only its own self-interest. Virtually everyone thought the AMA was entering the political battle simply to protect the pocketbooks of doctors. Talk of professional standards, charitable care, and the like made no impact on critics. It was all about money.

This was why the AMA entered the debate on the Clinton plan with extreme caution. The association did not want to be tarred and feathered again. It was tired of being viewed as an enemy of patients in need. It was also riven by internal dissension. Many AMA staffers were sympathetic to the Clinton proposal, some were deeply opposed, and others thought the plan was all right but didn't offer enough to physicians. These divisions virtually paralyzed the AMA throughout most of 1993, when the plan was being formulated behind closed doors. But by the end of the year the AMA had taken an action that effectively undermined any further support for the Clinton plan and gave political cover to conservative members of Congress on both sides of the aisle.

Everyone acknowledged the problem of the uninsured in the United States. The AMA had been watching their numbers grow for several years, and in 1989 the House of Delegates took the unprecedented action of endorsing an employer mandate—requiring employers to offer health insurance to their employees. For the first time the AMA was inviting the government into medicine, breaking a historic commitment to the voluntary system. But then, as would happen so often during the 1990s, it changed its mind.

The AMA followed up its 1989 endorsement of the employer mandate with the development of a program, Health Access America, to ensure universal access to health care coverage. Despite these remarkable changes in AMA thinking and policy, they were greeted by and large with public indifference or skepticism.

On a parallel course, the editorial board and staff of *JAMA* in 1990 independently voted to devote significant portions of *JAMA* and all nine AMA specialty journals to the subject of "Caring for the Uninsured and Underinsured." The many articles appeared in

May 1991, when it was clear that the worsening crisis of access extended far beyond the poor. Corporate downsizing and factory closings were placing more and more mainstream Americans at risk, as a result either of losing employment-based insurance or of gaining much less comprehensive insurance with a new employer. Some were left with no hope of gaining insurance because they had preexisting conditions and so were excluded from their new employer's group health insurance coverage. Taking these new realities into account, my *JAMA* editorial was titled: "National Health Care Reform: An Aura of Inevitability Is upon Us."

We announced the large collection of articles, with their many recommendations, in a press conference at Washington's National Press Club on May 14, 1991. In presenting the information, I repeated my editorial comment that

> it is no longer acceptable morally, ethically, or economically for so many of our people to be medically uninsured or seriously underinsured. We can solve this problem. We have the resources, the skills, the time, and the moral prescience. We need only clear-cut objectives and proper organization of our resources. Have we now the national will and leadership?

Our call for reform received extensive broadcast and newspaper coverage. It made the front pages of many newspapers, including the *Washington Post,* and the reporter Spencer Rich later told me that the story would have run "above the fold" if I had been speaking for the AMA. That was a question addressed at the press conference and in follow-up interviews. Reporters wanted to know whether I was speaking for the association. I explained that I was speaking as the editor of *JAMA,* an editorially independent publication of the AMA. In any event, it was now a political story, and it put the AMA, as publisher, in the middle of a fierce political fight.

AMA Executive Vice President Todd and other AMA staff learned just how fierce the battle was when they met with White House Chief of Staff John Sununu shortly after the headlines appeared. The AMA officials who were there to discuss some of the more technical problems affecting Medicare were caught off guard when Sununu began a rant about health care reform. Portly, short, and often breezy, Sununu was famous for his vituperative, sometimes scatological attacks on perceived enemies. "That's their issue," he shouted at Todd, referring to the Democratic Party's long-standing identification with health care and health care reform. "Stop stirring the pot," he warned, making the message clear by gesture and implication: if the AMA wanted its little technical difficulties addressed, it would have to keep its mouth shut about the big health care picture.

Sununu ran variations on this theme for several minutes, until Lee Stillwell, head of the AMA's Washington office, interrupted. A tough political operative, Stillwell had been press secretary for Republican Senator Bill Armstrong of Colorado for ten years and was in the running for the position of Bush White House press secretary before signing on with the AMA. He was used to political bullying and knew how to deflect it, or at least deal with it. It was the editor of *JAMA* stirring the pot, he said, not the leaders of the AMA. Stillwell in no way wished to alienate the Bush administration, since many issues involving Medicare regulations and reimbursements were in its hands, but he did point out that health care reform now was part of AMA policy.

Sununu may have been mollified, but he was not appeased. At that moment President Bush was set for a smooth sail into a second term. He enjoyed a 90 percent public approval rating following his brilliant management of international resistance to Iraq's invasion of Kuwait, and the last thing he wanted was a contentious, difficult, no-win debate on health care reform. His constituents were not interested. They wanted tax relief, especially on income derived from capital gains. Furthermore, they wanted freedom from government regulations, especially those that might adversely affect small businesses and insurance companies.

But the issue would not go away. It was brought home again by a special election in Pennsylvania in 1991, following the untimely death of Republican Senator John Heinz. The seat was filled temporarily by a Democratic appointee, Harris Wofford, an academic who had never been elected to public office. The Bush administration wanted the seat back, and Republican Attorney General Richard Thornburgh was handpicked to run. Thornburgh was a high-profile statesman with solid political credentials and wide name recognition in his home state.

Everyone expected a Thornburgh landslide, but Wofford came up with an unexpected strategy. Making health care reform the linchpin of his campaign, he traveled the state and repeated a simple question: If a convict is guaranteed access to health care services, why isn't a law-abiding citizen? The question resonated with voters, many of whom had been downsized or were concerned about "job lock," losing their health insurance if they changed jobs. That had become another issue in health care: many workers with preexisting conditions found that they couldn't get coverage in their new employer's group plan. The uncertainties about health insurance propelled Wofford into an upset victory and alerted the nation to the power of the issue.

Events quickly unfolded. Sununu left the White House, and the Bush administration packaged a plan for health care reform. Proposed were tax credits to help the poor purchase insurance, tax deductions to the middle class to pay for insurance, and large purchasing pools to help small businessmen buy affordable insurance. No mandates or sweeping changes were proposed for the traditional voluntary system.

One year after the confrontation between Sununu and the AMA in the White House, I was able to write of reform, "The Aura of Inevitability Intensifies," in the May 13, 1992, issue of *JAMA*. Five events had brought reform to the forefront of the national agenda: the recession of the early 1990s caused many politically active voters without adequate health insurance to join ranks with the politically impotent poor; the economic and tragic devastation of AIDS exposed the problem of underinsurance; physician support for reform removed political cover for members of Congress who had blamed doctors for blocking reform; the end of the cold war promised to mitigate our long-term preoccupation with expensive defense programs; and Harris Wofford was elected in Pennsylvania.

"The complex nature of reform is much better understood now than it was a year ago by the public, the profession, and the politicians," I wrote. "But national health care reform correctly has been called the most complicated issue to face U.S. policy makers since the Great Depression."

As the November 1992 election drew near, health care reform became the second most important concern among voters, immediately after the economy. On September 9, the AMA joined the American Association of Retired Persons (AARP) and the AFL-CIO in a call for a national debate on the issue, sending letters to both President Bush and Governor Clinton and holding a press conference to announce their action. Joining such a coalition was an unusual move for the AMA, which had quarreled with the seniors group and organized labor in the past over health policy, and it reflected the more progressive thinking of Executive Vice President Todd.

Although the three organizations did not agree on any specific proposal, the forum almost implicitly favored Clinton, who by then had published the outline of a determined effort to reform the health care system. Asked by reporters at an informal dinner meeting to name the candidate he thought was more serious about reform, Todd said, "Clinton." It was a classic Washington gaffe: a public figure was only publicly stating the obvious, but Todd's response exposed the AMA to the fierce political environment now surrounding health care reform. The following day the Bush White House warned that it would close its doors to the AMA if Todd didn't release a retraction. Todd complied, but his follow-up statement only gave the original statement another day's news cycle.

How the AMA Pulled the Plug on Health Care Reform

Clinton's November victory seemed to validate the serious need for health care reform, and by December the major stakeholders were offering positive assessments of the general outlines of Clinton's plan. The Health Insurance Association of America (HIAA), and the National Federation of Independent Businesses (NFIB), natural enemies of reform, indicated support for many of the Clinton concepts. The Health Care Leadership, representing insurers, pharmaceutical companies, and some hospitals, signaled its openness to the search for a consensus on reform. At that point no one wanted to be on the "wrong" side of reform. Political viability depended on a posture of reasonableness.

People were polite when Mrs. Clinton made speeches, and few questioned the apparent altruism of her motives. Moreover, no one questioned the need for an employer mandate, which was the crucial mechanism for gaining universal coverage. Democrats and Republicans alike voiced support for the mandate. And Mrs. Clinton's designated chief architect of the plan, Ira Magaziner, was treated with attentive respect.

For a moment it seemed that reform would prevail. On May 19, 1993, in our third annual *JAMA* issue devoted to health care reform, my editorial was titled "The Aura of Inevitability Becomes Incarnate." In the concluding paragraph I wrote:

> We stand at the threshold of reform. We shall soon see whether this administration and the Congress will confront the abyss of a widely divided electorate, spook at the potential political calamity that awaits, and rear up and retreat in disarray, allowing meltdown to loom ever closer. Or will the political leadership grasp a vision of our future, charge firmly and steadfastly ahead to bridge the abyss with eyes wide open in the interests of patients, the public, and the nation, placing narrow political vistas and rigid ideologies behind them, and plan and act strategically in all our best interests?

What I did not fully appreciate at that moment was that the largest health insurers had determined already that "health reform," which would rely on managed competition, would either be dead on arrival or open an entirely new market for them. These insurers, including Aetna, CIGNA, Prudential, and others, moved aggressively into the new market model of managed care. They forcefully entered markets, aggressively selling managed care to employers as the answer to cost containment. They recruited physicians, offering below-market fees with the promise of a steady stream of patients and warning of lost patients should they refuse to sign on. Insurers took similar contracts to hospitals and created interlaced provider networks at below-market costs.

Their assessment that the Clinton plan might be dead on arrival was correct. It was going nowhere because Mrs. Clinton and Magaziner deliberately kept politicians out of the process. Four prominent Democratic members of Congress had demonstrated their commitment to health care reform. In the Senate, Edward Kennedy of Massachusetts had been working on behalf of universal coverage since the early 1970s. His colleague John D. Rockefeller IV of West Virginia had taken over the Pepper Commission in the late 1980s and refined the concept of "play or pay," which would ensure coverage by urging employers to provide insurance or pay an excess payroll tax. In the House, Henry Waxman of southern California had been working for years to expand Medicaid coverage to children and low-income mothers. His colleague Fortney "Pete" Stark of northern California was an outspoken advocate of a single-payer system based on Medicare. A cantankerous and wealthy former banker, Stark, as chairman of the health subcommittee of the House Ways and Means Committee, had a deep and keen understanding of the intricacies of Medicare and was convinced that it could be extended to the entire population without risk. Medicare was tested, accepted, and manageable, he said.

Despite their commitment to reform, none of these leading legislators were included in the shaping of the Clinton plan. Nor were the major stakeholders—physicians, hospitals, and insurers. Magaziner wanted policy purity, but he would pay a steep price for this exclusion when the plan was ready for release. Since neither the key legislators nor the key providers had any stake in the plan, none of these parties could give it their blessing from the beginning.

With the 200-page draft ready for congressional review and input, Magaziner took the unprecedented step of making it available for review only in the West Wing of the White House. I was asked, as an independent observer, to review the plan. I did and found some elements that I liked and some that I criticized. At that point Magaziner did not want the plan released publicly until after review and revision; he realistically feared that copies sent to the Hill would almost immediately find their way into the hands of reporters and be picked apart in the press. This was the capping insult for Congressman Stark, who complained that it was demeaning to ask members of Congress to travel across town to view a document. Under fire from a potential friend like Stark, Magaziner had to relent. Copies were sent to the Hill, and almost immediately every health policy reporter in town had a copy as well.

The AMA also reviewed the draft and within days sent an analysis to every physician in the country, AMA member or not. The AMA analysis was also sent to reporters and received widely divergent comment. The *Los Angeles Times* reported that the AMA was generally supportive. The *Washington Post* said the AMA seemed to be here, there, and everywhere in assessing the plan, and according to the *New York Times,* the AMA was opposed to central elements of the proposal. All the stories were correct, and any apparent contradictions between them only exposed the internal dissension within the AMA.

If the AMA was paralyzed by the draft proposal, the NFIB was activated by it. The federation began a grassroots campaign against the central feature of the plan, the employer mandate. It contacted small businesspeople in key conservative states and urged them to tell their doctors to force the AMA to rescind its policy supporting the mandate. Accordingly, physician delegates from Texas, Louisiana, and New Jersey led the attack on the employer mandate at the AMA interim meeting in New Orleans in December 1993.

The rancorous debate was covered by the national press. Into the midst of it stepped Edward Annis, the old foe of Medicare and past president of the AMA for thirty years. He asked the delegates to rectify the mistake they had made four years before when they supported an employer mandate. The AMA chairman, Lonnie Bristow, forcefully defended the existing policy and asked delegates to retain it so that the AMA would have a viable place at the bargaining table when legislative language was written. Despite his eloquence, the House of Delegates voted to rescind the employer mandate policy.

Their action removed political cover for the key element of reform, and soon after every conservative member of Congress backed away from the mandate, perhaps with a sigh of relief. Then the HIAA organized a focused, expensive public attack on the Clinton plan, featuring its "Harry and Louise" television commercials. What was inherent in the Clinton plan now was being made explicit: our health care system handled different populations differently, and an enormously complicated system would have to be crafted to achieve complete equality. The ads suggested that those who had good coverage would see it degraded. They also suggested that those with at least some coverage had something better than anything government could devise. Finally, the ads implicitly suggested that those without coverage were safe to ignore.

"Scoring" Reform in JAMA

As the plan moved to Congress in 1994, it was met by several alternative plans introduced by members of Congress from both sides of the aisle. In its May 17, 1994, issue, *JAMA* graded all nine against a grid of eleven elements essential to reform. The elements were posed as a series of questions:

- Does it provide access to all for basic care?
- Does it produce cost control?
- Does it promote quality?
- Does it reduce administrative hassles?
- Does it promote prevention?
- Does it encourage primary care?

- Does it consider long-term care?
- Does it retain patient autonomy?
- Does it retain physician autonomy?
- Does it limit professional liability?
- Does it have staying power?

The proposal introduced by Stark won the highest score, 72 out of a possible 99. The Clinton plan scored 70, while the current system scored 55 and the Republican minority leadership plan scored 47. The lowest score, 38, was awarded to the plan of Republican Senator Phil Gramm of Texas, who went on national television to attack my rationing system. Publication of the grid once again stirred the ire of the AMA Washington office, which was trying to work out a compromise along the lines of the alternative proposal put forth by Sterns and Nickles (which scored 49). They thought my grid undermined their lobbying efforts.

The central element in the Stark proposal was a call for a Medicare Part C program to cover Medicaid beneficiaries, the uninsured, and firms with less than one hundred employees. As the year wore on, Stark took his proposal to the AMA leadership, seeking an endorsement. This was a rare event. In the 1980s Stark was highly critical of the AMA, asserting at one point that he was the only one standing between physicians and their attack on the U.S. Treasury. He also called AMA leaders "troglodytes" in public and something less printable in private. The AMA retaliated in 1986 by pumping $250,000 into an independent expenditure campaign on behalf of his bewildered challenger. Of course, Stark used the AMA's support for his rival to his own advantage and was handily reelected.

Relations between Stark and the AMA began to change in 1990, when James Todd became the executive vice president. Todd was a conciliator who thought it unwise to have a sour relationship with a member of Congress so closely associated with Medicare. He requested a meeting, and soon the two were on friendly talking terms. Both Stark and Todd were quick-witted, and both were committed to a program that treated patients, physicians, and other providers fairly under Medicare. They struck a deal on the implementation of a new payment system, and when Medicare threatened to undermine the deal, Stark and Todd fought side by side to right the program—and succeeded.

In meeting with the AMA leadership, Stark pledged his support for a fair Medicare system in exchange for the AMA's support for his plan, which some could view as a first step toward a single-payer system based on Medicare. Stark also suggested that working with him would be preferable to letting the commercial managed care companies take over the system, as their aggressive marketing tactics suggested they would. He said that doctors would get a better deal from him than they would from the managed care companies. Looking back, a lot of doctors would now agree.

Although Todd might have been tempted, he knew he could not take that deal to the AMA House of Delegates, especially in the wake of the employer mandate defeat. Meanwhile, the fractious AMA staff continued to battle. One side was led by John Crosby, head of health policy in the Chicago headquarters. The other was led by Lee Stillwell, head of the Washington office. Both were senior vice presidents, and both were former staffers for members of Congress, Crosby for Democratic Representative Richard Gephardt of Missouri, and Stillwell for Republican Senator Bill Armstrong. Both were determined advocates for their disparate visions of the AMA's goal. For Crosby, it was to promote the betterment of public health; for Stillwell, it was to promote AMA member interests.

Crosby was persuasive and persistent. He refused to believe that the AMA had backed away from its commitment to universal coverage, despite the vote against the employer mandate. He directed his shop to develop a plan that would encourage individual responsibility for coverage and carefully sold it to the board of trustees.

Stillwell smelled defeat in the Democratic proposals and urged AMA leadership to rekindle its ties to traditional allies in the Republican Party. He argued that after the collapse of health care reform, the AMA would have to go back to its main business of protecting physician interests in Medicare, and it would need its old friends on the Ways and Means and Energy and Commerce Committees.

The conflict between the two reached a climax during the final days of congressional debate on health care reform in the summer of 1994. Without consulting Stillwell (routinely done when Chicago officials planned Washington events), Crosby arranged another joint press conference for the AMA, AARP, and AFL-CIO in Washington to call for congressional action on health care reform. Once again the organizations did not specify which proposal to adopt, but their joint press conference was perceived by conservative newspaper columnists, especially Paul Gigot of the *Wall Street Journal,* as an AMA sellout to organized labor and Clinton. Republicans took a similar view, and the event marked the beginning of the end for Todd's progressive AMA leadership. It also marked the beginning of the end of Crosby's tenure at the AMA.

Todd was now persona non grata with Republicans, a status that became extremely meaningful after their triumph at the polls in November 1994. For the first time in forty years the Democrats were the minority party in the House of Representatives. Many blamed their defeat on the health care reform loss. The Democrats simply couldn't get the job done when, for the first time in a dozen years, they had controlled not only both houses of Congress but also the White House. And the job they wanted to get done seemed to impose complicated new government regulations that would be more harmful than beneficial.

Misguided Reform: Let the Patient Beware

In 1995 the number of uninsured Americans increased to 40 million. No one seemed to notice. The debate had shifted to incremental reform, much of it aimed at improving coverage for those who already had insurance. Legislation was passed to ban the insurance practice of excluding applicants with preexisting conditions. Legislation also was passed to mandate better coverage for mental health services. In the first case, insurers agreed to accept applicants with preexisting conditions, but at three or four times the normal premium. In the second, many employers dropped mental health coverage completely instead of enhancing coverage. The insurance companies, it seemed, were far more adaptable than the legislators. And every year the number of those without health insurance continued to increase, at about one million per year, to the more than 45 million Americans in 2000. The way to make money in the insurance business is to limit risk whenever possible.

In the May 17, 1995, *JAMA* issue on health care reform, I could no longer refer to an aura of inevitability. Instead, I had to write "Caveat Aeger—Let the Patient Beware." In my editorial I wrote: "Powerful economic incentives are transforming the profession of medicine into a business more than ever before, and there remain massive governmental regulatory factors as well, micromanaging every aspect of a physician's professional life." I added that physicians "must demand that professionalism means self-governance, self-determination, and self-policing, and then do it in good faith, inside or outside government or corporations, especially in managed care environments."

Finally, I warned that "if someday physicians and their organizations do become primarily self-interest groups, society—which has given them the privilege of being called professionals—will rise up and take that privilege away."

What we need is a reformed medical system for delivering care in a rationally rationed fashion. To do this, physicians must behave like professionals, not like entrepreneurs. The organ transplant problem that we began with could provide one model for a rational system. As I said earlier, the best outcomes come from centers with highly trained surgeons and support personnel. In 1989, when Thomas Starzl and his teams dominated the field of liver transplants, the University of Pittsburgh, where he practiced, performed 441 operations. Ten years later, following the opening of scores of competing liver transplant centers, Pittsburgh performed only 160 transplants. The other hospitals wanted a crack at the $250,000 price for the procedure as well as the enhanced prestige that goes with becoming a high-tech center. And transplant surgeons trained at large centers wanted a chance to run their own center, no matter how small.

That approach to medicine represents a tragic and insupportable misuse of resources. The physicians involved in opening marginal centers are not serving local communities, as they would argue. They are serving themselves, and indeed, they are putting their patients at risk because they are operating in centers that do not have sufficient volume to ensure a high level of expertise. Physicians should take the lead in supporting programs to rationalize high-tech medicine.

They should also consider following the lead of the state of Oregon, which has developed a rational system for rationing care for Medicaid patients. The state developed a long list of medical interventions, based on cost and efficacy. The more useful and effective the intervention, the more likely it is to be included. Pediatric immunizations score extremely well under the program, while cosmetic procedures score badly. The list itself is highly ethical, but the program is immoral because it applies only to the Medicaid population.

If we could succeed in determining what should be covered by insurance, I am convinced that we could reshape the entire health delivery system for the benefit of all. We can do it handily if we have the courage to pay only for care that really works. Coverage decisions provide the real key to health care reform.

3

The Coverage Circus

Why What You Need
Is Not Always What You Get

S OME YEARS AGO A PATIENT named Cynthia Herdrich of Urbana, Illinois, was forced to wait eight days for an ultrasound examination. Her health plan made the decision after her doctor examined her for abdominal pain. During the wait her appendix burst, and she underwent more complicated, extensive, and potentially risky surgery for peritonitis. Subsequently she filed suit against the health plan.

Inga Petrovich had to wait one year for an MRI when her health plan denied her physician's initial request. The delayed test revealed cancer at the base of her tongue, a cancer that eventually resulted in her death. Donna Marie McIlwaine of Scottsville, New York, was denied a proper diagnostic workup by her plan when her doctor examined her for chest pain and shortness of breath. She died within a week from pneumonia and a blood clot in her left lung—clearly treatable conditions.

Of course, in each of these cases the patient could have offered to pay for the test herself, or the physician or institution could have done the procedure without insurance company approval. However, patients typically don't pay for services out of pocket, and physicians and institutions typically don't move without insurance approval.

And that is precisely what is wrong with the current health care system. Insurance coverage decisions should be made by the medical profession and by a fully informed public. The profession should be responsible for restraining the overuse of expensive medical services, and proven preventive measures should be available without question. The profession and the public should be involved in establishing reasonable health care budgets and living within them in a regionally organized system. Instead, all of these decisions are being made by employers, insurers, managed care companies, and government officials.

How did this happen? It's a long story, very like the one about the development of health insurance. Like that story, it also is filled with good intentions and bad results. One of the worst results is that medical services and procedures tend to follow insurance coverage. That is, procedures covered by insurance generally are performed, while procedures not covered by insurance tend not to be performed, or at least not frequently.

That practice is at the core of the many problems that so many people are having with health care today. The massive number of insurance restraints on coverage now in place are rigorously enforced. Only a few years ago the doors to medical care seemed to be wide open. Now more and more of them seem to be closed, and almost every day we see another newspaper story about a disaster flowing from insurance denials of medical care. Even when UnitedHealth Group announced that it would no longer routinely require preauthorization for most physician orders, physician autonomy was not restored in any clear-cut fashion. We are beginning to understand, in an entirely new way, that health insurance does not always ensure access to needed services.

Of the more than 280 million people in the United States, all but 44 million are covered by some form of health insurance. Of the insured, approximately 39 million are covered by Medicare, 35 million by Medicaid, and the remainder by some form of employment-based insurance. But more than 30 million people who have insurance are seriously and significantly underinsured. They do not have the kind of comprehensive, in-depth coverage that studies have shown results in more timely medical care and better outcomes. Stated another way, the statistics indicate that only a minority of our population is covered by adequate, employment-based insurance.

People with comprehensive insurance are more likely to get what they need when they need it, and they are more likely to recover safely and quickly from medical interventions. By contrast, the uninsured and underinsured may delay seeing the doctor because they have either no insurance or a high deductible. They also may arrive sicker than those with good coverage, and they may experience more difficult and troublesome recoveries from medical treatments. Furthermore, they may bankrupt themselves if their lifetime insurance limits are too low.

But comprehensive insurance, such as that offered by traditional fee-for-service insurers, is hard to find today. In 1988, 71 percent of workers and families were covered by fee-for-service plans. That figure dropped to 49 percent in 1993, had plummeted to 30 percent by 1995, and continues to fall. The vast majority of those with insurance now are enrolled in some type of managed care plan.

Furthermore, more than 50 million people with managed care insurance are in plans that are not regulated by state insurance departments because they are preempted by federal law. Enacted in 1974, the Employee Retirement and Income Security Act (ERISA) was designed to protect pension plans, but employers who decided to self-insure also gained freedom from state insurance regulators under the act. Large multisite employers complained that their health benefits programs were uneven and difficult to manage because of variations in state regulations.

ERISA was supposed to ensure consistency, but what it really ensured was a free hand for employers and a significant loss of control over health decisions by employees. The latter soon discovered that they lived in a netherworld in which the rules were made, and changed at will, by their employers. This is a different kind of underinsurance because the limits of coverage are not spelled out in the insurance policy. Instead, they are determined by faceless administrators making decisions from remote locations about individual patients' medical needs.

Predictably, horror stories such as those at the beginning of this chapter emerged from this kind of insurance coverage and began working their way through the courts. Patients and physicians now seem caught in a new system of health insurance coverage that neither group likes. Both are keenly aware that insurance itself does not guarantee good patient care. What the patient wants and what the doctor thinks often no longer seem to matter, and resolution of this problem promises to be the focus of an intense political debate as the new Congress and new administration take office in the new millennium.

What they will discover as they dig into the issues of coverage is the deeper issue at the core of medicine: Is it a business, a profession, or some sort of ongoing mixture of both? Which set of values will guide decisionmaking about the coverage of medical services?

When Coverage Was Determined by Two Parties

The question was unimaginable when I entered medicine in the 1950s. Although health insurance had been around in this country for a couple of decades, decisionmaking in medical care hadn't changed much from the time of Hippocrates. Delivery of medical care was a private matter between the patient and physician. Indeed, no other professional, then or now, asks his client to disrobe and to respond to deeply personal questions. Patients have always complied because they trust their doctors and they want information or treatments that will make them well. In the past this private transaction was settled, often right down to payment for services, between the doctor and patient.

There were obligations attached to being a physician; these were overseen by organized medicine and controlled at the local level by county medical societies. To gain hospital privileges, a

physician had to be a member in good standing in the county society. That was the gateway not only to hospital privileges, crucial to
a practicing physician's career, but also to membership in the state
medical society and the American Medical Association.

Members of the county society were expected to participate
in hospital teaching programs and to devote another portion of
their time to clinical care for the poor. They also were expected to
follow professional ethical guidelines, which among other things
proscribed fee gouging, kickbacks for referrals to other physicians,
and solicitation of patients through advertising. To violate an ethical guideline was to risk expulsion from the society, and expulsion
could close down a physician's practice. It was a guild system in the
strictest sense of the term. Organized medicine set the terms for
practice, policed and disciplined its ranks, and allowed them to
compete on a relatively even playing field.

The system hadn't changed much in the 1950s from the early
1930s, before the widespread appearance of health insurance. The
obligations of the profession still were fairly well understood by the
public. The former AMA president Edward Annis explained them
once with a story about his early days in practice in Florida in the
1940s. He was called aside by a wealthy businessman who was a
member of his church congregation. The businessman told Annis he
was charging too little (two dollars for a visit, the norm at that time)
to his family and other well-off members of the congregation. He
also had heard that Annis wasn't charging poor people at all for his
services; the businessman told Annis that he had to start charging the
wealthier members of the community more in order to stay in practice. That was a well-known and highly accepted form of cross-
subsidization, involving only patients and physicians.

But that system had been challenged as early as 1932 by some
who expressed concerns about handling the medical needs of patients in this way. In that year the Committee on the Cost of Medical Care was independently founded and chaired by Ray Lyman
Wilbur, a past president of the AMA who became the president of
Stanford University. Among the committee's recommendations

was a call for group practice and voluntary health insurance programs. The *JAMA* editor Morris Fishbein quickly responded with
an editorial. As noted in the previous chapter, he called the committee report an incitement to revolution and to socialism and
communism, setting the tone of resistance of organized medicine
to any proposal to change the traditional, professional practice for
the delivery of medical care.

Despite Fishbein's rhetoric, the move toward voluntary insurance was inexorable. The costs of hospitalization were exceeding
ordinary patient ability to pay and local philanthropy to cover, even
though costs were relatively low. Back then the percentage of gross
domestic product spent for health care was in the range of 4 percent, compared with nearly 14 percent today. Something had to be
done, and from that conviction came Blue Cross insurance, which
quickly spread across the country in the 1930s.

The coverage was carefully designed, based on perceived
truths. First, there would be no "first dollar" coverage; instead, there
would be a deductible, which theoretically would discourage hospital admittance for care that was not deemed absolutely necessary
by the patient. Then there would be a co-payment, usually 20 percent of the charges, to encourage patients to leave the hospital as
soon as possible. Some physicians said that the co-payment provision speeded up the mending process: postoperative patients concerned about the daily mounting costs of their care, they said, truly
recovered more quickly than patients who were unconcerned
about costs.

By 1939 Blue Shield had been formed, essentially to cover the
costs of care provided by hospital-practicing physicians. Their fees
tended to be higher than those of family doctors, and it seemed
logical to cover them, since their services were delivered to already
insured patients who clearly required hospital care. Again, deductibles and co-payments were part of the package.

These insurance practices did not appear to threaten the traditional patient-physician relationship. Although some early plans
experimented with coverage for home and office visits, most soon

adopted policies of indemnity payments for physician services provided only in hospitals. Typically not covered were services performed by office-based primary care physicians. Also not covered were various diagnostic, laboratory, or screening tests, unless they were conducted in the hospital in conjunction with an acute illness or injury. Nor were the costs of prescription drugs covered, unless administered in the hospital.

There was a feeling that coverage should be extended only to almost catastrophic situations; the fear was that comprehensive coverage would lead to overutilization and abuse. The sizable population of the "worried well" might run up endless costs if preventive services were covered, even though such services could establish a baseline for a patient's health and possibly uncover a "silent" disease. People who wanted periodic examinations and were sufficiently concerned about their health should see their doctors and pay for professional advice out of pocket, the thinking went. People who did not want periodic examinations were assumed to be healthy and not in need of insurance coverage.

This concept of insurance coverage was challenged by prepaid group practice plans. They offered comprehensive coverage with few or only nominal financial bars to service. In fact, the whole idea of prepaid group coverage was to open the door to preventive services and make them more available to people who were ostensibly well. The point was to monitor a patient's health through periodic checkups and routine screens and to catch problems in an early stage, when treatment would be less expensive and outcomes would be better. Prescription drugs were covered, often dispensed from the plan's own dispensaries at little or no cost to patients. Furthermore, prepaid plans did most of their tests on an outpatient basis, saving the costs of hospitalization, which fee-for-service insurance required and more and more doctors were ordering so that their patients didn't have to pay for tests out of pocket.

A kind of idealism infected the physicians who joined the early prepaid plans, such as Ross-Loos and Kaiser Permanente in California and the Group Health Cooperative of Puget Sound in

Washington State in the 1930s and 1940s. They were on a mission to keep people healthy, and they enjoyed working within a large, multispecialty group, which facilitated consultations among physicians. One could walk down a hall, knock on a door, and talk to another physician about a difficult or puzzling patient problem. A camaraderie developed among physicians who were working together to keep their patients healthy.

They would need idealism to sustain them, for they were shunned by their colleagues in organized medicine, led by a very conservative AMA. Physicians were dropped from the membership rolls of the county society when they signed on with Kaiser or Puget Sound, and thus excluded from the AMA and deprived of hospital privileges in the community. The plans were able to survive because they built their own clinics and hospitals. They also survived because they worked in California, Oregon, and Washington, states that were open to innovation. A third reason they survived was that the name Kaiser was not a name that could in any way be attached to socialistic ideas.

A Private Builder of a Socialized System

Henry J. Kaiser was a colossus. He built dams, like the Grand Coulee on the Columbia River in eastern Washington. He built battleships and destroyers in the shipyards of Los Angeles, San Francisco, and Portland. Then he built automobiles, like the first American compact car, the Henry J., as well as the more luxurious Kaiser-Frazer sedan. He developed a high-end hotel complex in Honolulu, the core of what has become the Hawaii Hilton. He was the very model of an American capitalist, an entrepreneur extraordinaire.

Idealism had nothing to do with the formation of his prepaid plan. It began by necessity. He was moving scores of workers and families to the remote Grand Coulee site in the mid-1930s and saw that he had to include access to medical care as part of his support facilities. For advice, he turned to Sidney Garfield, a physician who had organized a medical staff and portable hospitals for the workers who built the Los Angeles aqueduct through the remote desert country of southern California. Garfield did the same for Kaiser's project, financing the program with voluntary, prepaid insurance and insisting that patients receive "red carpet" rather than "back-door" care.

Patients liked it, and they continued to like it when Garfield organized a similar program for shipyard workers. By 1945 more than 100,000 subscribers were enrolled. When the shipyards shut down after the war, many of the workers stayed in the Bay Area, and soon they were clamoring for continuation of the Kaiser plan in Oakland and San Francisco.

In response—and here he might have been idealistic, or at least proud of his accomplishment—Kaiser organized a three-pronged system for the plan. The Kaiser Foundation Health Plan enrolled members and administered the plan; the Kaiser Foundation Hospitals built and operated inpatient and outpatient facilities; and the Permanente Medical Group was an independent physician group that contracted with the Health Plan to offer medical services to subscribers. By keeping medical decisionmaking in the hands of physicians, the plans were protected from attacks by organized medicine. Owning their own hospitals further protected the plans.

The Group Health Association of Washington, D.C., had neither of those protections. Formed by employees of the Federal Home Loan Bank in 1937, Group Health did not own hospital facilities and did not insulate physician decisionmaking. Its governing board included layman consumers. The AMA called it a form of "unlicensed, unregulated health insurance, and the corporate practice of medicine." Then the AMA began a campaign, with the Medical Society of the District of Columbia, to deny hospital privileges to physicians participating in the plan, thereby cutting off hospital care for the plan's patients.

When the Justice Department responded by indicting the AMA for violations of antitrust law, Fishbein vowed that the AMA would pursue a legal effort to "establish the ultimate right of organized medicine to use its discipline to oppose types of contract practice damaging to the health of the public." A federal district court ruled in the AMA's favor, accepting the association's argument that medicine was a profession, not a trade, and therefore not subject to antitrust laws. Then an appellate court reversed the decision, ruling in favor of the Justice Department, and that decision was upheld by the Supreme Court in 1943.

By then it didn't matter. The AMA had worked on the problem at the state level. With the help of state medical societies, the association lobbied for laws barring prepayment plans that were not run by physicians. That effectively shut down the movement except on the West Coast, where doctors were running the medical plans. Physicians in the rest of the country showed little interest in forming prepaid group practice plans, with or without layman support.

At the time Fishbein was attacked as a reactionary, but looking back, he begins to sound something like a prophet. He thought it would be bad for patients if treatment decisions were made by corporate administrators, and he was essentially right. He thought that physicians should discipline physicians, not administrators looking at the bottom line, and he was right again. What he failed to appreciate was the unique nature of plans like Kaiser, in which physicians were in charge of medical decisions affecting the care of the plan's subscribers. He also failed to appreciate a new sentiment that would take hold in the United States. The idea that physicians should be responsible for "charity" care for the poor was falling out of fashion. There was too much noblesse oblige in the proposition, as well as too much paternalism and authoritarianism, critics said. They wanted an egalitarian system in which all patients were treated in the same manner.

The sentiment was given expression in 1965 with the passage of Medicare and Medicaid, the programs offering coverage for the elderly and the indigent, respectively. Coverage for Medicare was built along the model of traditional fee-for-service insurance, with deductibles, co-payments, and no coverage for outpatient prescription drugs or periodic checkups and preventive screens. The ever-attentive insurance industry discerned the public mood about coverage and offered Medigap policies aimed at filling these gaps and essentially offering "first dollar" coverage for care. Medicare beneficiaries who purchased the supplemental insurance would have the same comprehensive benefits enjoyed by subscribers to prepaid plans.

Soon it was apparent that everyone wanted comparable coverage, and more and more workers pressed their employers to expand coverage. They wanted immunizations, well-baby care, periodic office visits, and screens covered by fee-for-service insurance. This time there was scant opposition from physicians or the AMA. Office-based doctors had long noticed that there was little resistance to fee increases charged by their hospital-based brethren, presumably because patients did not have to cover the fees with out-of-pocket payments.

In fact, a curious pricing practice developed among surgeons. When most set their fees as high as they possibly could, that became the base fee under the "customary and reasonable" method for setting fees used by Blue Shield. Although surgeons were barred by law from fixing fees, they informally knew what the going rate was. When new surgeons entered the community, they learned what the prevailing fees were for given procedures, and then they set their fees at a higher level. Adam Smith might have predicted that a newcomer to a community would set lower fees in order to attract patients, but medicine was beyond supply-and-demand market rules. When new surgeons set higher fees, they not only got away with it but also drove up the prevailing fees for all surgeons.

By contrast, primary care physicians had encountered real resistance to fee increases, and they correctly perceived that it would recede with insurance coverage. However, the primary care physicians—allegedly the thinkers rather than the doers in medicine—either never were able to play the surgeons' game successfully or decided not to play it as relentlessly, and their fees did not catch up with those for surgeons and other technical interventionists.

Next in line for coverage were pharmaceutical companies, which silently welcomed it for outpatient drugs, which were covered by private insurance for workers and by Medigap for Medicare beneficiaries. Once payments were made by third-party payers, resistance to price increases diminished. Of course, prescription drugs for Medicare outpatients are still not covered, as of press time, unless the patient has supplemental insurance.

Price Escalation Assured by Coverage

Before these coverage expansions took hold, the costs of fee-for-service insurance and prepaid plan insurance were essentially the same. Once the expansions were firmly in place, the costs of fee-for-service insurance began to skyrocket. Medical procedures were following coverage, but in two entirely different systems. The difference was defined by incentives.

Prepaid plans lived within a closed system. Hospital facilities, outpatient clinics, and physician services were paid for in advance, creating an incentive to work with existing resources. In sharp contrast, fee-for-service insurance operated within an open-ended system. It would retrospectively pay for whatever was done. Furthermore, it allowed hospitals to include the costs of capitalization in their charges. The point was to support hospital modernization and development of new facilities. All this was done with goodwill. The fee-for-service insurers, the vast majority of whom were nonprofit Blue Cross and Blue Shield plans, hoped to promote better care for patients. No one foresaw what an open-ended system for covering comprehensive care would lead to.

The incentives created difficult ethical dilemmas. Here's one obvious example. A surgeon covered by fee-for-service insurance is confronted with a patient in the middle of the night who has abdominal pain. After an examination, the question for the surgeon is whether to operate. Somewhere in the back of the surgeon's mind is the understanding that if he does operate he will be paid, and if he does not operate he will not be paid. Either consciously or subconsciously, there was always a bias to intervene in fee-for-service medicine.

The same surgeon in a traditional prepaid plan knows that no matter what he does, his income is not involved. He is paid in the same fashion come what may, so he might decide to wait until morning and consult with other physicians about the patient's condition, or he might decide that an immediate operation is necessary. Either way, his income is not affected.

The fee-for-service incentives for hospitals created an explosion of new services, technologies, and programs, some of them questionable. I saw this firsthand at the University of California at Davis in the 1970s, when there was a huge growth in costly intensive-care unit (ICU) beds. The personnel and equipment needed for ICUs is many times more expensive than for regular hospital beds, yet more and more patients were being placed in ICUs. Money was pouring into the hospital, and of course it was being used to cross-subsidize some of the costs of research and teaching and most of the costs of charity care that the state of California did not cover. In fact, the benefits of ICU care then were only marginally greater than regular care in a number of conditions, according to many studies, but with everything paid for by insurance it was worth working for marginally better care, and for greater income to support the hospital's various programs.

The coverage incentives had a similar impact on pharmaceutical companies. Drugs moved from being a small part of the health care picture to the major role they play today. Now more than $90 billion is spent each year on drugs, a cost that has been doubling each decade since widespread coverage began. A private enterprise marvel of research, investment, and marketing, these companies provide a world model for product success. They conduct good research, plow the results of that research back into products, and then market the products to physicians and patients with stunning effectiveness. The fact that some of the new products are only slightly better, or no better at all, than their predecessors seems not to matter. The companies' marketing techniques are remarkably persuasive, even though sometimes questionable, as we will see in chapter 5.

Still, an amazing array of chemicals developed by the companies have allowed patients to control their blood pressure, cholesterol, diabetes, heart disease, cancer, and clinical depression, among many other diseases. Other substances have allowed women to control their reproductive cycle, and men to deal with erectile dysfunction. The companies have made revolutionary contributions to the quality of life and care for patients, and they have made lots and lots of money in the process.

The success of pharmaceutical companies underscores just what can happen when abundant resources are made available in the health care system. The major new advances in technology came from teaching and research medical centers, which were reimbursed by the open-ended fee-for-service insurance system. Stanford, Baylor, Johns Hopkins, Memorial Sloan-Kettering, Harvard, and Yale, among many others, led the way in new organ transplant techniques, open-heart surgery, ocular disease management, and cancer and stroke treatment. They were involved in the advancement of the art and science of medicine. By contrast, prepaid plan institutions were involved in practicing status-quo medicine and were much less focused on advancing medical science.

Impressive as the advances achieved at major medical centers might have been, they always came with huge costs and unpredictable outcomes. The problem is that many new technologies are based on uncertain science. All too often good clinical trials are not conducted before a new technique is almost universally used and coverage is forced. A fairly recent example illustrates the problem. In 1979 Gabriel Hortobagyi tried using bone marrow transplant technology in the treatment of metastatic breast cancer. The procedure was dangerous, debilitating, and expensive. Between 15 and 20 percent of the patients died from the drugs used in the procedure. Many others had permanent injuries, including heart damage and hearing loss. And the procedure cost upward of $200,000.

The initial remission rates exceeded 50 percent, and patients clamored for coverage, which was quickly though reluctantly granted; within a decade the number of procedures conducted increased tenfold, from 271 to 2,853. The cumulative number approached 16,000 in the late 1990s before it was acknowledged that the procedure had demonstrated little or no improvement over standard chemotherapy, which was far less costly. Even Hortobagyi conceded that his early work was overly optimistic. His results were based on a selection of younger, relatively healthier patients. They survived in greater numbers, he acknowledged, because they were healthier to begin with.

The procedure should have been subjected to controlled clinical trials, with patients randomly assigned to either standard therapy or bone marrow transplant therapy before widespread use began. Neither patients nor doctors really like that approach. Even if a new technology offers only the slightest chance of remission, patients facing death will reach for it, and doctors, highly motivated to try desperate procedures in hopes of saving a life, always will try something new. That's what they were trained for. We are also culturally biased to see a dying patient's valiant struggle to survive as heroic—the so-called rule of rescue. Newspapers offer accounts of heroic patients fighting terminal illnesses who refuse to participate in clinical trials and instead choose an experimental procedure that is unproven and has been put through little or no testing. I would suggest that the real heroes are those who consent to participate in clinical trials that may benefit not only themselves but also many others in society from that day forward. And frankly, patients in clinical trials generally receive better care than patients who are not in clinical trials.

Early Efforts to Control Coverage

Government officials became concerned about the costs of comprehensive coverage as early as 1970 and took a series of actions aimed at constraining the resources used for medical care. First came legislation that established professional standards review organizations (PSROs), whose purpose was to oversee and limit hospitalization for Medicare and Medicaid patients. Two years later came legislation that created health systems agencies (HSAs), which were to rationalize and slow the diffusion of new medical technologies.

In 1973 Congress passed legislation requiring employers to offer an HMO insurance option. (Prepaid plans now were called health maintenance organizations to underscore their commitment to preventive care.) The next year saw the enactment of ERISA, which freed employers from state insurance regulations and allowed them to set their own coverage standards if they decided to self-insure.

Then in 1975 the Federal Trade Commission (FTC) filed and pursued a complaint against the AMA and organized medicine, charging them with anticompetitive practices. The FTC wanted the AMA to abandon its restrictions against advertising, and it wanted organized medicine to abandon its practice of requiring county medical society membership in order to qualify for hospital privileges. Both practices were restricting trade and artificially increasing costs, the FTC asserted; the agency pursued that position through federal courts and finally won five years later with a 4–4 split decision by the Supreme Court.

Despite the policymaking intentions of this legislation and what was perceived as urgent need, none of these actions succeeded in restraining the rapidly escalating costs of medical care and health insurance, which continued to inflate in double-digit percentages each year. The PSROs may have reduced hospital lengths of stay, but they couldn't restrain the swift diffusion of new technologies. Nor could the HSAs. They were easily sidelined by patients and physicians, who convinced planning boards that a "rationally" planned distribution of new technologies could endanger patients. Seriously sick patients shouldn't be moved from one hospital to another for an MRI. Equipment should be placed where patients needed it, and the market rather than central planners should resolve the question of where that would be. No one was willing to acknowledge that there was no "market" for medical care covered by the kind of insurance that had evolved.

Similarly, the HMO legislation did little to convince health insurance beneficiaries to leave traditional fee-for-service insurance coverage. Most were comfortable with the old system, which allowed them complete freedom of choice among primary care and specialist physicians. It also allowed them to travel to whatever hospital they wished to enter for specialized care. And for most of the 1970s the cost of fee-for-service coverage was only slightly higher than the cost for HMO coverage.

Employers that self-insured generally retained standard coverage for their employees. What they escaped were conflicting state mandates, often won by powerful lobbying organizations representing paraprofessional practitioners. What they gained was consistent coverage for employees at their multistate employment sites.

By the early 1980s there was a general consensus that government regulations had failed and that only market forces would exert cost discipline in medical care coverage. When the market took over, with competing insurance companies "cherry-picking" insurance risks, more and more people lost insurance coverage, but costs nonetheless continued to rise. At the decade's end some 33 million people were without health insurance, but double-digit cost inflation marched on.

Something else was needed: someone willing to say no. Insurers were paying the charges, and employers were paying for the insurance, but neither party had effective control over coverage decisions. Almost without exception, whatever the patient needed or the physician ordered was covered. Patients liked it because they got their periodic checkups, received their screens, and had access to the newest technologies when they needed them. Physicians liked the system because it paid them well, provided them with excellent technical support, and gave them opportunities to explore new treatment methodologies. Neither had any incentive for saying no.

By the early 1990s commercial insurance companies had devised a strategy for saying no and constraining costs. The first step was to develop managed care networks of providers. Physicians were offered a steady stream of patients for signing on, but they had to accept below-market fees and abide by the strict contractual rules of the managed care plan. They had to gain preauthorization for patients they thought needed hospitalization or costly high-tech interventions. They had to admit patients to hospitals within the plan's network, and they had to comply with the plan's antidisparagement policies, which included not talking to patients about services the plan did not cover, even though the services might be helpful. That was the contract—take it or leave it.

Faced with those terms, the logical move was to discuss the contract with colleagues at the county medical society. That, of course, was proscribed. It was against the law for physicians to take any kind of collective action. As independent business practitioners, they could not "conspire" in any way to restrain trade. Despite the disagreeable aspects of the contracts, most physicians signed on, fearing a loss of patients if they refused. That is how physicians fundamentally lost their autonomy.

Patients lost choice because the HMO law required employers only to offer the managed care option. When the law was passed, it was inconceivable that fee-for-service would not remain the dominant insurance option. In the new environment, with commercial managed care plans aggressively soliciting employers, more than 60 percent chose a single managed care plan, often the least costly, for their employees. Those employers who included a fee-for-service option did so only with a defined contribution. They paid only so much of the premium for a given plan, and the employee had to make up the difference. This tilted the field toward managed care, since only older workers retained the fee-for-service option, increasing the insurance risk and the premium. With typical savings of between twenty and forty dollars per month by opting for managed care, many younger, healthier workers signed on.

Employers offering coverage through self-insurance often used insurance carriers to administer their plans, using the same restrictive networks and methods to constrain coverage. Their coverage decisions were protected by the ERISA law. Patient-employees could not sue for arbitrary denials of coverage or care. In a famous case involving a Houston employee whose lifetime benefits were slashed after he was diagnosed as HIV positive, the court ruled in favor of the employer. The ERISA law explicitly exempted employers from suits. In this environment, in which employers through their insurers could say no both to patients and physicians, insurance costs stabilized during most of the 1990s, with annual increases receding from double-digit to low single-digit numbers.

The New Coverage That No One Likes

What emerged from all this is the current managed care competition system, which is strikingly different from what was envisioned when the HMO law was passed in 1973. Although all managed care plans tend to be called HMOs, there is a fundamental difference between plans structured like Kaiser and managed care networks such as those formed by Aetna, Cigna, and other commercial insurers. In fact, there are a number of different ways to structure managed care plans. There are preferred provider organizations (PPOs), which establish pricing deals with hospitals and physicians, independent practice associations (IPAs), which historically were established by county and state medical societies, and staff model and mixed model plans, which rely on a core group of salaried physicians.

But the difference that defines all of these plans is whether they are nonprofit or for-profit. The ones organized to make money stand in sharp contrast to the more traditional nonprofit entities. Because they exist to serve their shareholders and investors, for-profit plans are punished on Wall Street when they fail. For example, a colleague recently pointed out that when Cigna reported disappointing earnings results, its stock price quickly dropped. But a publicly announced survey that gave Cigna low marks for the quality of care it offered didn't disturb its stock price at all.

An even more striking example comes from the recent experience of Aetna, which transformed itself from a large property and casualty insurance company, with some traditional health indemnity insurance, into the third-largest health insurance company in the United States. The transformation was managed by Richard L. Huber, a former banker who saw a way to hold down costs, gain new policyholders, and make more money. In 1996 he purchased U.S. Healthcare at a market high of $8.8 billion. Then he sold Aetna's old property and casualty business at a market low of $4 billion. In 1998 he bought NYLcare, and the following year Prudential Health Insurance of America, this time at the bargain price of one-third of the $3 billion initially sought when Prudential first put itself on the market.

With its many acquisitions, Aetna had managed to capture 21 million policyholders, one-third of them in HMOs and the rest divided into PPOs and traditional insurance. In addition, Aetna had some 700,000 Medicare beneficiaries. That was where the big money was supposed to be, and Wall Street investors were enchanted. By May 1999 they had bid the per-share price of Aetna stock up to $99.25.

However, even before the surge in its stock price, Aetna's high hopes were sagging. For one thing, the Medicare strategy never worked out. It was based on the fact that Medicare reimbursement levels were determined by region. In some areas of Florida, for example, reimbursement levels were set at a much higher rate than those in areas of Minnesota and North Dakota. With more money flowing into those regions, Aetna and other commercial insurers could afford to expand benefits, such as inclusion of outpatient drugs, and still make big money by clamping down on physician fees and hospital charges.

It was supposed to be a bonanza, but Health Care Financing Administration officials and members of Congress noticed. They decided the government was paying too much in some regions and scaled back reimbursements. Aetna responded by pulling out of some regions, cutting back on benefits, and petitioning for restoration of higher reimbursements.

Other things went wrong as well. Huber's battles with doctors were making nasty headlines around the country. He publicly denounced trial lawyers and called a California woman who won a $116 million punitive damage award from Aetna a "weeping widow." Through his various acquisitions, he had doubled revenues and positioned the company near the top, but he also seemed to attract litigation and negative press. Even the AMA joined the fray, charging Aetna with anticompetitive practices in the state of Texas.

Investors became restless. By February 2000, they had driven Aetna's stock price from its high of $99.25 to a new low of $38.50. One week later Huber resigned under pressure, and William H. Donaldson took over. Donaldson had been a member of Aetna's board of directors since 1977 and presumably had applauded all of Huber's high-wire moves, but as a former chairman of the New York Stock Exchange, he was perceived as a stabilizing influence. The stock price edged upward.

Then something entirely new developed. A Dutch financial company and a California managed care company announced a $10 billion bid to take over Aetna. ING Group NV, the Dutch firm, wanted to acquire Aetna's financial services unit, which marketed annuities, mutual funds, and pension products, and its international unit, which had regrouped Aetna's insurance assets in Latin America and Asia. The estimated worth of the units was $6.6 billion.

WellPoint Health Networks, the California company, wanted Aetna's health insurance business, with an estimated worth of between $4.6 billion and $5.8 billion. A market-respected firm, WellPoint already had purchased California Blue Cross, the health units of Massachusetts Mutual and John Hancock, and other health units in Texas and Chicago. The market response to Aetna's suitors was robust. Within days the stock jumped to $55. Within a month Aetna fought back, announcing its plan to split the company into separate health care and financial services companies, each with its own stock. So began the drama of Aetna, Inc.: Was the market value of its stock $56, $70, or $100? Meanwhile, the discredited Huber was given a $3.4 million severance package from Aetna.

It was a remarkable story of what had become of health insurance plans in the wake of growing commercial control. We ran an article in *JAMA* that divided managed care into the Dr. Jekyll plans and the Mr. Hyde plans, and the authors found that most nonprofits were on the Dr. Jekyll (good) side and for-profits were on the Mr. Hyde (not-so-good) side.

In fact, the Kaiser plan in California suffered losses in the mid-1990s resulting from the price competition of commercial plans, many of which, by limiting patient access to services, were able to offer their insurance at a lower cost. Kaiser complained and distanced itself from fellow members of the American Association of Health Plans (AAHP), formerly the Group Health Association of America (not to be confused with Group Health Cooperative of Puget Sound, or Group Health Association of Washington, D.C.). Kaiser supported more rigorous patient protections, which were anathema to the commercial insurers. The latter insisted that rules and regulations protecting patients would only add to the costs of health insurance, further burdening small employers and eroding health insurance coverage as the smaller employers simply dropped it.

The obvious problem with commercial managed care networks is that they lack an organizing principle other than financing. They manage profits, not care. Unlike the traditional nonprofit prepaid plans, in which medical services are organized and offered through a tight-knit group of multispecialty physicians, the commercial plans are organized by remote medical directors. They often base treatment decisions on abstract data and rely on technicians and usually nurses at the end of an 800 telephone line and "gatekeeper" primary care physicians to hold the line on coverage for specialized services.

Employee-patients who selected or were herded into the new commercial plans were quickly appalled by what they found, as scores of news reports have documented. Many were unable to continue taking their children to a trusted pediatrician when their employer changed plans or their plan dropped the doctor from its network. Then they discovered that they couldn't go directly to a specialist for a skin, ear, eye, or back problem. They had to go through the "gatekeeper" first, and they soon learned that physician service incentives had been reversed. Under fee-for-service insurance, physicians were rewarded for intervening. Under managed care, physicians were rewarded for not intervening.

The noninterventions rewarded under managed care, often in the form of a bonus, were prescribing fewer drugs, ordering fewer X-rays and lab tests, and making fewer referrals to specialists. In effect, gatekeeper physicians, as well as specialists, were getting kickbacks for constraining the use of resources. The traditional Kaiser physician, by contrast, was neither punished nor rewarded as a result of his decisions about the use of resources in providing care; his income was the same either way.

In practice, commercial managed care plans all too often prolonged the patient's illness or discomfort as the gatekeeper struggled to resolve the problem before doing the needed tests or making the requisite referral. Patients felt they were being hassled into forgoing what had long been identified as quality care by responsive, attentive physicians. In 1998 the movie *As Good as It Gets* made that point: when in one scene a mother complains about the HMO practices that inhibit care for her asthmatic son, spontaneous audience applause burst out in theaters all over the country, to the surprise and chagrin of the managed care industry. It was an unexpected, popular plebiscite.

Physicians also were deeply distressed by commercial managed care. They hated having their professional recommendations second-guessed by remote technicians at the end of an 800 telephone number. They resented the hours devoted to new paperwork requirements as well as the time spent on the phone. They despised being treated like small businesspeople instead of professionals, and many were appalled to see medical services hawked from ads on the sides of city buses.

As noted in chapter 2, the Clinton health care reform proposal failed in 1994 for a number of reasons—among them, it seemed too complicated and it also seemed to threaten that government would dominate health care. The Health Insurance Association of America made much of the latter point in its "Harry and Louise" television ads, which warned, "The government may force us to pick from a few health plans designed by government bureaucrats."

For a moment in the mid-1990s there seemed to be a consensus that government was not the answer but the problem. That idea energized the new Republican majority in the House and Senate, who took their seats in January 1995. What the country wanted, they said, was less government, lower taxes, and a chance to spend more of their money on the things of their choice.

Those ideas motivated Greg Ganske, a plastic surgeon from Iowa, to challenge Neal Smith, a Democrat who had held the congressional seat since 1958. Ganske toured the district in a 1958 vintage automobile, telling voters that Smith was as out of touch with contemporary life as the car he was driving. Yet despite his sympathy for smaller government, Ganske soon would be fighting for new government rules and regulations, in defiance of his party's leadership, to protect patients' coverage rights within the new managed care environment.

The Government Practice of Medicine

Almost universal discontent was being voiced by patients who had selected managed care plans or been herded into them by their employers. Particularly distressing was how these plans handled childbirth. Plans were zipping mothers in and out of hospitals for same-day deliveries, which were quickly labeled "drive-through" deliveries by newspaper reporters. The practice seemed barbaric, and there were reports of complications discovered at home that required readmittance of mother, infant, or sometimes both. Congress responded in 1996 by passing legislation requiring hospitalization of forty-eight hours for most births.

Patients also complained about the insurance practice of excluding patients with preexisting conditions from coverage. This either deprived patients of coverage outright or created "job lock": employees being forced to remain with their current employers because they feared loss of insurance coverage if they changed jobs and joined a new group. In 1996 Congress passed the Health Insurance Protection and Portability Act (HIPPA), which mandated coverage but did not address the question of premium rates. Insurers responded by offering coverage for those with preexisting conditions—but at premium rates two or three times the normal rate.

Limits on coverage for mental illness, a chronic problem, also became a focus of concern; Congress passed a measure as an amendment to HIPPA requiring parity. Insurers would have to cover services for mental health patients in the same way they covered patients with physical ailments. Typically, mental health care limits were a fraction of those for physical illnesses, in many cases limiting a mental health patient to one hospital stay while allowing diabetic or heart disease patients multiple hospital admissions. The law included an amendment, however, that effectively undermined the parity requirement. If parity inclusion increased a company's insurance costs by more than 1 percent, the law would not apply. That low threshold allowed most companies to ignore the law. Others simply dropped mental health coverage altogether.

Also under congressional debate was the practice of ushering breast cancer patients in and out of hospitals in one day for mastectomies, and lifetime insurance limits. Legislation was introduced banning same-day mastectomies, and testimony was heard in the summer of 1998 on lifetime limits. Among those who appeared was the actor Christopher Reeve, who suffered severely debilitating injuries following a fall from a horse. Paralyzed from the neck down, Reeve told members of Congress that his life could have ended had he not been able to personally pay for his own care after his lifetime insurance limit was exceeded.

The biggest congressional battle centered on legislation designed to protect patients and physicians from a number of abuses practiced by managed care companies. The centerpiece of the proposal crafted by the Democrats in 1999 was the right to sue managed care plans if their medical decisions resulted in the denial of care. This proposal was fiercely resisted by the Republican leadership, health insurers, and employers. It was fiercely supported not only by Democrats but also by Ganske, Charles Norwood, a dentist from Georgia, and a substantial number of other Republicans who crossed party lines to vote in favor of the Democratic proposal in the House.

Also supporting the legislation and every other federal intervention into medical care practice cited in this chapter was the American Medical Association. It was a remarkable role reversal for the AMA, which had long allied itself with Republicans, insurers, and businesspeople in the battle against government intrusion into medicine. Historically the AMA opposed most initiatives by John Dingell, a Democratic congressman from Michigan with a long record of support for a government-based insurance system. On the day of the winning House vote on the patients' bill of rights, two AMA officials stood side by side with Dingell on the steps of the Capitol in celebration. The Senate bill, considerably weaker, contains no right-to-sue plans for malpractice when they make medical decisions, and it affects only 50 million patients—those insured by large employers under ERISA protection—instead of the 161 million protected by the House bill.

In spite of the bill's good intentions, it does not solve medical coverage problems. Decisions about coverage should be made by neither the government nor the marketplace. They should be made by the profession and the patients. To make that happen, we need to reintroduce the responsibilities once shared by doctors and patients about health care delivery.

Later in the book I discuss at greater length the many options for health care reform, but here I can briefly describe one model that has seemed to work. The Singapore system has provided insurance mostly for preventive services or serious hospital (catastrophic) care. Virtually everyone in the system has a primary care physician who works in an outpatient setting and is mostly paid for services by patients out of their own pockets. (Nonpayment of physician bills is rare.) Singaporeans can go to specialists if they choose, but again, they have to pay for services out of pocket. (Some private insurance, however, has recently been developed to cover such services.) By contrast, preventive services are virtually free, as are treatments for catastrophic injuries or illnesses, which generally require hospitalization.

What I like about the Singapore system is that it retards overuse of medical services while also retarding overcharging by doctors and providing serious inpatient care without price or payment concerns for the patient. The system discourages abuse and encourages individual responsibility. People are careful about how they spend their own money, and doctors are attentive because they know people will be shopping around. There is price sensitivity when it comes to buying care, when it's available. We have seen that as little as ten dollars per month can drive a person out of one insurance plan and into another, and Singapore does this for between 3 and 4 percent of GNP.

In Singapore proven preventive services have been covered. Medical science has demonstrated the effectiveness of a number of procedures, including immunizations and well-designed screens such as mammograms and Pap smears. A system like Singapore's recognizes that preventive services have to be free of charge so that patients are motivated to preserve their good health. It is good for them, good for the country, and good for controlling costs. But the services also have to be professionally defined and based on sound, scientific research. Because service follows payment, we must remember that, unless new preventive methods are carefully studied before introduction, services will proliferate wildly if they are covered by insurance.

In fact, the most difficult coverage question relates to the use of emerging, extremely expensive technology for covered, catastrophic care. Coverage should not precede clinical trials, as the history of the bone marrow transportation for breast cancer clearly suggests. More than money is involved. Thousands of women underwent painful, dangerous, and very costly procedures that finally proved to be no better than less invasive interventions. Physicians should offer these patients something better than hope, and that should be hopeful expectations based on science.

That is the real challenge for the profession. Coverage decisions must not be made by employers, insurers, or politicians. These decisions must be made by medical professionals, who can document clearly the benefits of their interventions, and by fully informed patients, who are willing to undertake the risks associated with many invasive procedures. What is at stake is the state of the art of medicine. If the profession does not govern the development and diffusion of new technology, government and business interests will. In the process of holding down costs, a legitimate concern of third-party payers, government and business could very well retard advances in the state of the art and harm patient care in undreamed-of ways.

That process already is under way. The discount payment policies of managed care plans do not cover the costs of teaching and research at sophisticated academic medical centers. As far as managed care is concerned, all hospitals are alike. They are there to offer remedial care, not to investigate expensive, elusive cures for arcane diseases.

The profession no longer can merely complain about restraint of resources for teaching and research. It now has to define the resources needed to support productive scientific research, and it has to live within the limits of reasonable resource allocations. The profession must now do something it has long resisted: live within the limits established by sound regional planning, based on solid scientific research. If physicians fail to exert professional control over the delivery of care, they risk losing their professional status altogether. If physicians abandon their profession, they will become high-paid technicians, able to perform complex procedures on command but unable to give patients attentive and humane care. Cures are elusive, but the need for attentive care is widespread, and patients will abandon their doctors if they do not provide it.

4

There Is No Alternative to Medicine

Why People Buy Care Wherever They Find It

SOME YEARS AGO THE SON of Michael S. Goldstein, the author of several books on alternative medicine, suffered a severe burn injury to his foot. The consulting allopathic (conventional) physicians concluded that the only cure was a skin graft. When Goldstein and his wife learned that the procedure would require lengthy hospitalization, during the course of which their son would be tied to the bed to prevent him from touching the graft, they looked for alternatives. What they tried was fresh-cut aloe vera, carefully applied to the wound. They also used imagery, telling their son in soothing tones how the treatment would restore healthy tissue. "In about three months the foot had healed," Goldstein said.

Jeff Millison, co-founder of a "wellness center" in Maryland, had a comparable experience. As a sixteen-year-old he suffered an auto accident that left him with intractable pain and unsatisfactory healing of broken bones. In desperation, he turned to an acupuncturist and soon after witnessed a dramatic bone growth, with eventual complete healing. Millison now serves as an acupuncturist and certified herbal medicine therapist at his center.

The literature of alternative medicine is replete with many such tales of dramatic, spectacular, and even miraculous cures. All are individual anecdotes: none prove cause and effect. Now let me tell you another story, this one from Archie Cochrane, the British physician and epidemiologist. As a prisoner of war during World War II, Cochrane was the only doctor in a camp with 20,000 other prisoners. The diet was poor, and diarrhea was endemic. In addition, there were several epidemics of typhoid, diphtheria, infections, and jaundice. The only medications at his disposal were aspirin, some antacid, and skin antiseptic. He expected hundreds of prisoners to die, but only four did, and three of those succumbed to gunshot wounds inflicted by the German guards. This demonstrated, Cochrane said, "the relative unimportance of therapy in comparison with the recuperative power of the human body."

There seem to be some mysteries associated with wellness and health. We read about them from time to time, learning about the placebo effect and the self-limiting nature of most complaints that patients present to health practitioners. The body has a remarkable way of taking care of itself, but the mind seems to require chronic reassurance. Some lessons can be drawn from this: "first dollar" insurance coverage is not good for patient health; there is no alternative to proven medicine; neither allopathic nor alternative practitioners have controlled the major health problems of this country effectively; and some mischief is afoot in alternative practices, especially with respect to nutritional supplements.

"First dollar" insurance coverage has been a disaster for good patient care. Pressed for time, doctors seem more interested in filling out forms than attending to patients, and patients often feel that doctors are more interested in money than in caring for them. Despite this track record of distress, more and more people are petitioning for inclusion of alternative medicine and practitioners in conventional insurance coverage. Indeed, some health plans already are experimenting with inclusion, adding a number of alternative practitioners to their lists of providers. It's the wrong way to go. One of the leading advocates of alternative, or complementary, medicine,

Andrew Weil, a Harvard-trained physician, made the point when he stated that people rely on health professionals too much. "Prepaid medical plans make this worse by encouraging people to run to their doctor with every twinge," he has said.

Advocates for coverage point out that more and more people rely on alternative therapies. Estimates suggest that more than 630 million visits are made per year to alternative practitioners, compared with some 340 million visits to primary care physicians. Patient satisfaction is high, care is good, and costs are low, advocates for such coverage say. This sounds very much like what everyone was saying about allopathic therapies in the 1930s and 1940s, before the widespread introduction of health insurance coverage.

That is precisely the problem. As noted, insurance coverage tends to blunt price sensitivity. When a third-party payer steps in, practitioner fees start to rise, and attentive care starts to fall by the wayside. For the moment, however, alternative practitioners, most of whom live within an out-of-pocket payment universe, charge significantly lower fees for services, and people gladly pay them. It is estimated that more than $27 billion was paid for alternative therapies in the most recently reported year. People must be paying for something. The question is: What is it?

As best as I can determine, alternative medicine depends on a body of concepts linking thought processes, lifestyle practices, and certain remedies to healthful living and, in some cases, cures, such as those described earlier. But if Cochrane is right about the recuperative power of the body, the real question may be: Why do people go to any practitioner at all, allopathic or alternative? Most of their complaints are self-limiting. The symptoms disappear in time because of the body's recuperative power.

The answer is that they go to practitioners because they are either in pain or worried about some symptom. They need attention and care. If they have a bacterial infection, such as those that cause pneumonia, strep throat, or some sexually transmitted diseases, the allopathic doctor can cure it with antibiotics. Other problems, including the ubiquitous lower back pain, neck prob-

lems, anxiety, arthritis, headaches, and many others, are less suscep-
tible to curative care. What patients suffering those symptoms
want is attention, counsel, and caring, and what allopathic physicians have discovered is that more and more patients with chronic
problems are turning away from them and going to alternative
practitioners for help.

This trend prompted the editors of *JAMA* to begin examining
alternative medicine in the mid-1990s. By that time it was clear
that patients were taking alternative medicine herbs and often not
telling their regular doctors anything about it. This was a warning
flag because some herbs can interact negatively with pharmaceutical drugs prescribed by a doctor, and both the patient and the doctor can get into serious trouble.

Every year we convened a Delphi process: the editorial board
and staff nominated topics, stratified by repetitive balloting, for research papers to be featured in the next year. We wanted to identify
areas of research that required time and effort and would be helpful
to our readers. Alternative medicine began to show up as a nominated topic in 1995. At first interest was very low, but by 1997 interest in alternative medicine was high. In a brief time it went from a
position near the bottom of the list to one close to the top.

Driving the change was a readership survey in which we had
asked physician-subscribers what they wanted us to publish. The
survey listed an extensive number of topics, including cancer, diabetes, and heart disease, as well as alternative medicine and a number of other areas of interest. The survey went to both typical
physician readers and a panel of expert, academic physicians. The
experts ranked alternative medicine number sixty-seven out of
seventy, but the readers ranked it number three.

The readers were practicing physicians. Their patients, however
tentatively, were beginning to ask about alternative therapies, and
the physicians had no answers. Not only did they feel bad about
the situation, but they also felt they had to know what their patients were doing and whether they might be endangering their
health as well as their pocketbooks.

As a result of the survey, the *JAMA* editorial board voted to devote a large amount of space to alternative medicine, and we ended up with some ninety articles published in *JAMA* and the nine specialty journals published by the AMA in November 1998. The articles, submitted by all kinds of doctors, went through the usual peer review process before publication.

What Works and What Doesn't

There were some striking results. Among them was a convincing finding that an ancient Chinese practice corrects breech presentation for pregnant women about to deliver. The practice involves the burning of herbs to stimulate acupuncture points. Called moxibustion, the treatment is applied to stimulate an acupuncture point on the woman's foot for fifteen minutes per day during the thirty-third week of pregnancy. A control group received routine care without moxibustion. All 260 women in the study were pregnant for the first time, and all had fetuses in the breech position, determined by ultrasound. Results were dramatically better for treated women; 75 percent of their fetuses changed position, because of increased fetal activity, to the correct head-first position, compared with only 48 percent in the control group.

Another study demonstrated that a Chinese herbal formulation effectively treats irritable bowel syndrome. This study involved 116 participants, screened by a gastroenterologist, who were divided into three treatment groups. One received an individualized Chinese herbal formulation; another received the standard Chinese herbal formulation; and the third received a placebo. Results were evaluated by both patients and gastroenterologists. In the first group, those receiving individualized formulations, 42 percent of the patients reported improvement while gastroenterologists noted improvement in 40 percent. Percentages for the second group, who received the standard herb formulation, were 44 percent (patients) and 59 percent (gastroenterologists), while the placebo group percentages were 22 and 19.

Other studies noted failures in alternative practices. The widely used herbal compound *Garcinia cambogia* was found to be ineffective for weight loss. The study involved 135 overweight but otherwise healthy men and women who were divided into treatment and placebo groups. All followed a high-fiber, low-energy diet, maintained normal physical activity, and took a caplet thirty minutes before meals. Weight loss for the treatment group was seven pounds while weight loss for the placebo group was nine pounds, clearly demonstrating the ineffectiveness of the herb.

Spinal manipulation for control of tension headaches also proved ineffective. In this study, one group received soft tissue therapy and spinal manipulation and the other received soft tissue therapy and a placebo laser treatment. After seven weeks the first group reported a reduction in daily headache hours from 2.8 to 1.5, while the placebo group reported a reduction from 3.4 to 1.9, demonstrating no significant differences.

Without question, these articles and the many others published by the journals captured the imagination of the public and press and produced some positive results. First, they demonstrated to the world at large that the AMA journals were not actively against publishing material on alternative medicine. To the alternative medical community, we proved that we would give them a fair shake just like all other researchers and practitioners. To allopathic physicians, we stated that it was all right to talk to their patients about alternative medicine, and to the scientific community, we demonstrated that it was acceptable to conduct research on alternative medicine, and that such research could be done. By strong implication, we suggested that it was something they could take seriously.

Through one tour de force publication in November 1998, the articles clearly showed that some alternative methods worked and some did not. There was a noisy backlash. This was quackery, many physicians asserted. *JAMA* never should have published such junk. We were legitimizing something that was not at all legitimate. Had we forgotten the AMA's historic mission to combat quackery and promote scientific medicine? This stuff belonged under the rug, and we were wrong to lift it.

Others later speculated that because I had given official recognition to the field I had sent shudders through the AMA corpus. This was a thought shared by many physicians, many media reporters, and very many advocates of alternative medicine.

Of course, the AMA has long been identified as an antagonist to nonscientific therapies. In 1906 *JAMA* hired a physician named Arthur J. Cramp to head a program that became known as the Bureau of Investigation to look into nostrums, patent medicines, non-approved propriety medicines, and other substances that proved to be useless, deceptively advertised, or dangerous. In 1907 he published his first edition of *Nostrums and Quackery;* nine more editions would be published by 1936. There was a lot to warn people about: nostrums typically contained a large amount of alcohol as well as opiates, narcotics (whose sale was not controlled until 1914), and other substances that could depress heart and liver function. The products were heavily advertised and enjoyed brisk sales.

But the biggest, most long-lasting battle the AMA fought was against chiropractic. The association considered the theory unscientific and wrote into its code of ethics a ban against physician contact with chiropractors. It lobbied against allowing licensure for chiropractors and resisted extending insurance coverage for chiropractic. But state by state the AMA lost its battle against chiropractic. In the 1970s the association was sued by chiropractors and enjoined by a federal judge from taking any action to restrain chiropractors from doing their work. (The AMA had already eliminated its ban on association with chiropractors from its code of ethics.) However, the order did not restrain the AMA from speaking out on behalf of a scientific test for the basis of chiropractic.

Critics of the AMA's campaign against quackery complained that it was simply a turf battle. They charged the AMA with attempting to block access to all caregivers other than physicians, asserting that the issue had less to do with science than with money. My experience in medicine suggests that while physicians are naturally interested in income, they are preeminently interested in the scientific validity and effectiveness of their therapies.

The Difference Between
Chiropractic and Chiropractors

Chiropractic became a focus of scientific discussion during my medical school studies of pathology. That discipline defines the basic study of disease, what is it, how it creates illness, what the various processes are, and what the essential anatomy is. In studying the bone structure of the spine and the nerves it protects, my fellow students and I brought up the issue of chiropractic.

Our pathology teachers told us that the theory of chiropractic, as originally propounded by D. D. Palmer of Iowa in the 1890s, was that all disease is a result of insufficient nerve supply to target organs. Theory held that this is caused by pressure on nerves as they leave the spinal cord resulting from subluxations of vertebrae-squeezing nerves. We also were told that there is in fact no such thing as "subluxation of a vertebrae" that would squeeze a nerve, cut off nerve supply, and result in end organ disease. There was no scientific evidence that it had ever happened.

The theory, in short, was fundamentally fallacious. Cures were supposed to come from identifying the subluxation, applying adjustments, and attaining organ health when the spine was under control or in alignment. That would allow nerves to function normally. Basic anatomy tells us that nerves are necessary and useful, and that when pressured or pressed they cause pain in sensory nerves, or damage or destruction in motor nerves. In either case, they do not function properly. That can be identified functionally, pathologically, and microscopically. In chiropractic, I believe, there have been no studies showing that the "subluxation" impinges on nerves or causes them to degenerate, with resulting multi-organic diseases. That was what I was taught, and that is what I still believe. I have never seen a shred of evidence to the contrary.

I should confess that my early experiences with chiropractic were unimpressive. I recall my parents talking about it because one of my mother's good friends was a chiropractor. My parents respected her, enjoyed her company, but thought that chiropractic was somewhat silly. They never went to her for care, but they liked her and remained friends with her for years.

Later, when I worked as an orderly at the Mobile City Hospital in 1951, I lived in a rooming house a few blocks away that was owned by a chiropractor. She had two roomers, me and another man, who also was a chiropractor. She maintained her office on the first floor of the house, and every morning on my way to work I would pass by and glance in at her expectant, hopeful patients.

That summer I developed a severe cold, and my fellow roomer said, "You've got a really bad cold. Let me adjust your neck." I asked whether it would do any good, and he said he thought it would. So I said, "Okay. Fine." I had never had an adjustment before and felt a little odd about the way he cracked and crinkled my neck. Afterward it was clear that while he didn't hurt anything, he didn't help anything either. My nose stayed stopped up.

About the same time a chiropractor moved into the little town of Fairhope, where we visited our family doctor H. C. Jordan, M.D. The chiropractor opened an office on the same street and hung a big sign with his name: M. D. Jordan. This created quite a flurry of interest, and a degree of confusion, since M. D. Jordan seemed not to identify himself as a chiropractor, and for a period of time people wondered whether he was a regular medical doctor like H. C. Jordan, M.D. This left a lasting impression on me about the marketing acumen of some chiropractors.

Putting aside my early bias against chiropractic, it is important for me to note the distinction between theory and practice. Chiropractic may be one thing, but chiropractors may be something entirely different. Many of the things that chiropractors are doing today, supported by their schools and licensing boards, have nothing whatever to do with the theory of chiropractic. As chiropractors have grown as a workforce, and as many people have come to believe in them for whatever reasons, they have adopted other methods of treatment, excluding prescription of drugs and surgery. Some of the treatments actually seem to ease symptoms. In fact, a study published in the *New England Journal of Medicine* showed that osteopathic manipulation, somewhat similar to chiropractic manipulation, relieves back pain as effectively as standard treatment with drugs. That is a significant finding, since many back pain drugs come with unpleasant side effects, and surgery can cause big trouble.

I had one experience with back pain that was managed successfully by an alternative intervention. It occurred in 1980, when I was in charge of a teaching program on addiction medicine for practicing physicians. The meeting was held at a hotel in the high Sierras, and I had brought along a projector and other equipment for my presentation. As I was moving the equipment from my car, I wrenched my back. It was a sudden back pain, something almost everyone has experienced at least once, and some many times. I went into the meeting room and tried to set up the equipment, in obvious pain.

A primary care physician named Vicky Fox, who was a friend and did a lot of work in addiction medicine, walked up and said, "What's wrong?" I said I hurt my back, and she said, "Where does it hurt?" When I pointed to the place, she said, "Let me try acupuncture for your back. I think I can help."

She had been experimenting with acupuncture for addiction and pain relief and said she had had some success with pain relief but was uncertain about success with addiction at that time.

I agreed to the treatment, and she went to get her acupuncture needles. When she returned, she asked me to pinpoint exactly where my back hurt. Then she checked out my ears and found the precise point on my ear that she thought would correspond with the area of my back pain. She inserted the needle and twirled it with her fingers. The procedure didn't hurt, since it was a very thin needle, and in a short time I felt warmth around the place where my back had hurt. A few minutes later the pain began to fade. Within half an hour the pain had disappeared, and I went through my presentation with no back pain whatsoever. I was impressed. I felt better, and thanked her.

That was my one and only experience with acupuncture, since I've been lucky enough to not have any serious recurrence of back pain. But I do occasionally use another alternative therapy, melatonin, for sleep. Melatonin is a naturally occurring hormone produced by the pituitary gland. As one ages the normal levels of melatonin decrease, and decreased melatonin is believed to be the reason so many older people have sleep disorders. I take about one-quarter of a milligram when I know I'm less likely to sleep well—when I'm in a different time zone, for example—or when I have to get up early for an important meeting and want to sleep soundly until the alarm rings. It seems to work for me, either on its own merits or as a placebo. There has been only one good study on its effectiveness in treating jet lag, but the results were negative. The study may not have been done correctly, but in any event, no harmful effects, such as toxicity, overdose, or addiction, have been described so far.

The Powers of the Placebo

The placebo effect can be remarkably powerful. It occurs when a patient is given a dummy pill that the practitioner says will help, or when a dummy therapy is applied with similar assurances from the practitioner. The effect comes not from what the practitioner says, but from what the patient believes. Above all, the mind matters when it comes to gaining a placebo effect.

The mechanisms are not precisely understood. The link between mind and body is mediated by the hypothalamus, a cherry-sized structure of the brain situated behind the eyes. The hypothalamus coordinates the functions of the nervous and endocrine (hormonal) systems. The fight-or-flight response is controlled by the hypothalamus. It also mediates body temperature controls, signaling shivering, sweating, thirst, and hunger. A woman's monthly reproductive cycle begins with signals from the hypothalamus, as does gonadal activity. This is the mind-body switch that may account for female infertility and the observation that infertile women who adopt children often become pregnant. Theory suggests that anxiety about mothering disappears once a woman rears an adopted child successfully.

Certainly, anyone who suffers from seborrheic dermatitis understands the connection between mind and body. Emotional distress can almost instantly cause an outbreak resulting in itchy scaling skin above the eyebrows and below the nose. Prolonged distress can cause severe dandruff. Any number of autoimmune disorders are influenced by mental perceptions, and it follows that any number of symptoms could be cured by mental beliefs.

In any event, "therapeutic touch" may rely on the placebo effect. Despite its name, therapeutic touch isn't touch at all. It is non-touch. It is about "energy fields": by waving a hand over a body, a practitioner is somehow able to detect distress and to ease discomfort. In something of a "The emperor has no clothes" story, it was a nine-year-old child who discredited therapeutic touch therapy.

The story began in 1995, when Emily Rosa, with her mother's help, designed a study on therapeutic touch for her grammar school science project. The study involved double-blinding patients and nurses who employed the therapy. Hands were inserted through cutouts in a screen, and neither patient nor practitioner could see what was happening. Of course, nothing was happening as far as therapy was concerned. Emily completed the project, presented it to her class, and got a good grade.

Then her mother, father, and a couple of other people urged her to extend the project, to embellish it and make it stronger. They wanted her to conduct a more rigorous study and submit it to a medical journal for publication. The project was completed by the following year, and the written article was signed by four authors, Emily and three adults, including her mother. They submitted it as a research paper to *JAMA,* where it was categorized and assigned by a subeditor who immediately considered it unworthy and rejected it without outside review. One of the authors called me and complained that the paper had not been given sufficient attention, saying it was a fantastically interesting paper that was very well done. Would we reconsider the decision?

As was my penchant as the editor of *JAMA,* I didn't let rejections stand automatically. I did consider appeals once in a while, with good reason. Not often, but now and then a reconsidered article would get published. I listened to the explanation of this paper and thought it sounded interesting—kind of quirky, but still pretty interesting.

"Send it to me personally," I said, deciding to handle it myself. I read it and sent it to the standard number of outside reviewers. The resulting reviews were favorable, including one from our toughest statistical reviewer who said the design of the project was beautiful, very clear and very simple. The study demonstrated that the concept of therapeutic touch was fundamentally flawed. It showed that if the underpinning theory behind therapeutic touch was flawed, the practice had no value. That was the message.

I brought the paper to our manuscript meeting and got it accepted, although only after a lot of discussion. By no means was there a unanimous opinion that we should publish the paper. It was on a strange subject (therapeutic touch), and the lead author was, by this time, only ten years old. In defending the paper, I pointed out that I never knew how old our authors were. We didn't ask them to send us their birth certificates. I couldn't care less how old an author was. What I cared about was the quality of the science, how well the paper was written, and what our peer reviewers said. So we published the article and then found our lead author on the front page of the *New York Times.* Her article generated huge publicity.

As I had guessed, many people found the lead author's age to be noteworthy and it attracted attention. Some thought we had gone too far, others said that we had done the right thing. Emily herself became quite accomplished at doing interviews. She wound up receiving the Harvard "Ignoble Award," presented by the society that publishes the *Journal of Irreproducible Results.*

Most people had never before heard of therapeutic touch, including most physicians. That was another reason for publishing the study. It was important because 70,000 American nurses were trained to do it and doctors didn't even know what it was. Emily's study showed that the science of therapeutic touch was groundless. The paper has stood up. No one has been able to challenge its results so far, and I don't think anyone ever will.

Although the nurses who make their living doing "nontouch" therapeutic touch vilified me, I would still never spend my money on it, and I would never recommend that others do so.

The theory of homeopathy falls into the same category. On the face of it, it's preposterous and totally absurd. The homeopath places in water a certain chemical substance that has something to do with the disease process or the symptom he is going to treat. This chemical is diluted in water so many times that no test can detect its presence. It is absent, but theoretically the water is supposed to have remembered that it was there somehow. The practitioner administers the water to the patient, and the patient gets better. Fortunately, the water doesn't hurt the patient, except in the pocketbook or in unfulfilled expectations. This "therapy" may help the patient because of the placebo effect, but it probably won't help, and in any case it's nonsense.

But having said that, just as in chiropractic theory, the homeopathic practitioner is different from the theory. Many homeopaths practice within the larger scope of holistic or "wellness" medicine. Although they call themselves homeopaths, they are prescribing vitamins, herbs, and exercise. Some of the vitamins, like E, may have been proven effective, and everyone clearly understands the therapeutic value of exercise, proven again and again by various studies. So homeopaths practice more than homeopathy, and some of the therapies they recommend may really work.

That takes us back to the central question of what works in medicine, either allopathic or alternative, and to Cochrane's observation about the remarkable recuperative powers of the body. Most illnesses are self-limiting; that is, they correct themselves when left alone. Between 70 and 80 percent of all complaints presented to primary care physicians, and probably alternative practitioners as well, are self-limiting. Many have a psychological component, but in any case they are distressing for the patients. They want their practitioners to do something, and so the practitioners prescribe a medication, advise a course of activity, or offer massage or manipulation. When they get better after taking the pill, doing the exercise, or accepting the laying on of hands, patients see cause and effect.

Most patients, however, get well by themselves no matter what is done or not done. Samuel Johnson observed this phenomenon in 1734 when he wryly stated, "It is incident to physicians, I am afraid beyond all other men, to mistake subsequence for consequence." Of course, what we then knew about medical science was all wrong, but nonetheless, Johnson correctly was concerned about cause and effect. One of my teachers from many years back, Juan del Regato, a well-known radiation oncologist, put it another way when he said, "Just because the frogs come out after it rains does not mean that it rained frogs." This is why we must have randomized, controlled clinical trials.

Some allopathic therapies clearly work. Bacterial infections are cured by antibiotics. Some viral infections, such as measles, are prevented by vaccines, while other viral infections, such as herpes, are controlled by medications. Lives are saved when diseased organs, like an inflamed appendix, are surgically removed. Such therapies are based on scientific evidence. Clinical trials have clearly established a cause and clearly demonstrated an effect for many interventions. It was discovered, for example, that when the pneumococcus bacterium was present, the antibiotic penicillin destroyed it. All therapies, whether bone marrow treatment for late-stage breast cancer or Saint-John's-wort for depression, should be subjected to scientific trials to establish their effectiveness. We need to find out what really works. We need to separate the frogs from the rain, as it were.

The Search for Science

A promising area of research in alternative medicine is Chinese herbs, which have a strong rationale for effectiveness. Pharmacology began with herbs. Two examples of natural substances used in allopathic medicine come to mind immediately. Quinine, which has long been used to control malaria, comes from cinchona bark, and digitalis, used to strengthen the heartbeat, comes from foxglove leaves. As mentioned earlier, the *JAMA* study on the standard Chinese herbal formulation to control irritable bowel syndrome clearly demonstrated its effectiveness. I'm convinced that continued serious study of Chinese herbs will identify more truly good and useful medications.

That is the task before us—to look into what works. Right now studies are under way at Vanderbilt and Duke on the therapeutic value of Saint-John's-wort. There has long been anecdotal information that the substance can ameliorate depression. Now it is undergoing controlled, double-blind trials, with informed consent and close monitoring. Some say that alternative medicine can't be subjected to scientific study, but that's not true. It can be done, and it is being done.

I have to confess that I've always considered alternative therapies quirky at best and downright garbage at worst, but like all allopathic physicians, I have to recognize and acknowledge that a lot of people are using alternative medicine today. It is painful to ask why, but the obvious answer is that people are not happy with allopathic medicine. Many don't have family doctors anymore, and they don't trust the men in white coats, who don't know them and spend so little time with them when they come for help with their problems. "First dollar" coverage has been bad for physicians and patients, for even when insurance covers their visits, patients think regular doctors are overpriced and overrated. Furthermore, the high-tech interventions prescribed by doctors often either don't work or even seem to cause more problems than they cure.

Alternative medicine offers a real alternative. It's relatively inexpensive. The practitioners are nice to their patients and communicate well. They listen carefully and may lay on hands to make the patient feel better. Some may do back manipulations that have nothing to do with subluxation but still ease lower back pain. One strong indication that people find great value in their encounters with alternative practitioners is that they reach into their own pockets to pay for such care, since insurance generally doesn't cover it. Alternative medicine is friendly and healing, even though there's generally no science involved. It also seems to appeal to a longing for "natural" remedies and to an almost mystical belief that, with guidance, patients can control their own destinies.

That's why the *JAMA* editors took alternative care seriously in the mid-1990s and planned and published special issues on alternative care. We knew that more and more patients were using alternative therapies and that their regular doctors knew nothing about it. We also knew that patients didn't trust their doctors with information about what they were doing. They were afraid their doctors would be skeptical, bemused, or disapproving. This was driving a wedge into the patient-physician relationship.

Another reason for taking alternative medicine seriously relates to the political support it has gained. Democratic senator Tom Harkins of Iowa has for a long time been a staunch advocate of alternative medicine. He pressured the National Institutes of Health to create an Office of Alternative Medicine in 1992. The first director was Joseph Jacobs, a pediatrician with solid academic credentials, who was quickly wounded in the political cross fire on alternative care. He resigned less than two years later, and the program limped along, although with greater funding support near the end of the decade.

A curious development in 1994, also probably politically motivated, was the decision by Congress and the Food and Drug Administration (FDA) to deregulate nutritional supplements. Overnight the United States became the easiest place in the developed world to get certain chemical products without a prescription, whereas it used to be one of the hardest places. Many European countries looked askance at what the United States had done. They thought it was crazy to declare that melatonin, creatine, and a long list of hormones were not drugs but nutritional supplements, purchasable without prescription and at will in health food and drug stores. But the nutritional supplements industry enjoyed sky-rocketing sales, from $8.8 billion in 1994 to about $16 billion in 2000.

It's not a healthy situation. There is little or no regulation of the safety and effectiveness of the dose levels that are sold, and there is little or no regulation of manufacturing processes and purity of product, no guidelines on contamination or quantitation. The FDA simply requires manufacturers not to misrepresent the product as efficacious for specific diseases. Although they have to stop short of mentioning specific diseases, the label language can do so indirectly. It can say that the product, for example, *might be* useful for arthritis or sleep loss. What the FDA did was proscribe false claims without proscribing false marketing. Make no mistake: these substances are drugs, not nutritional supplements, and the FDA should regulate them. The American Association of Poison Control Centers received 6,914 reports of adverse reactions in 1998, 64 percent of them involving children, according to the *Washington Post*. No wonder I'm breaking the law in the Netherlands every time I get off a plane with melatonin in my suitcase.

Proven or not, there's no question about the overall advance of alternative medicine. More and more hospitals are including "wellness," "integrative," or "complementary" programs in their mix of services. Andrew Weil, who has made a fortune writing about alternative therapies, designed the Program in Integrative Medicine at the University of Arizona College of Medicine, which is aimed at moving alternative medicine into the mainstream. More and more health insurers are offering some type of coverage for alternative care. But they are simply responding to market forces.

The integrative approach reminds me of my meeting many years back with Zhang Hong Kai, the editor of the Chinese edition of *JAMA*. As a Western-trained physician, he practiced both conventional medicine and Chinese medicine. When I asked him how that worked, he said that he used Western medicine when he encountered a patient with an acute medical problem, such as appendicitis. When he encountered a patient with a chronic symptom, such as low back pain, he used Chinese medicine for symptom control. His decisions were guided as much by constraint of resources as by ideology.

For all the talk of the naturalness of alternative medicine, there are dangers associated with its use. Don't forget that, if 70 to 80 percent of complaints are self-limiting, that means that 20 to 30 percent are not. A sharp, abdominal pain, suggesting appendicitis, untreated, could lead to a fatal outcome. Blood in the sputum or stool indicates the immediate need for allopathic diagnosis.

Anyone contemplating the use of alternative therapies should first have a good understanding of what they are doing. If they have regular doctors, they should let them know about the alternative therapies they are using. They also should have a doctor who will value their feelings, a growing likelihood since physicians are now trying to learn about alternative medicine. The Internet is another source of information for all kinds of health care, but patients should be extremely wary of books and sites on the Internet. A lot of really bad information is out there. If patients have serious symptoms, they should waste no time in seeing a regular doctor as soon as possible.

The Future of Alternative Care

Where do we go from here? Should we try to integrate alternative practices into mainstream medicine, or should we muddle along with two competing forms of medicine? A number of predictions about the future of alternative medicine were made by Tom Delbanco, a Harvard professor practicing in Boston, in "A Piece of My Mind," a section of *JAMA's* special issue on the subject. Among them is a prediction that media reporters will become disenchanted with alternative medicine. The rash of favorable stories about alternative treatments, along with unfavorable stories about errors in conventional medicine, may change. Stories about alternative practitioner failures, such as missed tumors, may be followed by stories about the successes of conventional medicine, such as the transformation of AIDS from a killing disease into a chronic illness with the advent of new drugs. New vaccines and genetic therapies could help scientific medicine rebuild public trust.

If alternative medicine were to gain enhanced insurance coverage, the practitioners would soon find themselves overwhelmed by the demand for comprehensive documentation. Furthermore, as alternative practitioners age, they will seek larger incomes. "Inexorably, time with each patient will shorten," Delbanco predicts. Meanwhile, conventional primary care doctors may reclaim time with patients who want to take a more active role in their own care.

He also points out that neither alternative nor conventional clinicians have improved most human conduct significantly. Obesity, stress, addiction, and other self-destructive behaviors continue to resist sound counseling. Delbanco predicts that new medications developed by scientists may offer conventional physicians superior methods for dealing with behavior problems that adversely affect health.

The placebo effect may play a growing role in conventional medicine, he predicts, looking forward to a day when conventional doctors may tell their patients, "This is a placebo. We have little idea right now why it works, but it often does. Give it a try." Given their safety, low cost, and efficacy, placebos may have a salutary impact on medicine.

A lot of the controversy surrounding allopathic versus alternative medicine would be sorted out in short order if the insurance issue disappeared. Many alternative practitioners, and many of their patients, carry a great deal of resentment over the lack of insurance coverage for alternative care. Lack of coverage tends to devalue alternative care: the withholding of coverage seems to say that the alternative therapies are not useful and, indeed, are unworthy. By contrast, insurance coverage for allopathic medicine tends to legitimize conventional therapies while also rewarding their practitioners more generously.

If insurance causes so many problems, why not get rid of it entirely for primary care services? Why not follow the suggestion I made in chapter 3 and have insurance cover only established preventive services and scientifically proven catastrophic care? We already know that patients will pay out of pocket for alternative care. We also know that they are dissatisfied with much of the care they receive from allopathic physicians, who seem to be as busy with insurance charts and forms as they are with patients.

In fact, if we want a clear picture of what "first dollar" coverage does to patient care, we need only look at what has happened to the patient-physician relationship during recent years. In a world without coverage for routine care, practitioners would compete for patients on the basis of their expertise as well as on the quality of their services. Costs of care would moderate, and satisfaction with care would increase. I know a number of physicians who would enjoy not having to fuss with forms and would find a great deal of pleasure in being liked and trusted by their patients again.

That would provide an interim correction, but in the final analysis we will discover that there is no such thing as "alternative" medicine. There is only medicine that has been scientifically tested and found to be safe and effective. That is the medicine worth using and paying for. Medicine that is tested and found to be ineffective or unsafe shouldn't be used and shouldn't be paid for. Any medicine that enjoys some plausible reason for working should be tested and put in one category or the other. That way, all safe and effective forms of what we now call alternative medicine would become mainstreamed. It is a long-term project, but it is worth doing.

5

Mouse Calls for House Calls

The Benefits, Deficits, and Promotion of Internet Care

I F SOME ALTERNATIVE MEDICINE PRACTICES seem questionable, driven by hucksters, dreamers, and kooks, some of the practices on the Internet seem as insane as the snake oil spiels of the late nineteenth century. Afflicted by arthritis, psoriasis, phlebitis, rheumatism, herpes, or cancer? Take shark cartilage for relief. A mere $500 to $1,000 per month will cure stage 4 cancer. Thousands have benefited, the claim goes, from the miraculous angiogenesis properties of shark cartilage, a nutritional product that the Food and Drug Administration has termed nontoxic.

Sounds fantastic, and such claims are indeed from the world of fantasy, now aided and abetted by the wonders of the Internet. With hundreds of sites on the Internet, shark cartilage is hawked in a way that typifies the kind of bad information available in cyberspace. There has never been any credible scientific evidence that shark cartilage is of any benefit to anything other than sharks, which have a cartilaginous skeleton that supports the skin and allows the animal to live.

Shark cartilage also supports the people who make their living from selling the product, largely on the Internet, but also in a lot of drugstores, pharmacies, and health food stores. Yet there is no evi-

dence that humans derive any benefit from ingesting shark cartilage. Despite this overwhelming lack of evidence, Internet sites
abound with opinions, information, and "scientific" articles on the
therapeutic properties of shark cartilage. Anyone can buy it. All
that's needed is a credit card number or the willingness to pay cash
on delivery. It's good for entertainment, titillation, and the profit
margins of the sellers. Other than that, shark cartilage is a total
waste.

What do we do about this? How do we proceed? The Internet
represents the most significant advance in human communication
since the printing press. It is more important than the telephone,
radio, or television, although Internet technology obviously draws
from these technologies as well as others. Although it's still new,
evolving, and difficult to understand, it represents a giant step forward. Anyone with an Internet-ready computer and a telephone
line can communicate with anyone else, anywhere else in the
world, almost instantly. Furthermore, we can communicate without government restrictions and few to no economic restrictions.
The Internet allows the exercise of freedom of the press and freedom of speech and the free flow of information at very low cost.
Words, ideas, sounds, and video images can be sent with the click
of a mouse.

It has got everyone scared—legislators, regulators, administrators, ethicists and physicians are all on edge. The open forum provided by the Internet is unprecedented. Never before has a
medium so successfully evaded control. My central concern about
the use of the Internet, as a medical journalist, is that people will
attribute more value to the information they receive on the Internet than it deserves. The power of the medium is so great that
people might be tempted to think that, if it's on the Internet, it
must be true. The quality of the technology, however, is much
greater than the quality of much of the information it conveys.

In fact, there is no guarantee that Internet information is any
better or worse than the information we might receive on a street
corner, at a bus stop, in a bar, or from a handbill or movie screen.

We are now experiencing a backlash. Some people tell me they don't believe anything they read on the Internet because so much of what they see there is suspect. To make a point, I respond that I don't believe anything I read on paper because so much of it is wrong.

The Internet is just a medium, no matter how powerful or how ubiquitous it is. Although most North Americans think that just about everyone has access to a computer, we should remember that only 1 percent of the world's population owns a computer, and only 30 percent of the world's population is literate. Similarly, not everyone in the United States owns a computer. The great potential to improve world health is thus limited by both the quality of Internet information and the ability of poor Third World countries to retrieve it.

Both of those problems are manageable. Free, high-quality medical and health information can reach people in Third World countries because it takes only one computer and one telephone line to receive the information. That computer could be placed in a post office, a public library, or a hospital, and it could distribute useful information to large numbers of people in a timely fashion. They could address a public health crisis immediately by accessing a single computer and downloading pertinent, helpful information.

That takes us to the second, more troubling problem with the quality of Internet information. No one knows exactly how many health sites are available. I have a friend in Copenhagen who says there are two million sites, but he's counting the home page of every physician and hospital in the world. Our best guess is that something like 20,000 health sites exist on the Internet. It should be remembered that anyone who knows how to use the Internet can be the author, editor, and publisher of the information on the site. What are they putting out, and why are they doing it? These are critical questions for the 98 million Americans—a number that is climbing steeply—who use the Internet for health information.

Many sites are filled with misinformation, some are very good, and a lot are in between. Many are managed without the traditional checks and balances of the medical journal world, where scientific articles are reviewed by peer scientists before publication, or even the fact-checking that is routine among newspapers, magazines, radio, and television. There is always some level of editorial control in the public media. Someone owns the publication or broadcast station, and someone, usually an editor or producer, is responsible for the information being made available. Thus, some kind of quality control prevails; it may not always be good, but it's always there.

On the Internet there is no quality control beyond that exercised by the person who puts the information on the site. That is our first line of defense. We used to say *caveat emptor* (let the buyer beware), but with the Internet we should say *caveat lector* or *caveat viewor* (let the reader or viewer beware). (I have to add that when I first used *caveat viewor* in a *JAMA* editorial, the Latin scholars objected: there is no such Latin word and I couldn't create a new word for a dead language, they said. If the ancient Romans had had TV sets or computer screens, however, we can be sure they would have had a word for "viewer.")

I prefer the caveat approach to censorship. First of all, censorship simply won't work on the Internet. There would have to be an international set of rules, and there is no reason to believe that all of the nations of the world would agree to a single set of regulations. The World Health Organization (WHO) took up the topic in 1997, when it convened a meeting to discuss regulation of the advertising, promotion, and sale of drugs on the Internet. I attended the meeting with Stuart Nightingale and others from the FDA to speak against the promulgation of rules that would outlaw drug advertising, promotion, or sale over the Internet. Our position was that we should try to educate people in how to use the Internet rather than enact restrictive laws. Most countries already have restrictive laws governing sales of pharmaceuticals, we argued, and those laws should be applied instead of trying to impose new laws on countries from outside. In any event, it was unlikely that 250 countries would agree to enact the same laws. After due deliberation, WHO agreed.

So we have to beware, and to that end we developed five basic rules, first published in *JAMA,* for anyone seeking health information from the Internet. Every health site should be put to the following test:

1. Who wrote what is on the screen? If a name is attached to the information, that is helpful. If no name is attached, that calls for immediate doubt. Without a name, the information can't be trusted. Writers who don't sign their names are worse than ghosts; they may not even exist. Certainly they are beyond question because the "author" can't be queried.

2. If the author's name appears, where does that person work? Does the author have a real job? Can he or she be e-mailed or visited? Is there an address, an institutional connection, and an endorsement from a reputable place?

3. Where does the information come from? If it wasn't written originally for the site—and a great deal of information on sites does not originate there—where did the information first appear? Look for attribution and consider the source.

4. Who owns the site? Where did the funding for the site come from? Internet sites cannot be created out of thin air. Someone has to have the wherewithal to fund it and to fund the information that appears on it. Whether the site is sponsored by advertising, subscription, or an owner's underwriting, disclosure should be readily and easily determined.

5. When was the information posted? Whether it was yesterday or five years ago, it should be dated. If the information has been updated, the day of update should be noted. In medical science things change every day. New information appears that invalidates old information, puts another angle on it, or balances

it. Information on the Internet may be invalidated, changed, or altered, but one would never know without proper dating.

Finding an Internet Site

If the forewarned reader has easily obtained answers to these five questions, he or she knows that the people running the site are reasonably competent. They know what they're doing. They at least understand the principles of journalism, something of the principles of medical ethics, and some of the principles of good business practices. But having such knowledge doesn't necessarily make their information valid.

The forewarned reader has to go further. The next step after answering the five questions is to find "brand-name" identification. If the information comes from the Harvard Medical School, the Mayo Clinic, Johns Hopkins Hospital, the Centers for Disease Control and Prevention (CDC), or the National Cancer Institute (NCI), chances are good that the information is valid. These and similar institutions put their reputations on the line whenever they put information on the Internet.

For-profit sites, such as Medscape, where I now serve as editor in chief, earn trust through the reputations and work of the people they use and through their own track record. In the new fast-forward Internet time, Medscape, launched in May 1995, is one of the older medical information sites around. We use authorities for all of our information, and our editing process is virtually as rigorous as the process I used at *JAMA*. Our authors are trusted names in their fields and write from the best institutions, which vouch for their work. Other commercial sites are newer and still finding their way. Some may be good, some are not, but Medscape has done what it takes to become a trusted site.

What about these many sites? How do we reach them, and how do they work? Anyone who enters the Internet has to use an access point, and most portals have search engines of various kinds.

Investors make money from the portals and from the search engines. Users are at the mercy of whoever put the search engine together. They can retrieve only what the search engine provides. Some search engines are put together very carefully so that users can reach the best sites available. Others put on anything they can find that has a key word. Some limit their searches, and others say they will search the entire Web—a little white lie because no one can search the entire Web, only subsections of it. In fact, I've heard that no search engine can search more than 30 percent of the Web. The largest, Google, claims to search more than one billion of the three billion–plus pages available on the Web. Searching the entire Web is a gigantic and impossible task.

So where does one begin? One good way to start is with the National Library of Medicine site or with www.healthfinder.gov. These sites offer a mass of government information that is amazingly easy to navigate and offered free of charge. An excellent source of peer-reviewed information is offered by Medline, which is produced by the National Library of Medicine.

Medline has 4,000 of the best medical journals of the world in various languages online, and its list goes back to 1967. One can enter the database, search with key words, and come up with dozens, hundreds, or thousands of articles from the journals. Only abstracts are published on the site, not full text; full texts can be retrieved from libraries or reference sources cited on the Internet. Medline is a treasure trove of information: many articles detailing obscure research in areas few people would recognize are carried in its database.

But few people need that wide a range of information. Although some 30,000 medical journals are published in the world, the vast majority of the best, most frequently quoted and cited new information in medical literature comes from less than 500 of the 4,000 journals carried by Medline.

At Medscape we followed the concept that most people are searching not for huge volumes of information but rather for the best information they can obtain quickly and easily. We identified the best 269 journals of the 4,000. We used several methods to make that cut, including the popular method of identifying the journals that physicians like best as well as more esoteric methods, such as determining which journals are most referenced by research scientists. The result, Medscape Select, provides the best answers to the most frequently asked questions of medical literature. We have separated all of the wheat from most of the chaff in a time-effective manner. That is what the competition is all about on the Internet. We're all competing for readers' time, and we're seeing more and more physicians and consumers turn to the Internet for quick, reliable information, using it effectively, and coming back for more.

The Long, Slow Path to Cyberspace

I began working with computers in 1963, when I was stationed at Letterman Hospital in San Francisco as a captain in the U.S. Army and was assigned by my chief to automate the California Tumor Tissue Registry. He told me to put it on a computer, and I asked how I would do that. "Go over to that building," he said, pointing. "They've got a huge machine in there called a computer. Talk to those folks, and they will tell you how to take this information off these cards and put it onto a different set of keypunched cards. You can then feed the keypunched cards into a computer, and it will print out information in an orderly, sorted-out way."

Sure enough, the computer people taught me how to do the keypunch business, and I took the California Tumor Tissue Registry and put it onto punched cards, thereby automating it in 1963. Two years later the army sent me to the IBM education center in Poughkeepsie, New York, to take a one-week course called "Computing for Physicians." There I met about one hundred other physicians learning how to use computers, and one of our main teachers was Donald Lindberg, an assistant professor of pathology at the University of Missouri, who was becoming an expert in computer medicine. Don and I were about the same age, had almost identical last names, and were both pathologists; we became lifelong friends. He later became a full professor at Missouri and soon was known as the best computer pathologist in the United States; he was a pioneer of the American Medical Informatics Association and became the director of the National Library of Medicine at the National Institutes of Health in Bethesda, Maryland. When I established my editorial board for *JAMA,* he was among the first physicians I asked to join. He did, and when I was fired, he was the only board member to resign in protest. When I joined Medscape, he was among the first I asked to join our editorial board, and, with government approval, he agreed.

With the information I gained at IBM, I went to the William Beaumont General Hospital in El Paso, Texas, as chief of pathology and started to automate the hospital's clinical laboratory. In the process, I became the first military pathologist to use computers in a hospital lab. I also learned that computerization is complicated and expensive, but from 1965 on I have tried to apply computers to medicine wherever I was working.

Ever since 1965 I have said that physicians will use computers in a big way in the practice of medicine, and I have been wrong in that prediction again and again. A subset of physicians now use computers: pathologists like me, who use them in labs; radiologists, who use them in CT scans; and anesthesiologists, who use various computerized monitoring machines. But aside from billing functions, computers haven't been used by physicians for the decades they have been available, no matter how many of us in medicine have exhorted them to do so.

In the early 1990s some of us once again predicted that physicians would use computers in a big way, and this time we were right. In 1995, for example, only 3 percent of U.S. physicians knew how to access the Internet, according to my own data. By 1996 the percentage had increased fivefold, to 15 percent. The following year it doubled again to 30 percent, and in 1998 it reached 60 percent. In 2000 good data from several different sources suggests that more than 90 percent of physicians access the Internet for some purposes. And they do it themselves, not relying on their nurses, office managers, children, or spouses. We can't say exactly how physicians use their computers, but we do know they understand how to use the technology and do access it for something. About half seem to use it to gain medical health information.

Now at last we are positioned to make "mouse calls" in lieu of house calls. When we started using computers in clinical labs, one of our main purposes was to connect the lab result with the physician at the bedside. With information in hand, the physician could quickly make the proper judgment and treat the patient appropriately. Today that is done routinely everywhere.

Where we go tomorrow is clearly mapped. We could have a lab test done in Austin, Texas, for a patient in Johnson City, a big geographical gap that can now be bridged instantaneously by the computer. Because we now have the technology that ensures this kind of connectivity, information transfers like this one are already happening. Here is another possible scenario: a patient enters a symptom into the computer and transmits the information to a physician who interprets it. A test of some kind may be ordered, and the patient is seen at a laboratory. The test results are instantly transmitted to the physician by e-mail or telephone or through a hand-held palm device. The physician then e-mails the patient directly with instructions to change the dosage of a drug, stop taking the drug, go directly to a hospital emergency room for immediate care, or go to the physician's office.

The vision of this kind of patient-physician relationship has led Mark Leavitt, who founded MedicaLogic in 1985 in Portland, Oregon, to dedicate his life to improving patient care by electronic medical records. MedicaLogic's Logician captures the health information that matters so as to decrease medical errors. We merged Medscape with MedicaLogic in 2000 to help inform patient-physician decisionmaking at the front end of the relationship where the decisions that matter are made and to also make trusted information available to patients through CBSHealthWatch.com.

In another scenario, a diabetic patient might do a glucose test at home and feed the results into a computer, which immediately transmits the information to the physician. The physician would get a printout or a graph on the office computer screen and immediately e-mail the patient to recommend a change in insulin dosage. The patient would never have to come in for a visit. This is wonderful for patients and doctors who know one another, but I generally would not recommend skipping the office visit for a patient and doctor who have never met.

There are services on the Web that provide "blind" hookups between physicians and "guests" (patients). On sites sponsored by hospital systems, doctors offer "medical information" rather than advice to patients in an interactive mode. The guest describes a symptom, and the doctor follows up with a question. After the back-and-forth session reaches a certain point, the doctor offers medical information free of charge. I conditionally would advise against this practice. In the long run it may be more prudent, and perhaps even less costly, for a patient to rely on the physician with whom he or she has an established relationship.

There is more to medicine than graphs and printouts. The seemingly more mundane practices of medicine, such as looking at the patient, noticing reactions to queries, hearing voice inflections, and feeling the pulse, can be critically important. Clinicians develop a sixth sense from dealing with patients directly, an experience no one can get off the Internet. However, once a relationship is established, significant benefits can be derived from e-mail exchanges between patients and physicians. Think of all the missed telephone calls. Now a patient can e-mail a query, and the physician can e-mail a response. That kind of connectivity cuts through voice mail frustration and documents the interaction.

One other issue in Internet medicine must be dealt with: without appropriate licenses, it is illegal for physicians to practice across state or national boundaries. But medicine can be practiced across state or national lines through doctor-to-doctor consultations. Then it is ethical and legal. Think of the patient in Kuwait with a complicated heart condition. The patient's Kuwait physician can transmit the EKG or cardiac-catheterization data electronically to Brigham and Women's Hospital in Boston over the Internet. A cardiologist there can interpret the data and then consult by Internet immediately with the Kuwait physician, who then makes the decision and implements the therapy, following information from this second opinion. The distance of 7,000 miles is reduced to zero by the Internet. This concept is practiced by a wonderful company in Cambridge, Massachusetts, called World Care.

The Internet also can be an antidote to managed care. In strictly managed care, administrators with MBAs from the best business schools determine the amount of time a physician is allowed to spend with any one patient, especially in an office setting. However, once a patient and physician have established a therapeutic relationship, they can expand the time they are in contact through the Internet, which is outside the reach of bureaucrats. A lot of information can flow back and forth with the click of a mouse, and it can be more thoughtful and better managed, to the greater satisfaction of both patient and physician.

Sometimes too much information seems to be floating about. A number of physicians have complained to me about patients who come in with reams of computer printouts. They are good patients who want to do the right thing, but it's frustrating for the physician because a lot of the printed-out information is garbage and a lot of time is wasted sorting through the data to determine what is trustworthy and what is not. Explaining everything takes an inordinate amount of time, a rare commodity for those in managed care networks. Some physicians say they wish they could pull the plug on their patients' computers.

But no one should stop patients from accessing the Internet, and no one can censor what they receive. What physicians need to do is direct patients to trusted sites. As noted earlier, there are a number of sites that give out trustworthy information, including those established by government agencies. The University of Pennsylvania maintains an "oncolink" site developed specifically for cancer patients. Harvard and Aetna have an "Intelihealth" site, and reliable sites are maintained by the Mayo Clinic and many other well-known institutions.

One of our marketing strategies at Medscape is to have a trusted site for both physicians—Medscape.com—and patients—CBSHealthWatch.com. Physicians can refer their patients to the site, and patients can refer their doctors to the site for information they have received. They can meet on Medscape for trustworthy material. We also provide physicians with their own home page on Medscape free of charge to promote patient-physician relationships.

Our consumer market model provides three levels of information: basic, intermediate, and "what your doctor reads." The first level provides the simplest information on all matters of health care and can be read with a fifth- or sixth-grade vocabulary. The second level presents information in a somewhat more sophisticated manner, with a twelfth-grade or junior college vocabulary. The third level presents information for physicians, using their professional vocabulary. Patients can move from one level to another, seeking the information they need, free of charge.

We learned our lessons on how patients access information some years back when *JAMA* established an HIV information site, with the sponsoring help of Glaxo. It was intended for physicians and was very sophisticated, but Bill Silberg and I discovered that more consumers than physicians were coming to the HIV site. These profoundly interested consumers became extremely sophisticated readers. That insight shaped our Medscape model. A layperson may want the highest level of information about a specific disease, such as HIV or diabetes, but the same person may know little about orthopedics and may want only the basic information on what to do if a parent falls and breaks a hip. With our model, patients can gain whatever kind of information they wish at whatever level of sophistication they need.

Gutenberg Time to Internet Time

One of the most important events in the history of science was the development about 300 years ago in England and France of primary-source peer-review medical journals. This new system checked the

validity and worth of new information. When someone wrote
something, another person in the same field reviewed the material and helped to decide whether the piece should be published.
Peer review established limits on the publication of scientific articles and led to the medical science editorial enterprise as we
know it today.

That enterprise was formalized in Vancouver, British Columbia, in 1978, with the founding of the International Committee of
Medical Journal Editors. Editors from *JAMA,* the *New England
Journal,* the *Annals of Internal Medicine,* and the *British Medical Journal* met to delineate rules of behavior for medical editors and authors. It had taken 300 years to initiate and elaborate an internationally accepted code of ethics, the "Uniform Requirements,"
thereby ensuring the trustworthiness of published information for
physicians, health reporters, and the public at large.

The Uniform Requirements address, for instance, the question
of authorship. Clarification was needed of a practice that had developed over time: having a famous researcher sign on to an article
by a junior researcher at the same institution. Often the practice
was a courtesy extended by a senior scientist to a younger one
struggling to gain recognition. Certainly the practice helped place
the paper, since the more famous name gained editorial attention,
but it came with risks, as Nobel Laureate David Baltimore learned
to his distress. A junior colleague in his lab was the main author of
a paper whose authenticity was challenged. As a co-author of that
paper, Baltimore found that his career went into eclipse for years as
charges of fraud were investigated.

The journal that published the paper had not yet signed on to
the Vancouver code. Had it followed code policy, it would have required a signature from Baltimore attesting that he was a bona-fide
author, that the work was done in his lab, and that it was done well.
He might have looked at the paper differently if he had been required to sign an authorship "affidavit." He probably would have
looked at the paper more carefully, and he may or may not have
chosen to become a co-author. Although his career was under a

cloud for several years, Baltimore was eventually exonerated when the charges were dismissed, and he went on to become the president of the California Institute of Technology.

In any event, while it took 300 years to develop rules for peer-review journals, it took only four years to codify rules for medical information on the Internet. The medical Internet began in 1995, and by 2000 rules had been written to govern behavior in the practice of Internet medicine.

The unfortunate lapses of C. Everett Koop, which were exposed by the *New York Times* in the summer of 1999, underscore the need for clearly understood and widely accepted rules of conduct. The very popular Koop Internet site was shown to be recommending hospitals that were paying for their listings without disclosures. That was a clear instance of what I call "medical Internet payola"—failure to disclose that a recommendation was made as a result of financial considerations. It was an embarrassment for the site and for Koop, who had become an icon of medicine during his years of good service as surgeon general of the United States. "Chick" has been a friend of mine since the mid-1980s and remains a close friend, so his lapse was personally and professionally distressing to me.

To his credit, Koop took immediate action by convening a meeting in New York of twelve Internet health information providers in October 1999 to talk about establishing rules for the industry. We discussed rules in four areas: privacy, content development, advertising and sponsorship, and e-commerce. At Medscape we had developed an advertising policy earlier that year and finalized it in August. I had planned to announce our policy guidelines at a meeting in October 1999, but because of the *New York Times* stories about Koop, we published our policy in the first week of September. We wanted to set the record straight that this was a long-standing issue of concern at our site, and that our policy had not been motivated by the exposé.

At the meeting convened by Koop we collectively based our decisions on material derived from the "AMA Principles of Medical Ethics," from the codes of the Society of Professional Journalists and the U.S. Chamber of Commerce, and from the International Committee of Medical Journal Editors and the Accreditation Council for Continuing Medical Education. The result of these deliberations, endorsed by twenty companies, is called "HIEthics" and was announced in San Francisco in May 2000.

In addition, the Internet Health Care Coalition met in February 2000 to develop rules. That coalition can do what industry cannot: bring together government officials, academia, the ethical community, the profession of medicine, and industry. It can establish overarching policy across the Internet, and it has done so. The result is called "eHealth Code of Ethics," also announced in May 2000. The hope is to develop solid rules that will inspire voluntary compliance. The additional hope is that once consumers understand that good Web sites comply with the code, they will rely on those sites.

Internet Privacy Concerns

Few things are of more concern to patients than the privacy of their medical information. People generally don't want other people talking about their medical problems, but privacy is difficult to maintain. As early as my premed days I learned that there are no secrets in hospitals. There still are no secrets in hospitals. The issue of invasion of privacy antedates the Internet, the computer, and the telephone. People tend to find it "interesting" if you have cancer, syphilis, or HIV. Some can be trusted with this information, and some cannot. Hospital elevators are a particularly important place where private information is often publicly shared.

The events that occur in the patient-physician relationship are themselves private, the business only of the patient and the physician. But they also become the business of the closest family members, and then to some extent they become the business of the insurance carrier if the contract allows access to information for billing and payment purposes. In fact, I know many psychiatrists with patients who pay for care out of pocket because they don't want any insurance records of their therapy.

Private information on the Internet presents a heightened problem. There is a dramatic difference between the old hospital system, in which there were no or few secrets, and the new era, with its technical capability of distributing mass information at the touch of a finger. What one person tells another in a cafeteria pales by comparison with what can happen to computerized information. We all have read accounts of computer hackers who manage to invade sites and steal information, including credit card numbers. In approaching the Internet as a therapeutic information transfer device, patients should be aware that private information could become public and be wary of what they confide about themselves in cyberspace. This delicate issue has to be addressed with great sensitivity. Yet the established rules must apply to both paper and electronic recording.

I'm reminded of a couple of ruses used to protect the privacy of celebrity patients. Some years ago, when I was a toxicologist-pathologist at the University of California at Davis, I was asked to review the medical records of Elvis Presley and as a consultant to give my opinion on the cause of his death. In looking over his hospital and autopsy records, I learned how Elvis's hospital in Memphis had successfully protected his privacy over the years: they had changed his name in the official records to Aaron Sivle. (Aaron was his middle name, and Sivle was Elvis spelled backward.)

In another example, friends of mine at Cedars-Sinai Medical Center in Los Angeles told me that there was a very tight clamp on information on the condition of Frank Sinatra during the last weeks of his life. The hospital refused to provide any information to the public, through the media, about what was happening. In fact, he was in terrible shape and was apparently kept alive in a vegetative state, with no mental capacity whatever, for an extended period. But no word of his condition leaked to the media, and no media "circus" sprang up at the hospital during his final days.

The Memphis deception may not have been legal, or even ethical, but it was proper. Similarly, the Los Angeles hospital did the right thing. There are times when celebrities deserve the same privacy that any other person enjoys. Of course, the dead have no rights.

Generally, information generated from the patient-physician relationship should be kept private. Much of it would stay private if we followed my suggestion about covering only preventive services and catastrophic care. That practice would return ordinary doctor-patient interactions to their historic norm: whatever happened in the encounter would be the business only of those two parties, and any third-party insurer would be excluded.

The only exceptions to this privacy practice would be certain celebrities, especially those running for high public office, and mentally ill patients who pose a threat to others. By now it's fairly well accepted that someone running for president of the United States has to surrender much of his or her medical file to the public. The power of the office is so great that the health of those who seek it is a legitimate and public point of concern. In the second example, a psychiatrist is obliged by law to break patient confidentiality if a patient says, for example, that he plans to kill his wife. The threatened person has to be warned. Protecting life is a principle that overrides the principle of privacy.

The Ubiquitous Pharmaceutical Sponsors

As the medical Internet is burgeoning, it is fascinating to watch the behavior of the marketing arms of the pharmaceutical industry adapt. They have been so successful over the years.

When I was a senior at the Medical College of Alabama in Birmingham, I received my introduction to pharmaceutical company marketing techniques. Married in August 1956, my wife and I were treated to a second honeymoon trip entirely paid for by Eli Lilly Pharmaceutical Company. Lilly then had a long-standing policy of paying expenses for senior medical students and their spouses for a train trip to Indianapolis. We were put up at nice hotels, treated to excellent dinners, and invited to tour the Indianapolis Speedway and its museum as well as many elements of the Lilly pharmaceutical manufacturing plant. At the end of the tour we were sent back to our medical schools with bags full of pharmaceutical products.

That was standard operating procedure for pharmaceutical companies working to influence physicians to prescribe their products in 1956. In one sense, those days are gone, but in another they are still very much with us. U.S. pharmaceutical companies remain a world model for creating devious methods to get physicians and patients to do what the companies want, whether or not it is in the best interest of the patient. The measure of their success is startling: U.S. spending on prescription drugs went from $5 billion in 1970 to an estimated $110 billion today. In fact, the health care inflation rate, which started escalating again in 1997, was principally fueled by the cost of drugs. The 6.5 percent increase in health care costs in 1998 was three to four times greater than the general inflation rate; prescription drug products and their prices were blamed for most of the increase. In the 1990s drug costs skyrocketed from $38 billion to well over $100 billion.

There are a number of reasons why pharmaceutical products are responsible for an increased percentage of total health care costs. First, a lot of new products are being released. Many of them are truly beneficial and can prolong life or improve quality of life. Others are simply new. Consider Relenza, produced by Glaxo Wellcome, and Tamiflu, by Hoffman-LaRoche, both approved in 1999 for treatment of influenza. Their approval was controversial, and in fact an expert panel recommended that the FDA reject Relenza. Studies showed that both drugs cut flu symptoms by one day, reducing typical disease duration from seven days to six. However, the FDA took the unusual and unelucidated step of ignoring expert advice. Later the FDA had to issue a warning advisory that physicians were relying too heavily on the influenza medications and missing more serious secondary infections that required antibiotic treatment.

The FDA action underscores the second problem associated with drug cost escalation: advertising. In the mid-1980s the FDA relaxed its rules on direct-to-consumer pharmaceutical advertising, and the response from the industry was almost instantaneous. By 1989 consumer advertising had hit $12 million, up from zero less than a decade before. By 1998 a report indicated that the ten drugs most heavily advertised to consumers accounted for 22 percent, or $9.3 billion, of the total increase from 1993 to 1998 in retail drug spending.

The companies had mounted aggressive marketing campaigns on television and in the print media, touting the benefits of their products, particularly oral antihistamines, antidepressants, cholesterol reducers, and anti-ulcerants. Other heavily promoted products were Viagra, for erectile dysfunction, and Xenical, for weight loss; marketing analysts forecast sales potentials of $1 billion and $3 billion per year, respectively.

For years pharmaceutical companies restricted the promotion of prescription drugs to physicians, and heavy marketing campaigns relied on advertisements in medical journals to influence physician-prescribing practices. Now the companies can promote their products directly to consumers, trying to influence human behavior with extremely creative and very expensive advertising campaigns. The new promotional techniques clearly serve the best interests of the pharmaceutical companies, the stock market, and investors, but only sometimes do they serve the interests of patients and physicians.

The AMA turned out to be terribly ambivalent about direct-to-consumer advertising. When the practice began in the 1980s, the association expressed concern, saying that such advertising would interfere with the patient-physician relationship. But then the AMA started its own series of television shows on cable TV. Although the series was aimed at physicians, consumers tuned in and saw the drug ads that were covering the costs of production. In 1993 the AMA altered its policy, saying that consumer advertising was all right if certain criteria were met; the drug companies easily complied.

I was involved with the TV programming from its inception in 1991 to its demise in February 1995. My primary interest was to maintain the professionalism of the medical education being offered on television. High-quality, peer-reviewed biomedical literature was preferable to "advertorials" and "infomercials," in my estimation. It seemed to me that drug advertising was a reasonable price to pay for the public consumption of reliable medical information. Unfortunately, the programming went, but the direct-to-consumer ads continued to appear in all forms of public media.

How the AMA Controlled Drug Advertising

During most of the twentieth century the AMA played a leading role in the control of drug advertising, and once again, Morris Fishbein was the principal actor in the drama. When he became editor of *JAMA* in 1924, the AMA already had exerted control over prescription drug promotion. Although the Pure Food and Drugs Act had been passed in 1906, it required only that a medical product be unadulterated. The AMA demanded more, and let pharmaceutical manufacturers know that it would accept ads only if the manufacturer restricted its advertising to physicians through medical journals.

The standard practice had been to hawk nostrums and notions to the public with newspaper and magazine ads, and then advertise prescription drugs to doctors in medical journals. The AMA said it would accept ads in its journal only if the company stopped advertising to the general public. The pharmaceutical companies complied because it was more profitable to sell drugs prescribed by physicians.

Fishbein formalized this practice in 1930 by having the AMA councils on pharmacy and chemistry, physical therapy, and foods and nutrition award "Seals of Acceptance" to new drugs that had passed the councils' tests for safety and efficacy. *JAMA* also had a strict advertising code that controlled the claims made by manufacturers about the benefits of their products. The publication in *JAMA* of a drug ad meant the product was useful. Although the FDA had been essentially sidelined by the AMA, change came in 1938, when a crisis developed with a new drug formulation and Congress amended the Food, Drug and Cosmetic Act, making the FDA ensure the safety of a drug if used as directed. The thalidomide crisis of the early 1960s led to further strengthening of the FDA, which was given authority to control advertising information.

In fact, all of the governmental regulatory initiatives were driven by public scandals. The 1906 congressional act that required purity in food and drug products was driven by revelations about the appalling conditions in meatpacking companies published in Upton Sinclair's novel *The Jungle*. The 1938 congressional amendments to ensure drug safety followed the "Massengill massacre"— the deaths of more than one hundred patients after using a new formulation of a sulfonamide drug. And legislation in the 1960s to strengthen the FDA was introduced after the thalidomide disaster, when babies were born with gross malformations to mothers who had taken the drug.

The new regulations insisted that drugs be more than merely pure and safe; now they had to also be effective. Every drug marketed was to be subjected to controlled studies to determine whether it was definitely, probably, possibly, or not effective. When the studies began in the 1960s, some 5,000 prescription products were being offered for sale. After they were studied, only 2,500 were found to be definitely or probably effective. The other 2,500 never saw market shelf life again.

While it lasted, the AMA's advertising policy was remarkably effective. The revenue generated by pharmaceutical advertising was sufficient to cover virtually all of the association's expenses, and from 1912 until 1949, the year Fishbein left, there were no dues for membership in the AMA. Membership was extended free of charge to any physician who already was a member of a county and state medical society.

It was a cabal that profited both the AMA and the pharmaceutical companies. Whether drug advertising in *JAMA* was good or bad for patients would have to be examined drug by drug, although I suspect that not much would come of such an inquiry. Most of the drugs being prescribed before World War II weren't much good anyway. The doctor's little black bag may have had a lot of things in it, but not much that was useful. Still, the advertising practices were nefarious, and they resulted in a crisis for me as editor of *JAMA,* when I was new to the job in 1983.

That year *JAMA* published a medical news article that told the truth about a particular line of products that were being marketed to physicians. The article indicated that there were adverse side effects in one version of the product line. The product manufacturer, Pfizer, objected vocally to the publisher of *JAMA* and then began withholding advertising for all of its products. The cost in lost revenue soon was counted in millions of dollars, a fact noted by the AMA publisher, executive vice president, and board of trustees. The pressure on me to retract, apologize, or publish some kind of countering article became increasingly intense.

I was a young editor, with only one year on the job, and I did the wrong thing. I didn't retract the article, because it was true, and I didn't apologize, but I did assign a new writer in the medical news section to write another article on the same subject. I told the writer nothing about what was going on and did not indicate whether the article should be positive, negative, or indifferent. My direction was simply to write another piece on the subject. The article was well researched and written and didn't say anything particularly good or bad about the Pfizer product; the company stopped withholding advertising money, and the AMA powers-that-be were mollified.

Then the story leaked to Howard Wolinsky at the *Chicago Sun-Times.* His front-page article exposed the sorry affair and put my editorship in jeopardy, as it should have. I should not have done what I did, but I learned my lesson and never did anything like that again. The lesson for the higher AMA officials was that they had better not pressure anybody like they pressured me again, and from that day forward I never again received any direct pressure from a pharmaceutical company, or from the AMA on behalf of any company.

But in the mid–1980s the pharmaceutical companies learned that there were new, and perhaps better, ways to influence physicians to prescribe their medications: by enlisting leading physicians in their communities to prescribe them. They discovered that doctors follow opinion and thought leaders. They don't necessarily do what the medical journals tell them, what medical research tells them, or even what the most creative ads tell them. They tend to follow their leaders.

So the companies created new programs called physician influence group seminars (PIGSs). They would pay a leading practitioner $5,000 to $10,000 for one speech about a given product in a given area. The drug the practitioner was paid to speak about was usually a scientifically sound product, but the big bucks were paid anyway. The speaker would be sent, all expenses paid, to a resort in Sun Valley or a Caribbean beach resort. Then practicing physicians in the speaker's community or field would be invited to attend, with their spouses or friends. They would spend an hour or two at the seminar, then stay on an extra two or three days, with all expenses paid by the pharmaceutical company. Free of charge, they would learn about new science in the field, new discoveries about the disease, and new medications, and they could also polish their water-skiing or snorkel skills.

A physician from Salt Lake City, John Nelson, telephoned me one day to complain about PIGS programs. He said they were awful, unethical, and damaging to physician reputations. I said, "Why don't you write about it?" He did, and after a few rounds of reviews it appeared as "A Piece of My Mind" in *JAMA:* "A Snorkel, a 5-Iron, and a Pen." Nelson described a meeting with a drug company rep who asked him to try a new delivery system for a well-known product. After several meetings Nelson agreed to try the new product a few times in selected cases.

Some weeks later Nelson encountered a colleague who described a wonderful Caribbean vacation with his wife, paid for by the rep's pharmaceutical company. The colleague had flatly refused, again and again, to try the new product. The invitation to the Caribbean came after one such refusal. Two months later Nelson encountered another colleague who had spent an extended weekend at a western golf resort, paid for by the same company, which extended the invitation after he had refused several times to try the new product.

"I feel betrayed by this company," Nelson wrote. "I believe I made a reasoned effort to use this new product, despite its much higher cost, and despite the fact that the literature has not shown it to have the long-term beneficial effects of the drug it is meant to replace." But, he added, the colleague who enjoyed the Caribbean retreat began using the new product routinely. "Could there have been something in the soft, romantic evening air that made this product's clinical efficacy look more attractive?"

Nelson's article and a different letter to the editor of the *New England Journal* at about the same time effectively blew the whistle on the PIGS-at-the-trough program. Shortly thereafter Democratic Senator Edward Kennedy from Massachusetts threatened to hold hearings about the practice, and the AMA's Council on Ethical and Judicial Affairs crafted policy, saying that physicians should not accept gifts from individuals or companies above a small dollar amount. Pens and key rings were okay, but trips to exotic places were strictly proscribed. Some time later we learned that one company was organizing yet another trip (to the South Pacific no less), and we assigned a medical news reporter to dig up the details and write a story. When it appeared, the exotic trip was canceled.

In discussing pharmaceutical company promotional excesses, I run more than a little risk of angering some people. Medscape derives revenue from advertising and sponsorship, but I do think the companies would run the greater risk if they tried to punish us for telling the truth. The truth is that they do conduct great research and enjoy high profit margins, and that they sell the same products in Canada and Mexico at much lower prices. They get away with this because those countries don't have the same kind of marketing cartels that run things in the United States. There are elements of truth in their assertion that they need high profits to reinvest in research and development, but it's not the whole truth. The way they earn their profits is simply quintessential capitalism.

We are in genuine danger of overmedicating ourselves in this country, at great cost and often with questionable benefit. It has been found, for example, that overuse of pain medication can rebound and cause the very pain the medication was designed to control. When people overuse products like Excedrin, Tylenol, and Advil, for instance, to control headaches—and some people take as many as fifteen tablets per day—the medication itself can cause headaches, yet another paradox in medicine.

People also encounter trouble with prescribed products designed to control conditions that may be better addressed by diet or exercise. Many patients have a strong desire to resolve all their health problems with a drop, a pill, or a plaster. That desire goes back to the days of nostrums and elixirs, only now the medications come with all kinds of scientific assurances. Think of those splashy magazine ads with great graphics and large type on one page, followed by another page of dense type with warnings, precautions, and listings of adverse reactions. The glamour is on one page, and the science is on the other. What looks easy in one place suddenly looks terribly complicated and difficult in another. How come? The answer is simple: there is no such thing as a "safe" drug.

Exogenous substances always are ingested at some risk, and physicians always have to weigh the potential risk against the potential benefit. Furthermore, the FDA trials of new medications typically involve hundreds, and sometimes even thousands, of patients. But when the drug is suddenly used by hundreds of thousands of patients, new and unexpected adverse reactions occur. This creates new problems for drugs that are widely advertised shortly after FDA approval. In the near future, because of the Human Genome Project, vast numbers of new drugs will appear, targeted for specific genetic situations. Companies will be seeking approval for many of them based on data from clinical trials involving dozens or scores of people rather than the usual hundreds or thousands. So the prospects for both benefits and risks have never been greater.

I confess that I am of two minds when it comes to direct-to-consumer advertising. Some days I would completely ban consumer ads because they are inflationary and exert pressure on physicians to prescribe expensive products. Other days I can see value in ads that educate patients about health, especially with respect to drug-use compliance and even motivation.

For example, when the FDA acted to remove Rezulin, a diabetes drug linked to sixty-three deaths from liver failure, drug companies with competing products ran large print ads. They warned of the dangers associated with the dangerous drug while also soliciting patients for their approved alternatives. In the process they educated patients about the FDA ruling.

In the end, however, we have to wonder whether less isn't sometimes more in medicine. Sometimes the best medicine may be to advise cautious waiting. Often, as Archie Cochrane so eloquently pointed out, the recuperative powers of the body are indeed more powerful than medications. Sometimes the very best therapy comes not from pills or procedures but from professional attention to a patient's distress.

6

A Terminal Profession

Why Medicine Is Under Attack

S O IF PHYSICIANS ARE SUPPOSED to pay close attention to their patients' problems, why don't they? And if patients can actually enhance therapy by trusting their doctors, why don't they? In fact, why is there a general perception that physicians cover up, close ranks, and sometimes even bury their mistakes? Why do people think that too many doctors are in it only for the money, and that their idea of self-regulation is to charge as much as they can get away with? Unhappily, these perceptions exist because too often they are true.

The sad state of affairs is that the profession of medicine seemed to lose its way during the flush days of unquestioned third-party reimbursement. It lost its overriding commitment to care for the poor without charge, and it lost its responsibility to self-govern its ranks. And the AMA offered little leadership. Time and again it resisted initiatives aimed at disclosure, self-referral, or higher standards of practice. It was perceived as solely concerned with protecting physicians' income, and the perception too often was the reality.

There were times when the association fulfilled its traditional ethical obligations, but it often moved slowly, with apparent reluctance. It was founded to strengthen physician education and training, monitor competence, and maintain high ethical standards. Today the public trusts the physician training system and believes most doctors are competent, but has little faith in the profession's ethical standards.

To be fair, the core of the AMA's problem relates to the ambiguous nature of medicine itself: it has always been a business as well as a profession. Two examples from my early experiences illustrate the tension between these poles. As a reward for being in the upper third of my class in medical school, I was allowed to choose an elective course in my fourth year. That was the way it worked in the 1950s. Now medical schools allow all students a lot of elective time in the fourth year.

In any event, I chose an elective in pediatric cardiology. Every day I worked with pediatricians and cardiologists, X-raying newborn infants in an attempt to diagnose congenital heart defects. This was not long after the breakthrough blue baby procedure, and medicine was just beginning to correct or ameliorate heart disease. So it was important to know exactly what the lesion was because some could be operated on and some could not. (Now, incidentally, virtually all such lesions can be corrected very early in life.)

During the course of my study I worked with other medical students, one of whom had just returned from an elective that included working with a practicing physician. I remember one day vividly. We were discussing the electrocardiograph (EKG) machine, and the question was whether EKGs should be used in an office practice. My colleague said, "These EKGs are important, but I'm not going to use one in my practice. I learned out there that you can't make any money off EKGs. They cost too much, and no one will pay you for them. It's just not worth it."

I was still an idealist then, and I was appalled by what he said. It was terrible. The question of money was decisive for him, not getting the equipment his patients needed and doing what was right. Until that moment I hadn't even thought about the economic consequences of equipping a physician's office. The idea that patients might be denied needed service because the physician couldn't make any money from it was brand-new to me. But it was a common phenomenon, and I have watched it ever since. There will always be some doctors who are attuned to new questions and new opportunities so as to be poised to capture the market and get rich even faster. Money is indeed a strong incentive.

Another experience offers a different view of physician motivation. When I joined the faculty of the Los Angeles County–University of Southern California (LAC-USC) County Medical Center in 1967, the largest hospital in the United States at that time, I expected to spend most of my time teaching and conducting research, primarily in the area of my longtime interest: diseases caused by drugs.

One year into my tenure, Hugh Edmondson, the chair of the Department of Pathology, asked me to become the assistant director of laboratories and pathology. I had spent three years as lab director at the army hospital in El Paso and readily agreed to become assistant director at LAC-USC County Medical Center. I occupied that role for the next nine years, becoming associate director under Nancy Warner when she became pathology chair and lab director—the first female chair of pathology at a coeducational medical school in the history of the United States, I might add.

I inherited a peculiar rationing system at this extremely active laboratory. The hospital, owned by the county of Los Angeles, was built in the 1930s and often used as a facade for television shows, like *Dr. Kildare* and *Ben Casey.* Its administrators proclaimed that no person would ever be turned away from its doors. To my knowledge, no one ever was turned away, and that created difficult funding problems. Too many doctors were ordering too many tests, and there wasn't enough money to handle the demand. So the hospital had established a rationing system for laboratory orders.

Every Sunday night the chief residents of the various specialties handed out an allocation of ration stamps to the younger residents, who cared for most of the patients and ordered most of the tests. Every chemistry lab request slip had to contain a ration stamp sticker, and the book of stamps had to last seven days. If one of the young physicians had an inordinate number of very sick patients, he or she was likely to run out of stamps by Thursday or Friday night, and then couldn't order another test for two whole days.

Predictably, late in the week I would start getting calls from physicians who had run out of stamps and desperately needed them for patients in trouble. All I could say was, "I'm sorry. Maybe you can borrow stamps from a colleague." Then they would say, "You're killing my patient. She's in diabetic coma, and I can't manage the coma without chemical lab tests." I knew they were right, and I knew the system was immoral, unethical, and probably illegal, but I had to say no during the early weeks of my tenure.

Then I began a personal campaign to wage war on the stamps. I told everyone that we were going to get rid of them, but that it would take me a while to figure out precisely how to do it. One year to the day after inheriting the rationing system, we celebrated its end by burning stamps at "grand rounds." Actually, we burned only a few and threw the rest away, but it was a joyous occasion.

We did it through the bureaucratic budget process: we put pressure on the hospital administration to provide more lab technicians and machines and educated doctors in how to use the lab more professionally and intelligently. We wanted doctors to stop scattershot ordering of lab tests. We developed a patient-focused laboratory system in which all tests were categorized as to how quickly the lab results had to get back to the doctor. The point was to take care of the patient properly, no matter what the test was.

It was an A–B–C–D system. If the doctor needed results in one hour or less, the test was categorized A and results in one hour were guaranteed. Tests whose results were needed in four hours were classified B. Results for C tests were required within twenty-four hours, and we could take longer than twenty-four hours to report results for D tests. That was the system, and it was in place twenty-four hours a day, seven days a week. It worked well because the first three test categories were conducted in the hospital laboratory and the fourth category was sent out to a commercial lab. In fact, we virtually built the commercial lab business in southern California. Dow Chemical's BioScience Labs were essentially built with Los Angeles County money for spillover lab tests.

As the old rationing system was going down, I learned about how the young doctors had dealt with it. Some had created counterfeit stamps; there were bogus stamps all over the place. Some had sold ration stamps to others, and some had traded stamps. In a sense, it was entrepreneurialism at its best to counter a rationing system at its worst. They had done anything and everything they could to help their patients. That is precisely what physicians are supposed to do, and it is a crucial part of being a professional. The old system of rationing was unprofessional; it created errors, it hurt patients and physicians, and yet the county and medical school had approved it until we finally blew the whistle.

It strikes me that some of the restraints on services put in place by managed care plans might be dealt with in similar ways. It's already known that doctors sometimes hedge in describing conditions to make sure patients receive needed services. What we really need is a better managed care system in which medical goals, reviewed by physician panels, are clearly understood and everyone complies with procedures to achieve them, with mechanisms for review of exceptional cases.

Why Do People Go to Medical School?

I have learned that there are four reasons for wanting to become a doctor.

First, people who aspire to become doctors want to take care of sick people. They want to be of service, to help people stay well, and to help them get well if they become sick. That is a real motivation for almost everyone who applies to medical school.

Second, people who want to become doctors are good at science. They are good students who have studied mathematics, biology, and other sciences and earned good grades throughout their primary, secondary, and higher education. Otherwise, they couldn't get into medical school.

Third, people who want to become doctors want to have a good deal of independence. They like being in charge of their own lives; they look forward to opening their own practices and making up their own minds about how best to proceed in caring for patients. They want to govern themselves, to not be intruded upon by others. This desire partially explains the huge physician anger at managed care.

Fourth, people who want to be doctors want to make money, something that has been assured since the emergence of health insurance in the 1940s, and especially since the implementation of Medicare in the 1960s. People who go into medicine often make a lot of money—certainly not as much as captains of business, finance, and industry, but well beyond the average income. Physicians usually can live in nice houses, buy good automobiles, and send their kids to good schools. They can go to the symphony when they want and rarely worry about the cost of a new camera.

The first three of these reasons—a desire to serve, intellectual strength, and an independent streak—are critical elements in the makeup of any professional, but there is more to medicine. The essence of medical professionalism is self-governance and self-regulation, both of which rely on ethical standards. It goes all the way back to the Hippocratic oath.

The American Medical Association was founded in 1847 to create higher standards for medical education, standards for medical practice, and a code of medical ethics. It should be remembered that back in the 1840s people could take a three-month course, less than a high school diploma, complete it, and call themselves medical doctors. Admittedly, something of a guild mentality guided the creation of the AMA—if you couldn't meet the standards, you couldn't practice medicine—but the association can and should be proud of its history, especially of its commitment to high ethical standards. Its original code of ethics was so powerful that it almost tore the AMA asunder two decades after it was formed. A code of ethics can be volatile because it strikes at the heart of how people behave.

The association quickly established the Judicial Council (which lasted for many decades) to rule on AMA membership and member behavior. The council determined whether a member should be thrown out of the association for questionable behavior. As it adjudicated these cases the council created a body of knowledge and a body of principles as to what constituted ethical behavior.

When Kirk Johnson, one of the great general counsels of the AMA, joined the association in the 1980s, among the first things he wanted to do was redefine the scope of the Judicial Council. He wanted a nomenclature acknowledgment that the Judicial Council was more than a judging body, and that it was deeply concerned with medical ethics. Accordingly, he worked to change the name to the Council on Ethical and Judicial Affairs (CEJA), and after succeeding in that endeavor, he led the effort to strengthen CEJA's ethical standards opinions for physicians, whether AMA members or not. In fact, CEJA's standards are referred to by state medical licensing boards; if physicians repeatedly violate CEJA ethical standards, their licenses can be put on probation, suspended, or revoked.

Despite CEJA's power, most people are more familiar with the AMA's self-protective proclivities than with the good works accomplished by its ethics council. When I teach, I often ask medical students, and sometimes faculty, what they know about CEJA. Most know nothing at all. Then I ask whether they can recite the seven ethical principles established by CEJA, as detailed in the 150 pages of opinions and standards published in the council's "Code of Ethics." Again, they often say they have never heard of these principles.

It's a basic failing and a basic frustration for me. I think that all medical schools should have a required course in medical ethics. Most schools have such courses available, but many do not require participation. In fact, medical ethics is a growing field in academic medicine, and many schools have distinguished academic ethicists.

For the record, the seven ethical principles adopted by the AMA in 1980 are:

1. A physician shall be dedicated to providing competent medical service with compassion and respect for human dignity.

2. A physician shall deal honestly with patients and colleagues and strive to expose those physicians deficient in character or competence, or who engage in fraud or deception.

3. A physician shall respect the law and also recognize a responsibility to seek changes in those requirements which are contrary to the best interests of the patient.

4. A physician shall respect the rights of patients, or colleagues, and of other health professionals, and shall safeguard patient confidences within the constraints of the law.

5. A physician shall continue to study, apply, and advance scientific knowledge, make relevant information available to patients, colleagues, and the public, obtain consultation, and use the talents of other health professionals when indicated.

6. A physician shall, in the provision of appropriate patient care, except in emergencies, be free to choose whom to serve, with whom to associate, and the environment in which to provide medical services.

7. A physician shall recognize a responsibility to participate in activities contributing to an improved community.

Once again, the essence of professionalism is self-governance and self-regulation, which start with ethics. At its center, medicine is a moral enterprise grounded in a covenant of trust. That is what separates learned professionals from all others.

The Learned Professions

Today we call almost anyone who wants to be so called a "professional." We have professional wrestlers, professional writers, professional undertakers, and professional flight attendants. The modern use of the word implies a degree of commitment, training, and competence, but it does not encompass the special responsibilities and obligations of the learned professionals.

Traditionally there have been three learned professions: law, religion, and medicine. Practitioners in these areas became professionals because they were working with profound, ubiquitous, and unequivocal human needs. Attorneys, clergymen, and physicians must be trusted with the most private and intimate secrets of a person's mind, soul, and body. The client, parishioner, or patient must trust the professional to use the information to his benefit, not to exploit him. That is the social need and compact that led to the development of the learned professions. They are service professionals responding to deep human needs.

Edmond Pellegrino, director of the Kennedy Institute of Ethics, succinctly defined the essential characteristic of a learned professional some years ago. He said that "at some point in the professional relationship, when a difficult decision is to be made, you can depend on the one who is in a true profession to efface his own self-interest."

Christine Cassel, another physician with a deep commitment to medical ethics, elaborated by listing ten characteristics of a learned professional, and we published them in *JAMA:*

1. Self-governance individually and as a group
2. Service to the poor without expectation of compensation
3. Deliverance of quality
4. Not ripping people off
5. High level of learning
6. Autonomy of activity
7. Altruism
8. Self-sacrifice
9. Heroism as needed
10. Ethical practice with public accountability

There is no question in my mind that if physicians universally lived up to these standards and the ethical principles of CEJA, the trust they have lost would be restored almost immediately. If patients truly felt that physicians regularly efface their self-interest when dealing with difficult decisions, their belief in the efficacy of prescribed treatments would be enhanced substantially, and that would be good for patient health as well.

I began writing in *JAMA* about professionalism in 1985. In 1990 I developed the rocking-horse metaphor to illustrate the dilemma faced by physicians from time immemorial: medicine, with its high ethical standards, is nonetheless both a profession and a business. Physicians perform services that are valued, and that value is expressed in dollars, the coin of the realm, or sometimes in services in kind. That is what has kept the whole process going.

What disturbed me then, and disturbs me even more today, is that the balance between business and professional values has tipped dangerously toward the business side. I expressed this in a bell-shaped top and rocking-horse bottom, with money-grubbers and altruistic missionaries at opposite ends of the curve and businesspeople and professionals in the larger central portion of the curve. Any physician in any community can quickly identify the money-grubbers and the missionaries.

Unfortunately, we have always had money-grubbers, and probably always will. More alarming, however, has been the shift in the middle tilting physicians toward the business side. Of course, a pendulum swings and a rocking horse rocks. My concern is that, if the rocking horse rocks too far toward the business side, it may tip over and the profession of medicine may be lost; all trust and respect will disappear. Doctors will be fancy technicians, and patients faceless cases. That would be bad for patient health.

After my 1990 editorial was published, it seemed that the rocking horse was righting itself. In the early 1990s medicine did behave more like a profession. From 1991 until 1994 organized medicine worked very hard to devise a way for all Americans to be insured so that everyone could have at least basic medical care and receive free, or deeply discounted, care if they were in financial need. When reform didn't occur, the balance tipped again toward the business side, but by the late 1990s medicine, again following *JAMA*'s lead, had begun working on patient safety and patient protection programs. The profession once again was working strongly on behalf of patients.

But most of the 1990s witnessed a losing battle for professionalism as business concerns tipped the balance toward money-grubbers. At the beginning of the decade two-thirds of physicians gave free or deeply discounted care to patients in need. That is the sine qua non of a learned profession. As noted, free care had begun to erode with the introduction of Medicare and Medicaid, when many doctors decided they didn't have to attend charity clinics or hospitals anymore. With the growing numbers of uninsured patients in the 1990s, one would have expected an increase in free care, but to my own great disappointment, the percentage of physicians offering it did not budge upward one point.

The good news is that that percentage apparently didn't erode any further, and it easily could have (and may still do so). Managed care leaves little room for cross-subsidization. Doctors are so harassed by time-study business administrators that the time available to them to provide free care is constrained severely. The discounted fees of managed care also exert constraints. So the fact that the percentage of physicians offering free care remained the same is commendable, but it is still disheartening to note that one-third of American physicians intentionally offered no free care at all.

Today there is a real concern about medical professionalism. In the next decade we in the United States may lose it entirely and medicine may become unequivocally dominated by business interests. Eventually the pendulum would swing in the other direction, because medicine must exist as a learned profession. The need is too deep, historic, and pervasive to be ignored. In the meantime, however, the chasm between patients and physicians could widen as patients watch their doctors scramble for money and increasingly avoid them in favor of alternative practitioners.

Disciplining Doctors and Finding Good Ones

Finding a good doctor seems to be a chronic problem in medicine. Where does one turn for guidance? I'm commonly asked: "Which doctor can I trust? Where can I go for ordinary care as well as the best care?" The methods available for choosing a doctor are extremely limited, and even for a professional it's difficult to determine whom to recommend.

When I was in medical school, most students held that, if you wanted to know whom to choose for your own care, or for your family, asking the interns or residents in the emergency department was the way to go. You could ask them whom they consulted on the staff or faculty for their own care, they would tell you who was good and who wasn't, and more often than not they would be right.

This became an issue for me when my wife became pregnant and we had to find a good obstetrician. A little scouting around turned up the name of Ed Waldrup, a great obstetrician-gynecologist practicing in Birmingham, Alabama. It turned out that he was the one who delivered babies for almost all of the medical students and residents. Everyone went to him because he was so nice and did such a wonderful job. He had a substantial practice and of course gave away free care to the medical students. That was professional courtesy, a concept that goes back to Hippocrates. He enjoined physicians to teach each other, care for each other, and in times of necessity house each other. Physicians were to treat one another as family members.

This practice has eroded over the past three or four decades, and now the government and managed care companies say that the practice should be discontinued altogether. According to these parties, it's inappropriate, unfair, and based on a favoritism that should not be countenanced. Hogwash, I say. The practice of professional courtesy has deep and abiding roots and must continue. It's part of the practice of a profession.

The problem of finding a good doctor has become even more frustrating in the age of managed care, when many patients are asked to pick from a list of unfamiliar doctors. How do they know whom to trust? How do they know whether a particular doctor on the list is good or bad? In the light of horrendous malpractice complaints, with multimillion-dollar awards resulting from horrible mistakes, how can they be sure that Dr. X or Dr. Y isn't one of those incompetent physicians?

This was precisely the kind of anxiety that led to the legislation, enacted in 1986, that created the National Practitioner Data Bank. The data bank lists doctors against whom actions have been taken. License suspensions and revocations are listed. So are hospital discipline actions and malpractice awards or settlements above a certain dollar level. State licensing boards and other entities seeking to credential a physician can gain information from the data bank, but no one else can. All of this information is available on a centrally organized government list that can be accessed only by accrediting authorities.

Initially supportive of the legislation, which was packaged with the authority to conduct good-faith peer review, the AMA learned to dislike it, especially after practicing physicians learned that they might be listed. They despised the data bank, and so the AMA began a protracted battle to limit access to credentialing authorities alone. That would protect the public by proxy, AMA officials argued. Every year the question of opening the data bank is raised, and every year so far the AMA has been able to sink it.

Massachusetts took another tack, which gained the support of the Massachusetts Medical Society. The state decided that the data bank should be opened, but that the information should be explained in reasonable ways so that reasonable people could understand it. The argument against opening the data is that it is not only bad doctors who get sued. Many good doctors who took patients with problematic diseases also are sued and sometimes settle out of court to avoid the expense of a trial, even though their chances of exoneration are high. And of course, insurance companies may settle a case just to cut costs, regardless of any merit of the claim. Neurosurgeons are a prime example of physicians who take on difficult cases and are often sued. Obstetricians have the same problem: when a newborn is damaged in any way, even when there seems to be no good reason to blame the neonatal care, the obstetrician is often sued.

As we know from good studies conducted in Tennessee and Florida and published in *JAMA,* there is little direct evidence of a relationship between the quality of a physician's practice and the frequency with which he or she has been sued or settled claims. Indeed, the likelihood of a doctor being sued has more to do with a bad result or with the doctor's poor communication skills than with his or her competence. Family physicians and internists are rarely sued, for example, probably because they know their patients, talk to them, and earn their trust. Anesthesiologists learned this, to their benefit, when they not only tightened their procedural standards but began to spend more time explaining those procedures to their patients. Subsequently, suits against anesthesiologists and malpractice insurance premiums plummeted.

The experience in Massachusetts affirms that patients can be helped to understand the information in the data bank. Nothing really bad has happened to the profession there as a result of giving people access to data bank information. Doctors did not lose their practices. Patients continued to see their physicians. Furthermore, the rare physicians who have been sued ten or twenty times and settled may indeed not be practicing medicine competently, and people should have a chance to know about their record.

The Tragedy of Errors

Who is to blame when things go wrong? During the major portion of my tenure at the AMA, organized medicine was deeply estranged from the U.S. legal profession and felt a need to attack it. For many years the AMA's attitude toward malpractice was that the problem was largely caused by trial lawyers and greedy patients who saw a chance to make a "killing" by going after doctors and their rich insurance companies. I'm not here to defend trial lawyers. They have plenty of problems within their profession, but the idea of getting rid of the malpractice problem by getting rid of the lawyers was flawed from the beginning.

Yet that was the basic approach followed by the association for years. Martin Hatlie, an AMA attorney, was put in charge of trying to change the tort system and spent years exploring various avenues to that end. He enjoyed his greatest triumph during the "Contract with America" legislative blitz in early 1995, when the Republican-led House passed legislation to limit awards for pain and suffering to $250,000. The AMA ballyhooed this "victory" ad nauseam, but the victory was short-lived because neither the Senate nor the White House would go along.

Just before that time, I received a single-author paper from Lucian Leape, a physician at the Harvard School of Public Health, who had some devastating information about the costs of patient errors. I had met Lucian some years before at the Rand Corporation in Santa Monica, when Rand put together a group of physicians—including Kenneth Shine, who is now the president of the Institute of Medicine, Robert Brook of UCLA, and the Stanford health economist Alan Enthoven—to craft suggestions for health system reform.

Lucian had talked to me about the paper, titled "Error in Medicine," before sending it along. He asked whether I would be able to take the heat for publishing something with that title.

"Well, what does it say?" I asked.

"It says that errors in medicine kill more Americans per year than would three jumbo jet aircraft crashes every two days at O'Hare Field," he said, indicating that the number approached 100,000. He added that he was using hard data from three different studies, one from California, one from New York, and one from Utah.

I knew the studies. The lead author of the first one was Don Harper Mills, a physician and attorney from California and a former colleague of mine at USC; he had published the paper in the *Western Journal of Medicine*. Don had told me about his study when

I was going to work at UC Davis in 1977, noting that the Sacramento Medical Center was one of the really bad hospitals in California. The second study, authored by Troyen Brennan and a group from the Harvard School of Public Health, was published in the *New England Journal of Medicine*. The third study, from Utah, was offered to *JAMA* but rejected on the grounds that it offered nothing new. A group of my tough *JAMA* editors said the Utah study just duplicated what the California and New York studies had already demonstrated. I went along with them, even though my inclination was to publish. The papers all supported the same idea: error in medicine was a critical problem, and we needed to deal with it.

The thrust of Leape's paper was that not only were errors killing patients but medicine was approaching them in the wrong way. This was not a problem of malpractice, ignorance, greed, bad doctors, or bad apples. It was a systems problem. We needed better systems aimed at preventing error. We needed a system that would have different names for different drugs instead of a system in which the names of different drugs were almost identical. We needed a better system to make sure that the right drug in the right dose was given to the right patient. Pharmacists needed to prepare and label doses ahead of time. Computer systems needed to identify fatal drug combinations before they were administered. We also needed something as simple as a systematic approach to labeling limbs scheduled for amputation to make sure the surgeon didn't cut off the wrong one.

This was strong stuff, and I told Leape I wanted the manuscript. When it arrived, I assigned it to Jeanette Smith, one of *JAMA*'s toughest and best editors. She had it reviewed by rigorous outsider peer reviewers. All said it needed to be published, and after some revisions it was accepted for publication.

Once accepted, I had to figure out what to do with it. The paper did not mince words, and I knew a lot of physicians and hospital administrators were going to object strongly to publishing the information it contained. Leape reported that 3.7 percent of patients in fifty-one New York hospitals suffered an injury severe enough to prolong a hospital stay. Of these, 58 percent were attributable to error, and 13.6 percent were fatal. Extrapolated to the country, this resulted in an estimated 98,000 deaths per year. The other studies used similar methods but reached a lower number of 44,000 deaths caused annually by medical errors. I wanted to publish the paper for the profession but feared that I would lose my job if the public media hit hard on it.

The solution came when I decided to publish Leape's paper in a late December 1994 issue. Little attention was paid to *JAMA* material during the holiday season; typically holiday issues are the least read and covered. The media usually pick up almost nothing during that time, and general readership is low. But it would be in the literature, and the people who needed to see it would because it was in *JAMA*. I wanted the paper in the medical literature, but I didn't want to create a lot of hoopla because I wanted to remain editor of *JAMA* a while longer.

At the time of publication, to my knowledge only one reporter, David Baron of National Public Radio in Boston, recognized the importance of the paper. He broadcast a long piece on it, but no one else seemed to notice. The following month Abigail Trafford, editor of the *Washington Post*'s weekly health section, picked it up, immediately identified its importance, and put it in the paper. Then everyone saw it, and all hell broke loose.

Hate mail began pouring in. I was accused of being on the side of the lawyers, of being a damned turncoat and traitor to the cause. An intensive lobbying campaign to get rid of me began. I withstood the firestorm largely because James Todd was still executive vice president of the AMA. He understood the information and knew it was correct, so he deflected the criticism, pointing out that *JAMA* was editorially independent while also being a moneymaker for the AMA. Furthermore, he thought it was time to change the whole approach to malpractice; he had fought the old war to change the tort system in favor of negotiated claims settlements and had not succeeded.

Not long after this, I met Marty Hatlie at the luggage carousel at the Chicago airport, quite by chance. He was returning from Washington and I from San Francisco. We greeted one another, and then he asked, "What do you think about this Lucian Leape thing?" I said, "I think he's right, and that we ought to stop trying to kill the lawyers and start trying to prevent errors in medicine." Hatlie agreed, and said he was going to start working on that within the AMA. The lobbying effort was going nowhere, everyone knew that Leape's information was correct, and it was time to work on preventing errors. Fortunately, he had an ally in Todd, and out of their collaboration came the National Patient Safety Foundation.

Systemic Patient Safety First

Within a year Hatlie had spearheaded the formation of the new foundation, in which the AMA was joined by the American Association for the Advancement of Science, the Joint Commission on Accreditation of Healthcare Organizations, and the Annenberg Center for Health Sciences. By 1997 the independent not-for-profit foundation had gained a broad partnership that represented consumer advocates, health care providers, health product manufacturers, insurance companies, employers, payers, researchers, and regulators.

All agreed that the foundation's core mission was to promote safety by supporting a fresh and honest discussion about risk, error, blame, and accountability. The foundation members agreed on a strategy: to promote research for the development of new knowledge about safety and human and organizational error; to implement applications for preventing avoidable patient harm; to foster communication to enhance patient safety; and to develop educational approaches based in part on collaborative relationships with other complex industries, such as aviation and nuclear power, in which human safety issues also are investigated.

There was already a model for a patient safety system in the state of Massachusetts. In 1987 its Board of Registration in Medicine implemented a program that required physicians, hospitals, managed care organizations, and others to participate in risk management activities as a condition of licensure. Facilities could lose their licenses unless they established a patient care assessment system and submitted quarterly reports on all unexpected deaths and major treatment complications. The reports had to describe the event, the results of an internal investigation, and corrective actions.

For its part, the Massachusetts board issued safety advisories, calling attention to hazards such as chemotherapy dose calculations and concentrated intravenous potassium chloride solutions. It also convened panels of experts to develop safety guidelines for intravenous conscious sedation, for potassium chloride administration, and for prevention of suicides by inpatients with psychiatric illnesses.

Several features of the Massachusetts program should be underscored:

1. It holds health care organizations accountable for having safety programs and for responding to accidents.
2. It calls for active participation in safety programs by physicians.
3. It places primary responsibility for safety on the only unit that can correct faulty systems—the hospital or managed care organization.
4. Reporting is nonpunitive. Hospitals need not identify physicians, and information is held confidentially, even from the board's own enforcement staff.
5. It carries a big stick. The board can prohibit physicians from practicing at noncomplying facilities, in effect closing them down.
6. It is responsive. The board becomes engaged if facilities do not react aggressively.
7. It is proactive. The board identifies pervasive threats to safety and issues policies to thwart them.
8. It is amazingly nonbureaucratic, functioning with only three staff members and three volunteer board members.

An Open System at the VA

The Veterans Health Administration, under the leadership of Kenneth Kizer, restructured its system to focus on error prevention with the centralized Patient Safety Registry and Reporting System. The VA system is the government's principal direct health care provider as well as the nation's largest provider of health care professional training; it includes 173 hospitals and some 900 other sites at which it delivers care. The VA also started a program to increase the emphasis on safety by rewarding frontline caregivers who identify adverse events or potential patient safety situations that lead to improved processes or practices.

The VA went a step further by releasing a report in December 1999 documenting that in less than two years at its hospitals there had been approximately 3,000 medical mistakes and mishaps, resulting in more than 700 deaths. The problems included medication errors, failure of medical devices, blood transfusion errors, improper insertion of catheters, and surgery on the wrong body part.

Commenting on the study in the *New York Times,* Kizer said, "When you seek out problems and errors, you find them much more frequently. But no one really believes that errors happen more frequently at VA hospitals. We must uncover and define the full extent of the problem before we see progress." He is precisely correct, and everyone knows it. A month before the VA report, the Institute of Medicine of the National Academy of Sciences released its report affirming the California, Utah, and New York studies, which showed that between 44,000 and 98,000 hospital patients die each year because of medical errors.

The *New York Times* put that figure in perspective by showing that, even using the lower number of 44,000, medical errors were the eighth leading cause of death in the United States, killing more people than either breast cancer or AIDS. At the head of the list is heart disease, with some 727,000 deaths, followed by cancer (539,000), stroke (160,000), lung disease (109,000), accidents (95,000), pneumonia and flu (86,000), and diabetes (62,000). Using the higher number, 98,000, makes treatment errors the fifth leading cause of death.

The report was given intensive media attention, and studies by the Kaiser Family Foundation and the National Academy demonstrated public recognition of the safety problem. Bob Blendon of Harvard told me that his research showed that in late 1999 people knew more about the Institute of Medicine (IOM) report than they did about the health plan proposals of either Al Gore or Bill Bradley, both of whom were engaged in heated primary debates on health care coverage. The media attention truly reflected the interests of readers and viewers, who were saying, "We know what's wrong, but we don't understand clearly how to correct it."

Correcting the problem involves engagement with the highest standards of professionalism. Physicians have to begin by embracing the Hippocratic admonition to "first, do no harm." What that entails today is nothing less than a major change in our culture. Increasingly, physicians and other health workers in the United States live and interact in a culture characterized by anger, blame, guilt, fear, frustration, and distrust regarding health care errors. The public and institutions have responded by escalating the punishment for error. Clinicians and some health care organizations have in turn responded with suppression, stonewalling, and cover-up.

That approach has been less than successful. Medical harm by and large has not been the result of the ignorance, malice, laziness, or greed of any person or organizations involved. The risk of error is ever-present, as in aviation, and just as in aviation, nonpunitive systems could be created to reduce the probability that these mistakes will occur, thereby preventing harm to patients. Air travel is as safe as it is because aviation personnel routinely report problems, including near misses, which can be corrected. No one is punished for reporting errors, no matter how embarrassing. All are committed to identifying and rooting out potential problems.

Pilots and other crew members submit confidential reports about observed mistakes voluntarily, not just because the Federal Aviation Administration (FAA) is watching. The reports are analyzed, and alerts are issued as indicated. The public recognizes that the entire industry is committed to safety and respects that commitment, which extends right down to the security guards at entrance gates. We need to bring that level of commitment to safety to medicine.

This places a strong obligation on physicians. For decades they have worked within a culture of blame and cover-up. The AMA board doesn't like to admit that and has testified before committees disputing that view, but we all know that physicians and institutions cover up. That has to change. Patient safety requires the clear light of day. It demands honesty, confession, disclosure, and protection for the people who made the mistake. That's the only way to produce a system that works to help prevent doctors, nurses, and hospitals from making the same mistake again, or anything like it.

It's a tough requirement because it means coming clean, letting the family know as quickly as the facts are known that a mistake was made. We have to disclose the error. We have to apologize. We have to tell exactly how it happened and then let the family know that we are putting in place a new method to prevent the mistake from happening again. Furthermore, we have to tell the world about it so that others can change their methods accordingly. In effect, we must tell the family that something more than death or injury will be the outcome of the patient's tragic ordeal. It will help other patients, who will benefit by the disclosure and thereby avoid harm.

In addition, we must offer a settlement, in whatever terms make sense. All economic damages should be awarded, figures that could reach as high as $1 million or more. But non-economic, punitive damages should not be offered, and experience suggests they will not be sought if those who made the unfortunate error come clean quickly.

Coming clean has demonstrated effectiveness in holding down malpractice costs. One VA hospital in Lexington, Kentucky, reported that its policy of disclosure resulted in lower malpractice costs over a six-year period compared with thirty-six similar centers. Payments ranged from $1 million to $12 million during the period. The Lexington VA paid $1.3 million. Only seven other institutions had lower payments.

Stephen Kraman, lead author of a study published in the *Annals of Internal Medicine,* said that revealing problems "diminishes the anger and desire for revenge that often motivate patients' litigation." The point is that the angriest patients, not necessarily the most injured, are the ones who sue for malpractice. The Lexington VA policy was to notify patients or family immediately upon identification of error and to offer settlement if the injury resulted in loss of life or earning potential. Many of the patients might not have known of the problem if the hospital had not informed them.

Despite this encouraging news, it will be difficult for doctors to change their culture because that change represents a paradigm shift. Physician ego is enormous. The God image has been around for ages, largely because physicians have to make God-like decisions, and offer God-like services. They don't like to make mistakes. It's even hard for them to acknowledge that they are capable of making mistakes. Every year 45,000 people apply for the 16,000 slots available in U.S. medical schools. These are young people who typically made straight As in grammar school and high school and almost straight As in college. By the time the 16,000 reach medical school, they are accustomed to being the cream of the crop and recognized for doing things right. And in a very real sense, they *are* the cream of the crop because they have worked hard and tried hard to do everything right. It's very difficult for someone like that to admit a mistake, to say, "How could I cut off the wrong leg? How could I be so stupid?" Well, the answer is, you're not stupid, but you need to have a system in place that labels limbs properly.

Physician ego is not the only factor: most patients have a strong desire that their physician be extremely competent. And most of them are, but no physician is perfect or infallible. What physicians need are better systems, and fortunately work is moving forward to put those systems in place. David Bates at Brigham and Women's Hospital in Boston created a computer system that has reduced serious drug errors by 55 percent, saving the hospital more than $500,000 per year and preventing countless numbers of adverse reactions in patients. Bar codes for patients are used at more and more hospitals to make sure the right patients are getting the right drug in the right dose. Full implementation of the electronic medical record could do wonders. And this is just the beginning. Professionals close to the issue see a new era and a new culture of error recognition, accountability, honesty, and rapid and fair settlement for injuries, a culture that addresses the risk of harm as a system problem and works to prevent recurrences of similar problems.

Controversies Involving Trust

When the Institute of Medicine released its report on error in medicine, it made a number of recommendations, including a call for federal legislation that would mandate hospital disclosure of mistakes and require public disclosure as well. Those recommendations met with resistance from federal health officials. John Eisenberg, the physician who heads the Agency for Healthcare Research and Quality in the U.S. Department of Health and Human Services, suggested a cautious approach to mandatory reporting. He pointed out that a number of states have mandatory laws, and that it would be prudent to wait until evidence on their effectiveness is documented. The AMA endorsed his position.

The concern was that mandatory laws would intensify the culture of cover-up. Doctors and hospitals might work even harder to deny blame if they were required to report errors. Furthermore, the livelihood of community hospitals might be threatened if the public learned of serious mistakes committed within them. These are concerns that US Air, TWA, United, American, and every other airline live with every day. They cannot draw a curtain over an airline crash, and in fact they work rigorously with federal aviation officials to uncover the cause of crashes. They can survive such catastrophes because the public trusts them. The public believes in their commitment to safety and is assured that they are doing everything imaginable to protect air travelers—and with good reason, it turns out. In 1976 the risk of dying in an airplane accident was one in two million. As a result of error analysis, that risk today has dropped to one in eight million—a fourfold increase in safety for travelers.

Physicians are on the threshold of rekindling patient trust, if they accept that paradigm shift. Unhappily, physicians lost much of that trust during the 1960s, 1970s, 1980s, and 1990s when too many were tempted by the new ways to make money in medicine. The thinking of that medical student colleague of mine who worried that he couldn't make money on EKGs seemed to grip the profession during those decades.

The problem began when physicians stumbled over their ethical obligation to self-govern and self-regulate. Of course, no one likes being regulated, and everyone prefers self-regulation, but when people don't regulate themselves, they create problems that can be solved only by others. If an individual fails, the group has to regulate the individual. And the question of self-governance among medical professionals keeps coming back to the issue of how they make money. When one doctor doesn't do the right thing, other doctors, especially those in organized medicine, are obliged to respond appropriately.

Self-referral provides one example of the problem. In the normal course of events, physicians perform services and bill for them. That's a very straightforward transaction. The physician sees a patient with clear-cut strep throat and orders an antibiotic. It becomes more complicated when physicians order laboratory tests and X-rays. Then they have different options: they can send the specimen or patient to an outside facility, or they can send the patient to their own on-site facility. Early in the game physicians learned that by owning on-site facilities they could not only get results quickly and conveniently for their patients but also charge for this service. What researchers looking at this kind of self-referral learned was that, if physicians had a financial interest in a lab or X-ray facility, they were more likely to refer their patients for tests than physicians who did not have such a financial interest. The financial incentive clearly was wrong.

Surgeons have long worked under the cloud of this conflict of interest. The surgeon is the one who decides whether to operate, and one significant outcome of that decision is always whether the surgeon himself will earn a substantial fee. It is unclear how often surgeons have taken advantage of this, but there is no doubt that many of them have, and that a lot of missing tonsils and uteruses shouldn't have been removed.

The situation with laboratory testing is entirely different. It's easy to study because control groups can be identified and physician ordering can be tracked. That was how the conflict of interest of physicians self-referring to facilities in which they had a financial interest was demonstrated. When this came to the attention of the AMA Council on Ethical and Judicial Affairs, the council wrote guidelines proscribing the practice. It simply wasn't ethical. Even so, the doctors who were doing it protested loudly. They claimed that they weren't guilty of unethical practices and that the studies were flawed, but even though the council had to rewrite its opinion and bring it back to the House of Delegates more than once before it was approved as AMA policy, it stood firm. The impasse was broken by the federal government, which passed legislation denying Medicare and Medicaid payment for services ordered by self-referring physicians. Unhappily, too many physicians had violated the ethical guideline, and laws had to be enacted.

Although the laws were directed toward outside facilities in which physicians had a financial stake, physician office labs (POLs) were not all that different. The same principle applies even when the lab is on-site: if the physician has a financial interest in it, he or she will order more tests. In addition to volume, there also were quality problems associated with POLs. As a pathologist, I have a long-standing interest in the quality of lab testing. It goes back to my days in college, when I was a premed student and hospital lab technician. We didn't do much quality control then, but such practices were beginning to take hold, and by the time I was the editor of *JAMA* it was clear that there was a real potential for quality problems in physician office labs.

By then studies were emerging that compared the quality of tests done in POLs with tests conducted in referral labs, reference labs, and hospital labs. Good data, developed by good researchers and published in prestigious medical journals, demonstrated that the quality of POL tests was significantly deficient. Furthermore, that deficiency correlated with the level of education of the people working in the POL. Often a physician spouse or a high school student, typically with no technical training, would be the lab technician. Just as often the physicians lacked any technical lab training themselves; such training isn't offered in medical school or residency training. They relied on "cookbooks," or the manufacturing company that sold them the device. Fortunately, the devices and their manuals got better over time.

Then the exposés began. In the mid-1980s the Washington, D.C., media focused on the low quality of lab tests, especially Pap smears. Once again, the federal government took charge, passing the Clinical Laboratory Improvement Act (CLIA), which for the first time put many laboratories under government control through the offices of the Health Care Financing Administration. POLs were spared largely because of AMA lobbying aimed at keeping the government out of doctors' offices as long as possible, even though the rigorous standards CLIA applied to reference labs and hospital labs resulted in documented, unequivocal quality improvement. This was another instance of the AMA protecting doctors' income at the expense of protecting patients' care.

The unregulated POLs did not do as well. In the early 1990s *JAMA* published hard data showing that the likelihood of seriously erroneous lab results was three times higher in POLs than in reference or hospital labs. This study gained a great deal of media attention, garnering a big story in the *Wall Street Journal* and a lot of television airplay. As a result, Congress amended CLIA by bringing physician office labs under federal control.

There was hell to pay. AMA officials complained bitterly, and doctors screamed and yelled, claiming I was a "tool" of the pathologists. True enough, I am a pathologist, and in a sense I suppose I was their tool. But in publishing this information I was a better tool for the patient. I wanted my own children, my own family, to have access to better lab test results, whether done in a POL or a hospital lab. The quality differential the *JAMA* study identified was a hazard to patient care.

Although the AMA's lobbying effort in Washington managed to slow down the regulation-writing process for the CLIA amendments, the quality of POL test results did improve. They became more costly because more physicians had to employ professionally trained technologists and certain tests now had to be sent to outside laboratories. This requirement inconvenienced some patients who had to wait longer for results. There is, after all, a point to be made for the speed and convenience of POLs, which, by giving quicker results, can lead to quicker treatment decisions. In the best of all possible worlds—which may be on its way with improved testing techniques—doing lab tests as close to the patient as possible is the optimal way. But not if the results are wrong.

The truth of the matter is that POLs can be a lucrative part of a physician's income. Even when physicians sent out specimens to referral labs, many managed to derive extra income from the tests. If the lab charged two or three dollars for the test, the physician might charge the patient, or insurance company, fifteen dollars. It was a send-out business in which the physician became the middleman—ordering the test, procuring the specimen, sending it to the lab of choice (often a low-cost lab), getting the result, paying the lab and then charging an inflated fee. Though it has gone on for decades, this practice is not ethical and not the right way to practice medicine. Some new laws have interdicted this process.

The profession let itself down by not blowing the whistle on this and other questionable income-enhancing practices, and organized medicine failed its members by not taking them on. Self-governance means group governance when individuals don't comply, but the AMA and other physician membership associations did not act appropriately on this issue. Their members were making too much money from the practice; it seemed crucial to their business.

Sometimes membership organizations like the AMA feel compelled to act on behalf of their members when their interests come into conflict with those of the patients the profession is ethically bound to serve. But that is the moment when, as Edmond Pellegrino so eloquently observed, the true professional effaces his or her own interest. Disclosure, honesty, and truth are essential to the ethical practice of medicine. To lose sight of that is to lose it all.

7

Uninformed Consent

When Disclosure Is Incomplete, Misleading, or Nonexistent

DISCLOSURE BEGINS WHEN THE PHYSICIAN fully informs the patient about prescribed diagnostic and treatment interventions. That includes telling the patient not only what will happen but also what could go wrong. To not explain the consequences of an intervention, even of a "simple" lab test, constitutes unethical behavior, in my opinion. It also opens an avenue for distrust, especially when one test leads to another and all kinds of expensive procedures are undertaken.

Think of the complications that could flow from a blood sample whose test includes a screen for predisposition to a genetic disorder; this kind of screen is already possible and in a very short time will become commonplace. The insurance coverage and employment implications from that one test are enormous. The patient should know about the possible consequences and should have the right to refuse such a test.

Also think of the complexities associated with new medical technologies, including the growing use of the Internet. We may need new ethical standards to govern this area. Greater disclosure is also needed in our courts when they handle medical disputes. We have experts testifying for the plaintiff and experts testifying for the defendant, but where is the expert testifying for the truth? What we need are court-appointed experts whose only concerns are disclosure and truth. Moreover, the best strategy for keeping government and insurance out of the practice of medicine is for the profession to have unimpeachably high ethical standards that include full disclosure and informed consent.

Do we have that now? Anyone who has undergone a surgical procedure or invasive diagnostic test knows that we do not. Too many of us are familiar with the ritual that takes place, sometimes just before anesthesia is administered. A form is presented and a signature required. That is the "informed consent" document, which seems to be designed more for the benefit of the hospital attorney and the physician than the patient.

This happened to me recently when I underwent elective abdominal surgery. Sure enough, the form was presented in a routine manner, but with little interest in ensuring that I understood the ramifications of the procedure. Since I am a physician, I understood most of the information presented and did not choose to challenge the unenthusiastic manner of presentation. In addition, I considered myself a guinea pig in the informed consent routine.

Of course, I just went ahead and signed the form, as patients routinely do. The process was no different from the many times I've observed it over the years in serving on hospital medical staffs as a pathologist. The form and the process document truly uninformed consents because no real effort is made to help patients understand what might happen to them. The signatures are gained for legal and documentation purposes, and no member of the hospital staff seems to really care what the patient knows, thinks, or understands.

Why do we go through this charade? Why compel health care workers to make gestures that have no genuine content? The answer is historically simple: some terrible things have been inflicted on people in the name of scientific experimentation. This was brought home in gruesome detail at the Nuremberg war crime trials immediately following World War II, when evidence of bizarre and cruel human experimentation by Nazi doctors was presented. Although the goal of the Nuremberg trials was to determine the guilt or innocence of alleged war criminals, the trials spurred development of the concept of informed consent. A Michigan court had done some work on the concept in the 1930s, but its work was little known to most people, despite its importance.

The Nuremberg trials dramatized the problem in an entirely new way. From that experience came the belief that no human being should be experimented on by a physician or others without being informed in advance of the nature of the experiment and its risks as well as its potential benefits. Only with that understanding should an approval be sought and obtained. That was the ideal. Gaining such consent was practical and doable, but it generally wasn't being done.

The concept became a reality in the late 1940s, though few recognized it at the time. The medical research establishment paid it some lip service but didn't implement informed consent with any real degree of penetration for a very long time. Evidence has come to light that throughout the 1950s and 1960s humans were experimented on in hospitals and medical schools in many parts of the United States and not informed at all that they were the subject of research; neither was any kind of consent obtained. Recent journal articles and news reports have revealed that radiation experiments were performed at some of the best institutions, sometimes at great hazard to the patients, with no explanation or acknowledgment. I know myself that this kind of thing was happening because I saw it personally during those years.

The casual use of experimentation grew out of the very nature of this country's medical culture, which has relied on traditions that reach back to the eighteenth century. A curious quid pro quo concerning charity care also played a role in human experimentation. There is no constitutional or state requirement that medical care must be provided for all U.S. residents, though of course there have always been many people without means who nonetheless have needed care. The response to this need in the United States was the charity hospital. Typically funded by churches or county governments, these were hospitals like the Philadelphia General Hospital, the Boston City Hospital, the Detroit Receiving Hospital, the Charity Hospital in New Orleans, the Cook County Hospital in Chicago, the St. Louis City Hospital, the Los Angeles County General Hospital, the San Francisco General Hospital, and the City Hospital of Mobile, Alabama, managed by the Sisters of Charity of the Roman Catholic Church, where I first worked in medicine.

These institutions became highly valued because they cared for people in medical need without charge; in large part they were funded until the mid-1960s, and somewhat still, by county property taxes. They also were valued because they provided the principal training grounds for young U.S. doctors. The charity patients thus automatically became teaching cases. Medical students and residents traditionally learned by literally practicing on charity in- and outpatients. This practice was widely followed during my early days in medicine, and many institutions still adhere to it today.

That was the quid pro quo. If the patient wouldn't, or couldn't, pay for care, it was only reasonable to expect payment in kind by having the patient serve as a guinea pig for teaching and research. The patients didn't have much to say about the practice because they had no place else to go. Poor people with neither means nor insurance who were hospitalized at an academically affiliated charity hospital routinely became subjects for human teaching and experimentation. They weren't being told about it, but they also weren't being charged for care, and for a long time that seemed like a reasonable exchange.

The practice should have been abandoned after the enactment of Medicare and Medicaid, which were designed to pay for care for the elderly and poor and in doing so change their patient charity status to that of an insured patient. In theory the charity hospitals were no longer needed, and some, such as those in Philadelphia and St. Louis, were phased out or closed. One might expect that the Medicare and Medicaid caseloads were picked up by private hospitals or university hospitals, and to some extent they were. In fact, most "public" hospitals continued to function as before, following the old quid pro quo, albeit with new revenue streams.

This began to change in the 1970s, when much greater attention began to be paid to the issue of informed consent for human experimentation, even in the charity hospitals. Hospital ethics committees were formed, reviving a field that had been virtually dormant for decades. Also during this period, the concept of informed consent expanded to include routine surgery and other invasive procedures. Not only should people undergoing experimental treatment understand all the ramifications of the procedure, but so should people undergoing any kind of invasive intervention.

The new concept held that patients should be informed about even established and almost routine therapies. They should understand the nature of a procedure and its potential risks and benefits. Fully informed, they should then be offered the right to approve or disapprove of subjecting themselves to the intervention. Informed consent would be extended to hospitalized and ambulatory patients for surgery, anesthesiology, and all other invasive procedures.

This was a hotly debated topic in the early 1970s. As a member of the *JAMA* editorial board, I got into a long discussion with another board member, Robert Veatch, a prominent ethicist from Georgetown University. My point was the one I have been making here: the informed consent procedures that I witnessed in the hospital where I was working were really uninformed consents. No one made any effort to make sure the patients understood what could happen. The signatures were gained essentially for legal and procedural purposes.

Last year I conducted an informal survey to determine whether any progress had been made. I made a point of collecting informed consent forms from a variety of institutions and found little improvement in the process. The information was couched in legalese. The documents were wordy and not very clear. The average person would find them difficult to understand, although I'm sure that hospital attorneys would find them extremely clear and helpful.

The problem is even more acute in physicians' offices, where informed consents are rarely presented, or even considered, and quality control is virtually nonexistent. There's very little supervision in physicians' offices; in the privacy of their offices, physicians can pretty much do as they please.

As a pathologist, I'm particularly concerned about the lack of informed consent in laboratory testing. No one even thought about gaining informed consents for lab tests until the AIDS epidemic. Then health care professionals finally began to worry about what might happen to someone if his blood were drawn and a test for HIV performed. If the result were positive, indicating the presence of the infection, what would become of that information? To whom would it be conveyed? What if an employer learned of it, or an insurance company, or friends, family, and acquaintances? An entire series of factors concerning discrimination was raised. Not surprisingly, informed consent for drawing blood for an HIV test became a requirement, by law, in the 1980s.

That was a hopeful development. I thought it might encourage behavior changes with respect to all diagnostic tests. Surely now there would be an outpouring of support for truly informed consent for all lab tests, but it didn't happen. In the United States today, whether in hospitals or physicians' offices, patients are almost never asked for a truly informed consent prior to providing a lab specimen, whether blood, urine, stools, or whatever else. The only common exception is the informed consent obtained when a patient exhibits any untoward effect of the blood drawing, such as fainting.

Obvious consequences can flow from the taking of specimens. A South Carolina public hospital tested the urine of pregnant women for evidence of illegal drug use. When positive evidence was found, the information was turned over to the police. In Charleston thirty women were arrested, some taken from their hospital rooms in leg chains and handcuffs. The city maintained that its program was needed to protect the health of fetuses and newborns. Critics of the program asserted that it was counterproductive and that women would not seek needed prenatal care if their drug abuse were treated as a criminal rather than a medical problem. One of the women involved sued the city, and the case slowly worked its way up to the Supreme Court.

Less dramatic but no less problematic difficulties can flow from a number of other lab tests. There are many tests that can get the patient involved in a cascade of follow-up procedures, such as the stress test, which, if abnormal, almost inevitably leads to angiography, then angioplasty or open-heart surgery. A proper informed consent would let patients know what might be done to them because of the results of the diagnostic test. In the case of the stress test, the patient should be informed of the possible cascade of further procedures. In taking blood, the technician should give the patient a list of specific analytes for which it will be tested. Furthermore, if an abnormality is found, the patient should know that a series of procedures are indicated. They should be identified clearly, along with information about the associated risks and benefits. Some of the follow-up procedures can be expensive and hazardous, and some can lead to major surgery.

The prostate specific antigen (PSA) test provides a telling example. Now very popular, the PSA quantifies specific antigens, and if they reach a certain number they trigger, almost without exception, an additional string of diagnostic tests. Prostate cancer is the second most common cancer in men, and it most commonly occurs in the elderly, although it sometimes affects middle-aged men. Diagnosis can be confirmed by ultrasound scanning and prostatic biopsy. Treatment may be prostatectomy or radiation therapy. Sometimes orchiectomy (surgical removal of the testes) is performed to reduce testosterone levels. Impotence and incontinence are common risks of these treatments, and many men are unable to have sex after the prostatectomy.

Sometimes this aggressive approach is desirable, and sometimes it is not. At least one urologist I know maintains that many elderly prostate cancer patients, if untreated, will probably die from other causes associated with advanced age. In any event, for many years the ramifications of a high PSA reading have not been routinely explained to patients prior to the drawing of blood to perform the test.

New Pressures for Real Informed Consent

A new phenomenon in medical research may change all that. The new field of diagnostic human genetics may raise concerns about possible discrimination that will dwarf those posed by AIDS. It is now possible to diagnose many kinds of predispositions to diseases through lab tests. Patients can learn that they have a high probability of contracting a given disorder long before symptoms arrive. In some instances, the probability will approach 100 percent, but in all instances the probability will be high.

What will we do with information like this? When the Human Genome Project is completed in the very near future, we will have mapped the entire genome. We will know a great deal about specific genes and gene combinations, which, when related to specific environmental conditions, stand a substantial chance of resulting in specific diseases for given individuals.

How are we to handle this capability? Should we allow individuals to refuse the test by means of an informed consent prior to the drawing of a specimen? That strikes me as a reasonable option. Another might be to establish a procedure by which, if the testing is done and the results become known, the information is utterly, totally private. Only the patient and physician would know. The patient's family, employer, insurance company, friends, and the public would not be privy to the information unless by explicit permission from the patient. That's another option I would endorse, but it would require strict adherence by patient and doctor and others.

Some might argue that the insurance company has a right to the information. If the insured individual the company is covering for life or health should become incapacitated or die within one or five years, the company could claim a right to protect its other policyholders and stockholders from preventable losses. Others might argue that an employer has a right to know whether a job applicant is likely to develop cancer within a year or two, especially if the employer intends to enroll the new hire in an expensive, time-consuming training course.

I would be opposed to allowing insurance companies access to patients' genetic information. In a country without universal health insurance, how could we possibly allow insurers information that would result in price or coverage discrimination? How could we stand by and watch as one person after another was essentially denied needed medical services? It simply shouldn't happen. Employers also should be denied such information, since they too would naturally want to discriminate against people apparently destined for expensive illnesses.

Aware of the potential problems, President Clinton, in his final year in office, issued an executive order banning genetic discrimination by federal agencies. Wendy R. Uhlmann, president of the National Society of Genetic Counselors, commented on the need for such action in the *New York Times*. She said that a study by the Genetic Alliance showed that 13 percent of 332 support group respondents said they or their relatives had been denied jobs on the basis of familial genetic conditions. The same study reported that 9 percent said they had refused genetic testing because of concerns about discrimination.

The concerns are real and the mandate is clear. Central to the entire question is the privacy of a human being, the dignity of all individuals, and our right to give our consent prior to undergoing any procedure that might seriously harm us. The informed consent issue is somewhat like the Miranda rule, which protects a person from self-incrimination and was recently reaffirmed by the Supreme Court. Some institutions are improving and providing more variety in their consent procedures. They and many individual patients have placed a high premium on correctly gaining informed consent and are willing to spend the time and effort to do it right. But in the prevalent managed care environment, not much time is allowed for physician–patient interactions, and neither party may be willing to "waste" it on explaining informed consent.

Once again, the Internet may help expand time for patients and physicians. Certainly, it's possible to construct detailed informed consents to cover every imaginable service situation. These could be placed on the Internet and shared by patients and physicians. A patient recommended for a colonoscopy, breast biopsy, or any other invasive procedure could go online and call up the consent form for the procedure. The patient could query his or her physician, and the two could decide what to do and electronically document the decision, thereby creating a paperless medical record, retrievable only by those specifically designated. This would provide shared medical record keeping, and patients would have access to their own records with the touch of a key. They also would control access to their records through informed consent. No one could see the record unless the patient allowed it.

As I said earlier, there are no secrets in hospitals. Anything on paper or on a chart can be read by almost anyone walking by, and it can be copied and distributed without a trace. Although there are concerns about the privacy of electronic records and record keeping, when it is done right, the Internet provides greater safety than paper records. It also offers a new level of control of documents for patients, as noted later in the chapter.

The Ethics of Informed Consent

A number of ethical problems were exposed by the untimely death of Jesse Gelsinger, the young man who died in 1999 during an experimental gene therapy procedure at the University of Pennsylvania. When the FDA ordered a suspension of the experimental program, the university responded with a twenty-eight-page report challenging the charge of serious deficiencies in its program. Among the FDA charges was that there had been serious lapses in documentation of the university's explanation of risks and benefits while gaining informed consent. University officials maintained that every patient in the program had given clear and unambiguous consent.

Three months after the program's suspension, the National Bioethics Advisory Commission declared that serious changes were indicated for the monitoring of research on human beings.

Commission Chairman Harold Shapiro of Princeton University said, "One problem we have heard again and again is that, once an experiment is approved, there is a failure to follow what's going on with the patients. I think there is a growing consensus that something must be done."

Among the changes needed, the commission said, was better reporting of serious adverse effects. The National Institutes of Health earlier had reported 691 adverse events to date involving the use of adenovirus as a vector in gene therapy, but scientists had reported only 39. The role of patients in gene therapy research began to look suspiciously like the role of patients in the old charity hospitals. They were being experimented on without full disclosure.

Poor reporting, poor disclosure, and poor judgment were casting a cloud over one of the more promising new developments in medicine, and at the heart of the problem was an apparent lapse in the application of medical ethics. Ironically, this controversy arose at a time when the field was blossoming. When I attended medical school in the 1950s, I had one lecture on ethics, at the end of which the professor said it wasn't all that complicated. "It's mainly a question of applying the Golden Rule," he said: "Do unto others as you would have them do unto you."

The Golden Rule is not a bad place to start, but it's not that simple today. The field of medical ethics has become more and more dynamic ever since hospital ethics committees were established in the 1970s. It is now one of the most elaborate, most heavily populated, and most interesting fields in medicine—and one of the most deeply engaged in turf and concept battles. Truly a burgeoning field, it fits the mold of Jimmy Durante's old adage that "everybody wants to get into the act."

In my first year as editor in chief at Medscape, after I left the AMA, I learned that more people wanted to write columns or articles on medical ethics than on any other subject. We have medical ethicists everywhere, and all of them want to write, speak, and persuade. Some are physicians, but most are not. Many have a Ph.D. in one or another field of the humanities. Some are bona-fide doctors of philosophy, with a Ph.D. in that discipline. Others have divinity degrees or law degrees. Most are literary and relish writing and speaking about ethics.

There is no science of medical ethics, no accrediting agency, and no board certificate for clinical medical ethics. Nonetheless, ethical behaviors can be based on scientific evidence. Once scientific information has been accumulated on a particular treatment procedure, diagnostic method, or program, ethical decisionmaking takes over to determine how to apply the new science. How should the new information be implemented? Who should receive it? How should it be paid for? And how should people be informed about it?

Nonphysician ethicists may face difficulties related to their lack of clinical experience. They may not have been with patients in a responsible position when tough decisions were necessary. They may not have been exposed to the level of distress that can follow when a hard call has to made. What physicians learn practicing medicine day in and day out cannot be learned in any other way and may give them an edge over nonphysicians as ethicists.

The gene therapy offered to eighteen-year-old Jesse Gelsinger provides an example. Gelsinger had a form of ornithine transcarbamylase (OTC) mild enough to be controllable by diet and drugs. Severe OTC deficiency is devastating, allowing a toxic buildup of ammonia in the blood and causing coma, brain damage, and death. Newborn infants with a severe form of the disorder typically fall into a coma within seventy-two hours after birth. The disease occurs in one of every 40,000 births, and half of those born with it will die in the first month of life. The other half die within five years. It might seem reasonable to try the new treatment on newborn babies with the disease, but the University of Pennsylvania's resident ethicist advised against it. Arthur Caplan, a highly regarded Ph.D. ethicist (and a former member of the Medscape editorial board), thought that the parents of these infants would be incapable of giving an informed consent. "They are coerced by the disease of their child," he said.

Certainly, Gelsinger knowingly and willingly entered the experimental program. His stated purpose was to help babies born with the disease, but would it have been unethical to talk to parents of newborns about the experimental program? Obviously, they have been devastated to learn about the disease itself, but would they be incapable of making a rational decision about an experimental treatment? I don't have the answer for that particular question, but I do know that practicing clinicians develop a sense of how individuals will react to distressing news; they learn that different people react differently. The typical experience of a clinician adds a dimension to ethical thinking, which at its core may well be no more than a matter of applying the Golden Rule, as my medical school professor asserted.

When we discuss ethics, what we're really talking about is human behavior—what constitutes good behavior and what describes bad behavior. Five factors are involved in the governance of human behavior, starting with the least intrusive and building up to the most intrusive. The most important factor is the first, our genetic makeup. We don't know much about this yet, but we are learning that a great deal of our behavior is predetermined by our genes. What we received from our forebears in various combinations of DNAs is now increasingly perceived as a basic determinant of how we act.

The second factor is nurturing. It has been well documented that what happens to individuals in terms of bonding, education, and love, particularly before the age of three or four, has a great deal to do with their behavior. Nurturing is typically offered by parents and usually supports "good" behavior. If a gene-directed child takes a "wrong" turn, presumably a gesture, word, or nudge will set him or her right.

Beyond those two factors is personal morality, defined as a quality or action conforming to or deriving from the right ideas of human conduct, goodness, or uprightness of behavior. After morality comes ethics, defined as the principles of conduct governing individuals or professions, the ideals of character manifested by a people.

Then comes public law, defined as a rule or mode of conduct or action that is formally recognized as binding by a supreme controlling authority and made obligatory by a sanction.

If personal morality were deep enough and widespread enough, there would be no need for societal ethics. If ethics were strong enough and sufficiently ubiquitous, there would be no need for public law. Alas, neither is the case, and so we have thousands of laws. Legislators are elected in cities, counties, states, and countries to convene in councils, legislatures, and congresses to make laws acceptable to mayors, governors, and presidents that can be signed and implemented.

More often than not, laws are aimed at fixing problems. I believe that the existence of a law points to the failure of the principal governors of human behavior in that domain. Even the discussion by members of Congress of the problems of patients' rights and protections signals the failure of the major controllers of behavior in that area. If our genes, education, morals, and ethics were working properly, laws to protect patients' rights would not even require discussion.

The Ethics of Information Management

Perhaps the field of medical ethics has grown so dramatically in response to the explosive growth of information. It truly may have been simpler to do the right thing when there weren't that many things that could be done. The basic Hippocratic ethical dictum is to "first, do no harm." Before the advent of sophisticated and invasive new procedures, that dictum was easier to follow. Physicians couldn't do much, so they couldn't do much wrong.

Early last year I attended an assembly of some sixty people who had gathered at the Pan American Health Organization building in Washington, D.C. They represented the medical profession, industry, academia, government, and the ethics community. The meeting was titled "i-Summit," and the topic under discussion was the ethics governing the medical Internet. Just as electricity slowly and then dramatically changed the ways in which Americans worked, lived, and played in the last century, so the Internet will change American lives in deeply significant ways in the new century. That was at the heart of our discussion at the i-Summit. We spent two days developing principles we could recommend to everyone dealing with the quality of medical content, the personal protection of data, commercial behavior relating to sponsorship, advertising, and ownership, disclosure, and the use of the Internet in the practice of medicine.

My position in the discussion of medical practice was that we are at a watershed moment in the definition of medical practice. Much of what physicians do is being redefined. Consider what they do today, for example. They listen to patients and their families. They observe and examine patients. They identify problems, stratify those problems, and order tests to attempt to further clarify the problems. This leads to a differential or probable diagnosis, which in turn leads to a diagnosis.

The diagnosis was the principal goal when I began the study of medicine in the early 1950s. Today the diagnosis itself probably is not important. It's the problem that's important. Even more important is doing something about the problem. As Tinsley Harrison, one of my medical teachers, once said, "Patients aren't concerned about diagnoses. They are concerned about symptoms."

Having clarified the problem by coming to a diagnosis, the physician institutes interventions of various kinds. The physician monitors the course of the patient's recovery and then may institute preventive measures to prevent a recurrence or the development of other diseases in the future. The thread holding all of this together is information. A majority of the dollars spent in medicine and health care in developed countries today is expended on gaining information, including tests. When we think of dollars spent, we think of drugs, surgery, radiation, physical therapy, and bricks and mortar in hospitals and clinics, but these expenses are relatively small in comparison to what physicians and patients spend most of their time doing—seeking and using information.

The quest is for information, and physicians pursue it by observing, gathering bits and pieces of data, assimilating and interpreting them, and then dispensing their conclusions—telling the patient what is wrong and what to do about it. During the course of treatment further information is elicited. The physician encourages feedback from the patient on how the treatment is progressing and thereby monitors the course of therapy through information exchange. In fact, the entire process is almost nothing but information. Lab tests may be ordered, but only for information. If they're not needed, they're not ordered. It's all information. Do this. Don't do that. Take this drug. Stop taking that one. That is what the practice of medicine is all about today.

The question has been raised as to how much of this might be done over the Internet. Remarkable amounts of information can flow back and forth over the Internet. Hand-delivered notes can be replaced. So can letters, brochures, certificates, and even printed lab results. Test orders can be placed and results can be handled expeditiously over the Internet. The only information-gathering action that can't be done, it seems, is the drawing of specimens, but after the test is ordered, the patient can stop by a designated facility to give a specimen. If pharmaceutical agents are required, they can be ordered over the Internet, and the pharmacist can make them available or deliver them to the patient. Verbal communications can become electronic, eliminating the factor of distance and reducing the factor of time. Copies can be provided immediately. The new digital X-ray technology attached to a medical record offers protection against loss or misplacement. Typically, about 10 percent of film X-rays at hospitals are misfiled, and an additional 2 to 3 percent are lost. The Internet is perfectly designed to straighten out all of these information snafus.

Given these remarkable possibilities and opportunities, the i-Summit group determined that, in the practice of medicine over the Internet, physicians and patients should follow the basic principles of medical ethics. They should adhere to concepts first articulated by Hippocrates and codified and updated by the AMA

Council on Ethical and Judicial Affairs. Practitioners of Internet medicine should preserve patient privacy, disclose their financial interests, and gain informed consent. In addition, research about Internet medicine should be promoted, with control groups and randomized trials and publication of solid research results.

One question that remains unanswered is whether medicine should be practiced over the Internet between patients and physicians who do not have an existing therapeutic relationship. The group felt that some things could be handled over the Internet in the absence of an existing relationship, but that many other things probably could not. This is an area that requires further research. The question has to be studied and subjected to risk-benefit ratio analysis for different circumstances and different diseases. At the moment there is little or no information in the published literature on which diseases could be so handled, but this is a case in which ethics could follow science. Once we know what can be done safely and effectively solely on the Internet, an ethic for that practice will become clear.

During the past year I have made many public presentations on Internet medicine, and the audience response has been powerfully supportive. People keep saying how good it is to hear someone talk about the ethics and morality of Internet medicine rather than just the details of how it can be conducted. Everyone seems to suspect that scoundrels may live by detail legerdemain—the devil is in the details.

Disclosure Difficulties in Courtrooms

Few things cause more confusion and consternation than expert witnesses who take the stand and contradict one another on findings of medical fact. Indeed, according to news stories, some expert witnesses travel from one state to another testifying on this subject or that for well-heeled plaintiffs or defendants. It seems to be a system in which truth is for hire, in direct contradiction of ethical principles.

The CEJA opinion clearly states:

> The medical witness must not become an advocate or a partisan in the legal proceeding. The medical witness should be adequately prepared and should testify honestly and truthfully. The attorney for the party who calls the physician as a witness should be informed of all favorable and unfavorable information developed by the physician's evaluation of the case.

As a pathologist, I often served as an expert witness when I was in practice in California and Texas (prior to my employment at the AMA). I served as a paid consultant in both criminal and civil medical-legal cases. This experience taught me to appreciate the persuasive power of money. Of course, attorneys for both the plaintiff and the defendant want the truth, and a good expert witness will provide it. There's no question, however, that attorneys seek out expert witnesses who support their client's version of the truth. There's also no question that attorneys will not go to court with an expert witness who does not support their client's position.

Furthermore, attorneys often do not solicit an expert's early opinion in writing. Such a document would be subject to the discovery process, in which both sides theoretically have access to all pertinent information before the trial. So the system encourages attorneys to work with prospective physician-consultants in a somewhat clandestine way. The attorneys receive information verbally and privately before making a decision about whether they want a particular expert to appear in court.

Once on board, the physician-consultant tends to become a "team" player, as would anyone who grew up playing team sports. Competition matters in team sports. Once on the team, everyone works for it. No one expects to work against his or her team. As consultants, expert witnesses work with lawyers trying to construct a defense or with prosecutors or plaintiffs trying to coordinate an attack. The goal on both sides is to influence the jury. People understandably get caught up in tactics.

Quite honestly, it can be exhilarating. I well remember the charge I felt being sworn in, taking the oath, and then bracing for the attack from the opposing side's attorneys. Their goal was to tear me (my testimony) apart limb from limb. Their job was not to destroy me as an individual, but to destroy my testimony completely before the judge and jury. If they had to destroy me too in pursuit of that goal, they would try to do it. My job was to not let them destroy my testimony. It was the next best thing to playing football. They were responsible for fighting for their clients. Truth had little to do with the matter.

Sometimes the discrepancy between the testimonies of the plaintiff's expert witness and the defendant's expert is so great that it's abundantly clear that someone is not telling the truth. Against apparent evidence, one of the experts has come down on the side of the munificent client. The current rate for expert testimony is $450 per hour, which is paid not just for court time but also for extensive preparation time. It's a lucrative business, with few dangers. I cannot recall a single instance in which an expert was prosecuted for perjury, even when it seemed perfectly obvious that the expert was lying.

There are other ways to seek the truth, as I discovered while practicing forensic medicine in Sweden in the mid-1970s. There I discovered the extent to which a written record of a forensic autopsy was accepted by the court without the pathologist even having to appear. The doctor did not have to be sworn in and subjected to examination or cross-examination. The record was enough.

Later I practiced forensic medicine at the London Hospital College of Medicine in Whitechapel. In England the written record hardly mattered at all. The pathologist was expected to go to the coroner's court for lower-level determinations and to the crown court for higher-level determinations. Doctors routinely were examined and cross-examined. It was a fascinating contrast in how two different societies dealt with expert opinion. In Sweden few if any expert witnesses were called by the various sides for court cases. Instead, any expert testimony submitted was obtained by the court. The judge secured the expert witness, who reported fully to the court with or without remuneration. How civilized, I thought. How truly superior to what I had experienced in the States.

While it rarely happens, there are circumstances in which the court can secure its own expert testimony in the United States. However, one of the limitations of that rare practice is that the court pays comparatively little because of taxpayer constraints. U.S. courts are in no position to buy the expertise that some plaintiffs and defendants can afford.

The U.S. Constitution guarantees many rights, including those that ensure that criminal defendants can defend themselves in a court of law. The court will even routinely assign a public defender to indigent defendants. As previously noted, the Constitution (and all of its successor laws) does not guarantee a right to medical care, perhaps because it was written by lawyers rather than doctors. In any event, under the Constitution expert witnesses cannot be prohibited. Legally, expert witnesses for either side cannot be eliminated, and few would want to see that right denied. But it seems clear to me that balance could be added to deliberations by allowing the court to use an expert witness. In routine cases the court could rely on its own witness. In more difficult cases both sides could have their experts, and the court could have its expert. Instead of having to pick one side or the other, the judge and jury could also turn to a third, independent source of information.

It could help to have an unbiased expert for the court, especially in highly visible trials such as the criminal cases in which the defendant pleads not guilty by reason of insanity. The public and the profession have been dismayed time and again as well-paid mental health experts come down on this side or that, more for money than for truth it often seemed. I confess that twenty-five years ago I felt strongly that human behavioral science was not a science, and hardly even an art. Since then I've changed my view and now believe that the neurosciences are legitimate science, but behavioral issues still seem to me to be based in a fairly soft science. Often that softness is exposed in embarrassing contradictions between plaintiff and defense experts.

High-profile trials such as the murder trial of O. J. Simpson also could benefit from a third party—a court-secured forensic pathologist expert. The experts for the prosecution in the Simpson trial were, at base, employees of the county of Los Angeles. They had been working at the coroner's office, where it appeared that a rushed environment caused something of a mess, compared with optimal forensic measures. The defense, on the other hand, secured the testimony of Michael Baden, a longtime friend of mine from New York and a well-known forensic pathologist who once served as chief medical examiner of the city of New York.

Baden's powerful testimony did much to establish reasonable doubt, but his testimony was profoundly different from the testimony of the prosecutor's forensic pathologists. One could only wonder how presumably qualified professionals on both sides could be so far apart. The testimony of a third expert, not paid by either the prosecution or defense, might have been very helpful to the judge, the jury, and the public.

In the low-profile cases heard day after day in thousands of courts, expert witnesses-for-hire often testify as to the competence of a local physician in a malpractice case. I use two definitions of competence. First, competence is the ability of a person or a system to perform a task to achieve a satisfactory outcome for the person involved, whoever that happens to be. Many accept that definition, but there is a downside if the physician's practice is wholly incompetent but the patient's body is strong enough to recover anyway. Since the patient has a good outcome, it may appear that the physician is competent when there's no scientific evidence to support that conclusion.

The second, and more complete, definition of competence is the ability of a person or a system to perform the task at hand, for which he or she purports to be competent, in order to achieve an outcome that is satisfactory to the person or persons involved. In addition, the task is performed in a way that is acceptable to a reasonable group of peers. This means that the peers would say the attending physician did the right thing, and the persons involved would include the patient, family, insurance company, and employer, among others.

Judging competence can be complex. The outcome of surrendering it to competing hired experts is truly less than satisfactory. An expert friend of the court might turn out to be a friend to all.

When Disclosure Doesn't Work

There are times when no amount of disclosure, truth, or honesty can correct an unhealthy practice or activity. Cultural bias, indifference, and lack of political will preserve lethal environments clearly described by science. I encountered a spectacular example of the phenomenon in January 1983, after I published an editorial titled "Boxing Should Be Banned in Civilized Countries."

The editorial was prompted by new science, as well as by my conviction that policy should follow science. A study that appeared in the *Lancet* on fourteen boxers who had been national champions in Finland reported that four of six who had been professionals and one of eight who had been amateurs showed evidence of brain injury on CT scans. Another study, published in *JAMA,* reported that test results on thirty-eight boxers examined by CT scans and other tests showed a significant relationship between the number of bouts fought and the degree of brain damage. The most predictable and permanent reward of boxing is chronic brain damage, the *Lancet* authors concluded.

My editorial conclusion was that boxing is wrong at its base. "Boxing seems to me to be less sport than is cockfighting; boxing is an obscenity. Uncivilized man may have been bloodthirsty. Boxing, as a throwback to uncivilized man, should not be sanctioned by any civilized society."

That editorial provided my first collision with the AMA board of trustees. They had just approved a Council on Scientific Affairs report that made a number of recommendations based on the assumption that boxing could not be stopped. The AMA House of Delegates had adopted the report's recommendations one month before publication of the CT scan studies, and the board seemed to feel that I had challenged its authority and was developing AMA policy on my own.

The public hullabaloo that followed my editorial was massive and prolonged. It included major network television coverage, newspaper articles and editorials, magazine stories, letters of support, debate and criticism of *JAMA,* and many media interviews for the authors of the CT studies. A congressional hearing was held, and several state legislatures considered actions. In June 1983 the AMA House of Delegates passed a resolution encouraging the elimination of boxing from amateur scholastic, intercollegiate, and governmental athletic programs. In December 1984 the delegates called for a ban on both amateur and professional boxing, a position the AMA has reaffirmed many times since.

The problems associated with blows to the head are multiple. Acute brain damage may be produced by rotational angular acceleration, linear translation acceleration, carotid injury, impact deceleration, cerebral edema, ischemia, and herniation. The results of brain damage include speech difficulties, clumsiness of movement and disequilibrium progressing to disabling ataxia, dementia, spasticity, and extrapyramidal disturbances. The intensity of changes in nerve cells with neurofibrillary tangles in the cerebral cortex exceeds that seen in Alzheimer's disease and senile dementia.

If ever a case of disclosure, truth, and honesty were made about the deleterious effects of boxing, it was made during the 1980s. Something should have happened, but nothing did. The congressional hearings on boxing lasted more than a month. Many illustrious witnesses testified on the problems with a bill that would have established a congressional advisory commission, but the subcommittee didn't approve even that. Many states looked into the matter, but few acted on the medical recommendations—at least, not to the extent of banning either professional or amateur boxing.

Meanwhile, the violence only escalated as "ultimate" and "extreme" fighting were introduced. In ultimate fighting, opponents may be of any weight and can therefore be extremely unevenly matched. They wear no headgear, no mouthpieces, and no gloves. Any part of the body may be used as a weapon except the teeth, and blows may be delivered to any part of the opponent's body. No holds are barred, and no rounds or rest periods are designated. It's a fight to the finish.

Extreme fighting is a variation on ultimate fighting. There are four weight classes, five-ounce gloves, mouthpieces, groin protection, and a referee with authority. The fighters engage in a combination of boxing, kick boxing, wrestling, judo, and various other martial arts. The TV promoters for pay-per-view cable telecasts celebrate its "brutal" and "barbaric" nature.

How do they get away with it? Why do we tolerate this barbarity? Probably because most of us don't care about the motley bunch of characters who make so much money from managing boxing and fighting events. These "sports" don't have much to do with most of us. The people who fight are struggling to pull themselves up from the lower rungs of the economic ladder. The people who watch are hardly much better off, and the people who govern are content to let well enough alone.

For a long time that environmental indifference seemed to apply to gun violence, which seemed to happen only in inner cities and to involve mostly inarticulate, poor, and disaffected minority youngsters. Middle-class Americans felt relatively secure, and members of Congress felt reasonably safe in ignoring the problem. In August 1991 I made a call for papers on any aspect of interpersonal violence, hoping to gain scientific information on the scope and depth of violent behavior in this country.

The response was extraordinary. *JAMA* received 131 papers for peer review, of which 12 appeared in a special issue in May 1992. The AMA monthly specialty journals also received many manuscripts, and a total of 50 papers were published in their June issues. Once again, the papers on violence received extensive media exposure, resulting in significant publicity about a major public health emergency.

The findings were stark. While the population of the United States increased by 26 percent between 1960 to 1980, the homicide rate due to guns increased 160 percent. Gunshot wounds were the leading cause of death not only in black but also in white teenage boys. Firearm deaths were seven times greater in the United States than in the United Kingdom, while the death rate from trauma in France was 66 percent of the U.S. rate, and the rate in the Netherlands was only 39 percent. One-third of students in thirty-one Illinois high schools brought weapons to school for self-defense.

In addition, one study demonstrated that firearm-associated family and intimate assaults in Atlanta were twelve times more likely to result in death than non-firearm assaults. Another documented that large numbers of handgun owners kept their guns loaded in their homes and that many were not locked up, even in homes with children. One-third of Seattle high school students reported easy access to handguns, and 6 percent owned a handgun, while another 6 percent had carried a gun to school, according to another research report.

C. Everett Koop and I co-authored an editorial in the special *JAMA* issue on violence, making a number of recommendations aimed at regulating gun ownership in the United States. The regulations we recommended were analogous to those that Americans accept for ownership and operation of motor vehicles. We noted that drivers must meet age and physical-mental standards, be identifiable as an owner or operator, have demonstrable knowledge and skill to operate a vehicle safely, agree to performance monitoring, and be prepared to forfeit the right to drive if responsibilities are abrogated. We recommended that gun owners meet the same standards through a system of gun registration and licensing for gun owners and users. Our goal was to apply the public health model to the study and control of violence. I find it gratifying that much of the debate in the 2000 presidential campaign about the control of gun violence seems to stem from, and agrees with, our work of ten years ago.

Some things have changed and some have not during the intervening ten years. Fortunately, the homicide rate in major U.S. cities decreased by 36 percent between 1991 and 1998. San Diego led the list, with homicides dropping from 14.7 deaths per 100,000 population to 3.4, representing a 76 percent decline. New York went from 29.3 to 8.6, or 70 percent; Boston from 19.7 to 6.0, or 69 percent; and San Antonio from 21.7 to 8.0, or 62 percent. Interestingly, police strategies in the major cities differed dramatically, from tough enforcement to community and problem-solving policing, but all cities showed major declines. Also of interest is the fact that this decline began about the same time we began to focus public attention on gun violence as a public health problem, not only one of law enforcement.

Meanwhile, high-profile gun killings moved from the big cities to the suburbs and smaller cities. Among the most heart-wrenching were those involving schoolchildren killing fellow students in random acts of violence. This major cultural shift put ordinary middle-class people at risk in their "safe" neighbor-hoods, schools, and homes. Nonetheless, legislators seemed less sensitive to growing public concern than to the traditional gun lobby, and even modest gun control proposals went nowhere in Congress.

Another area in which scientific disclosure and truth have had little impact relates to drugs. Individual behavior has as much to do with the drug problem as public indifference and legislative apathy, or skullduggery for that matter, although when it comes to tobacco some skullduggery is involved. We kept a campaign alive in *JAMA* for years on the adverse health effects of tobacco use. One of the most famous findings we published was a study that showed children could more readily identify Joe Camel than Mickey Mouse.

In a 1985 editorial I traced the history of AMA and *JAMA* with respect to tobacco. Beginning in 1934, the AMA accepted tobacco advertising in its journals. In 1952 *JAMA* published a study on bronchogenic carcinoma, driving a nail in the coffin of tobacco use, so to speak. The AMA then decided to discontinue tobacco ads, effective January 1954. In 1958 *JAMA* published a landmark study by Hammond and Horn, linking tobacco use with many additional diseases, and in 1964 the AMA called cigarette smoking a "serious health hazard."

For three years running in the mid-1980s, *JAMA* published theme issues containing evidence of the long-term harm caused by tobacco use, and the AMA took a number of policy decisions affecting tobacco. The association called for the elimination of federal price supports, the rotation of health warning labels on cigarette packs, an increase in cigarette taxes, and a ban on all tobacco advertising. Members of Congress were not impressed and complained to AMA lobbyists about all the noise the association was making.

Then in 1995 *JAMA* published information that demonstrated tobacco industry misconduct and mendacity. The industry had marketed its products for years in the full knowledge that they caused serious disease and death. It had long known that nicotine is addictive but kept its findings secret and consistently denied the only conclusion that could be drawn from the evidence. In a 1998 editorial, C. Everett Koop, FDA chief David Kessler, and I advocated FDA authority to regulate nicotine, federal statutes to protect children from tobacco use, funding of programs to help nicotine-dependent individuals quit, and expansion of regulation of environmental tobacco smoke, among other recommendations.

Despite our efforts, members of Congress resisted any moves directed at curbing big tobacco companies year after year. In fact, the real movement against tobacco came from local and state governments, which enforced clean air legislation and won multibillion-dollar settlements from tobacco companies for the costs of covering the health care consequences of tobacco use.

The problem with tobacco is that one of its active ingredients, nicotine, is an addicting drug. There was a time when there were virtually no restrictions on the purchase and use of drugs in the United States. In the early years of the twentieth century heroin was an over-the-counter health remedy, laudanum was readily available, and the use of alcohol and tobacco was widespread. Just before World War I federal laws were enacted to make the use of narcotics illegal, and just after the war federal law prohibited the use of alcoholic products. One law took, and the other was repealed a dozen years later.

It seems to me that human beings, or at least many of them, have wanted ways to alter their consciousness almost from the time they first gained their consciousness. Certainly, the history of alcohol and other drug abuse is as old as recorded history itself. What we are dealing with here is addiction, which operates on varying levels, affecting some people more deeply than others. A growing body of research suggests that addiction is more of a medical problem than a criminal or behavioral problem. From this perspective, what an addict needs is not handcuffs but help.

Education offers the best defense against tobacco addiction. One reason it's important to prevent teenage tobacco use, for example, is that, according to studies, early addiction seems to lead to deeper addiction. People who start smoking in their twenties seem to have less difficulty quitting than those who started in their teens. Information about the impact of alcohol could help prevent the auto accident fatalities caused by those driving under the influence. Everyone should understand the concept of blood alcohol concentrations and accept the standard of 0.05 percent as "per se illegal for driving." Most states today accept the much higher standard of 0.10 percent, although there has been movement toward establishing 0.08 percent as the standard.

Young people should be encouraged to learn about a number of other effects of alcohol. For example, it's well understood now that pregnant women should avoid alcohol use to prevent damage to their babies. Alcohol assistance programs for impaired individuals should be adopted by all businesses and public and private institutions. Medical schools should require courses in alcoholism and other kinds of drug dependency, emphasizing recognition of symptoms and treatment for addicts. Physicians should inform their patients that movement from social to regular use of alcohol as a tranquilizer is an early warning sign of potential dependency.

A more open approach toward alcohol abuse and alcoholism, including recognition of alcoholism as a disease, has led to beneficial treatment programs. Addiction does not go away and cures do not exist, but credible recovery rates as high as 50 to 90 percent have been demonstrated. This is a remarkable advance from the days when alcoholism was considered solely a character flaw.

A most intractable problem associated with disclosure centers on the use of illicit drugs. No amount of solid information seems capable of shifting our failed policies for containing illicit drug abuse. Year after year the U.S. and local and state governments spend hundreds of millions of dollars on interdiction, policing, and incarceration to stamp out drug abuse, with astonishing lack of success. It's a grim game in which no one wins. Drugs keep flowing into the country. Police keep breaking in doors and stopping cars. Courts keep sending people to prison. But the drugs keep coming.

Four years ago an august new group of physicians called Physician Leadership for National Drug Policy met at the New York Academy of Medicine to discuss alternatives to our failing U.S. illicit drug policy. Addiction to illegal drugs creates impaired health, harmful behaviors, and major economic and social burdens. Addiction is a chronic illness, and treatment requires continuity of care, including acute and follow-up strategies, management of relapses, and satisfactory outcome measurements.

All of the physicians assembled were impressed by the growing body of evidence that enhanced medical and public health approaches are the most effective way to reduce the harmful use of illegal drugs. The new approaches clearly offer great opportunities to decrease the burden on individuals and communities, particularly when integrated into multidisciplinary and collaborative strategies. All were unimpressed by the prevailing emphasis of the criminal justice system on interdiction to reduce illegal drug use and the harmful effects of illegal drugs.

The physicians agreed that it is time to refocus our policy by investing in the prevention and treatment of harmful drug use. Such a change of focus would require reallocating resources toward drug treatment, using criminal justice procedures that are demonstrated to be effective in reducing supply, and reducing the disabling regulation of addiction treatment programs.

In addition, they agreed that concerted efforts to eliminate the stigma associated with the diagnosis and treatment of drug problems are essential. Substance abuse should be accorded parity with other chronic disorders. Furthermore, physicians and other health professionals should be responsible for training themselves and their students to be clinically competent in the area of substance abuse.

Community-based health partnerships are essential to solving these problems, the physicians agreed. We should expand our investments in research and training and exploit the new research opportunities produced by advances in the understanding of the biological and behavioral aspects of drugs and addiction, as well as research on the outcomes of prevention and treatment programs.

At virtually the same time the AMA adopted a policy to encourage greater efforts to prevent the initiation of drug use, to aid those who wish to stop, and to diminish the adverse consequences of drug use. It also advocated expanding opioid maintenance programs so that opioid therapy could be available for any individual who applies. Treatment should be driven by patient needs, medical judgment, and drug rehabilitation concerns.

The association also recommended needle and syringe exchange and distribution programs, with modification of existing laws, to maximize the availability of sterile syringes to help contain the epidemic of HIV infection. It reaffirmed its opposition to drug legalization and encouraged state medical societies to initiate state legislation to modify paraphernalia laws to permit purchase of syringes without prescriptions.

I'm still optimistic that policy will follow science in this crucial area. Billions of dollars could be saved. Thousands of lives could be spared or improved, and law-abiding citizens could enjoy significantly enhanced security. But I'm not holding my breath. In the year 2001, our cultural bias on drugs has yet to be moved by disclosures from science.

8

Disclosures on Death

Why Doctors Should Help Patients Die

B Y THE MEASURE OF CURRENT standards, I would be accused of "pulling the plug" on both my father and my mother. I was an intern at Tripler Hospital in Hawaii when I received word in 1957 that my father had suffered a heart attack. It seemed impossible to return—this was before jet travel—but I quickly learned that he was okay. He had survived and did recover.

Over the next two or three years he had a series of heart attacks, and each time he recovered less well. In the days before Medicare, he, as a self-employed music teacher, and my mother, an Alabama elementary school teacher, had no significant health insurance. They paid the costs of his care, which were substantial and difficult to manage, out of their meager budget and resources.

He was hospitalized at a small facility called the Thomas Hospital in Fairhope, Alabama, some ten miles from our home in Silverhill. Fairhope is in the tiny sliver of the state that touches the Gulf of Mexico between the Florida panhandle and Mississippi. He was under the care of Claudius Jordan, a general practitioner who had been our family doctor ever since his father, Henry C. Jordan, had died. Henry C., a GP in Robertsdale, was one of the principal reasons I went into medicine. As a friendly country doctor who made house calls when I was sick as a preschooler, he was an inspiration.

His son Claudius, having graduated from medical school twenty years later than his father, was more up-to-date on modern medicine. In those days before Hill-Burton had funded the Thomas Hospital, "Dr. Claudius" owned the hospital that he practiced in at Fairhope. Privately owned hospitals, I might add, existed long before the creation of for-profit mega-hospital chains like Columbia HCA. They were owned by people in the community who saw a need, had some money, and built them. They functioned as doctors' hospitals, and some retained that name.

The last time I saw my father conscious was in the Thomas Hospital, when I was able to drive from south Texas with my family in 1961. He had seen the two older grandchildren but not his new granddaughter. Since children couldn't enter hospitals as visitors then, I stood on the grass outside and held my daughter up to the window next to his bed in the one-story facility, and he looked out and smiled. My father told me later that the doctors thought he would make it through the hospitalization, and he did, but after returning home for nursing care he continued to decline.

Dr. Jordan called me some time later and told me my father's death was imminent. I flew from San Antonio to New Orleans, then took a train from there to Mobile. My cousin picked me up in the middle of the night and drove me thirty miles across Mobile Bay to my family home. There I discovered my father in a comatose state, breathing hard, unresponsive, and under the care of an incompletely trained but helpful nurse's aide. My mother was beside herself.

The attending physician and I really didn't know what the main problems were with my father, except that he had received the best care they could provide in the hospital and, of course, my family had run out of money long before. There was no hope for recovery, but we didn't know what his blood chemistries were, we had no chest X-ray, and we knew nothing about the state of his brain or anything else by objective measurements. Because nothing was being done, it was expected that he would die. He was given fluids when he could swallow, but he could not handle food. No IV fluids were administered at home. Though incontinent, he was cared for at home in a hospital bed bought by friends.

The doctor suspected that my father's kidneys were in bad shape, but he had no laboratory test to support that suspicion, and there was nothing that could be done at that point in any event. The kidneys probably were nonfunctioning. The doctor asked whether I thought we should give him a blood transfusion, but I couldn't see any point in that. We agreed not to. My father was watched expectantly by the nurse, and he died in the night. As far as I could tell, he was comfortable. He seemed not to be experiencing pain, and in the end he probably died from dehydration.

That was the way it was before high-tech medicine. There were no laws or courts involved in questions about what kind of care should be given to terminal patients. Nor was there a government payer willing to cover the costs of various expensive interventions. I can easily imagine what would happen today: we would put him in the ICU, do his blood chemistries, take X-rays, do brain scans, perhaps do hemodialysis, and probably needlessly prolong his death—or possibly make him better.

By the time of my mother's death ten years later Medicare was in place, but not in the place it now seems to be. She had retired from her school teaching job, although she still taught music. She lived alone and occasionally had a companion stay with her. She drove her own car, took care of herself, lived independently, and seemed fine. One morning, while in the bathroom, she developed a sudden headache, which resulted in hospitalization in the same hospital in Fairhope. There it was determined that she had broken a blood vessel in her brain while straining at stool, and the broken vessel had produced a partial incapacity.

Covered by Medicare, she was transferred to a private community hospital in Mobile for further evaluation, namely arteriography, with the possibility of neurosurgical clamping of the blood vessel or excision of the aneurysm, if one were found. Her care was assumed by two of my medical school classmates, the internist Ivy Williamson and the neurosurgeon Frank Cope.

They examined her and determined that she had indeed broken a blood vessel in her brain and was in bad shape, but not near death. High-tech diagnostic intervention showed a point of rupture of an artery, but in a place that was not amenable to neurosurgical intervention. So my mother was treated supportively. She did not die and was not unconscious, but she had sustained substantial cerebral damage. When I visited her at the Mobile hospital, she would come in and out of recognition of who I was, or who anyone else was for that matter. She was able to eat and drink, and it soon was determined that she would not benefit from further hospitalization.

With my approval, she was transferred to a nursing home near Daphne, Alabama, again about a dozen miles from our old home, where she was cared for by another classmate of mine, Tom Yancey. She remained in her severely altered, not fatal, state of brain function for many weeks. One day I got a call from my friend Tom, who said, "Your momma's doing about the same way as she was with the brain, but she's come up with an infection. It's a urinary tract infection, and we're trying to figure out whether we should treat her or not. Sometimes they take care of themselves, and sometimes they get a lot worse and spread. We're concerned about that."

I asked whether she was in any condition to have an opinion on her treatment. He said, "Naw. She's pretty much out of it." Then I asked what he thought, and he said, "Looks to me like we ought to not treat it. Let nature take its course, whatever that is." I told him I agreed.

A day or two later he called and said that the infection had spread and she was in a lot worse shape. He didn't know for sure, but he thought she would die from the infection, and she did. I did not see her in the final days because she wouldn't have known I was there and there was no close family for whom I had to offer emotional support since I was an only child.

I never saw the bills associated with that hospitalization or the nursing home care, and no collection agency ever came after me, so I imagine Medicare and/or Medicaid paid the vast bulk of the cost of her care and the rest was written off.

By current standards, Tom Yancey and I helped my mother die, though we never would have called it that. We were still very close to the way medicine had been practiced from time immemorial: physicians stood by and eased their patients' natural passage toward death. That was a much more humane way to practice medicine, and we have to recapture it. Patient and family trust is involved.

Let's face it, no one wants to die but everyone must. That is the way of the world, and upon consideration, no one would want it any other way. We have to make way for our progeny and understand that we live through them when we die. That is our immortality. We are the custodians of our DNA, which we received in an unbroken chain of life from the first living cell.

Despite this overwhelming reality, we continue to chase the illusion of life everlasting. We devise elaborate "scoop and run" procedures, rushing emergency medical technicians (EMTs) to retrieve people who have suffered outpatient cardiac arrest, giving them wonderful treatment, all the while knowing that only 3 percent will ultimately leave the hospital with a decently functioning brain. We ignore living will instructions and routinely apply "heroic" measures, essentially not even listening to our patients and their families. Too often we withhold needed pain medication for terminal patients because we fear the loss of our licenses or we're concerned about addicting them or speeding their deaths.

It's all terrible nonsense, and it's got to stop. We need to train physicians not only to fight for life but also to accept the end of life. We have to train physicians to be humane caregivers, to listen to their patients, and to ease their way to death. Honest disclosure doesn't mean telling the patient, "You have inoperable cancer," and then leaving the room (I've heard such stories, even recently). Honest but humane disclosure means sitting down and talking to patients, explaining what has been found, answering questions, and carefully moving toward a discussion of what to do, even if it takes time to do so.

There is a way, as we shall see, for physicians to help patients die. It is ethical, and although it hasn't yet been tested in court, it should be legal. If patients so decide, we should allow them to refuse all nutrition and hydration. Their discomfort can be eased by medication, and a peaceful death shortly comes.

The Modern Bias to Intervene

What would happen today with a patient like my mother? A lot, and a lot of it would not be in her best interest. These days even a person with advanced Alzheimer's disease who gets a serious pneumonia is generally treated. My mother did not have Alzheimer's, but she did have vascular disease that had damaged her brain in a similar fashion. Today the pressure from doctors, from family, from lawyers, and from the culture we have created in much of the United States would force intervention, even though it would be purposeless and possibly harmful to both the patient and the family. To some extent, the threat of a malpractice suit forces treatment, even when it seems to make no sense.

But there is no single reason that accounts for the changes that have transformed the process of dying. Obviously it's natural to want to stay alive. It's natural to want loved ones to stay alive. No one wants to lose precious connections with those they care for deeply. Yet that is something we all have to accept, and in an earlier time most of us turned to religion to help us reconcile ourselves to, or at least deal with, our loss.

That attitude of acceptance began to change when the technical capacity to keep someone alive became more sophisticated. One of the first steps in that direction came with closed-chest cardiac massage. A landmark *JAMA* article in 1960 described the life-restoring technique. When someone drops dead of a heart attack, pumping on the chest can bring him or her back to life. Other techniques were added, such as mouth-to-mouth respiration and then a host of sophisticated devices used by emergency medical technicians.

What is not commonly understood, however, is that if a person drops dead in the street and somebody does closed-chest cardiac massage, administers mouth-to-mouth resuscitation, and calls 911, even if the EMTs arrive quickly the chances of that person walking out of the hospital with good brain function are very, very low—something like 1 percent. In cities with extremely responsive EMT systems that respond to 911 calls in a matter of minutes and provide wonderful care in the ambulance on the way in, the percentage of people who leave the hospital with a decently functioning brain may reach 3 percent.

Yet people continue to believe in the "lifesaving" effectiveness of cardiopulmonary resuscitation (CPR). In a study published last year, 96 percent of the people surveyed believed that CPR works at least 65 percent of the time. The problem with CPR is that, while it may maintain oxygen flow, it may not restart the heart. If there is ventricular fibrillation, only a defibrillator can do that, and even defibrillators have limitations. Only half of the 250,000 cardiac arrests each year can be treated by defibrillation, and it has to arrive fast. Survival chances drop 10 percent for every minute that goes by before the defibrillator is used.

The human limitations of many of these high-tech interventions, such as treating pneumonia or kidney failure in an Alzheimer's patient, are daunting, yet they continue. An unhappy part of the picture is that the medical system is rewarded for prolonging lives. For example, the costs of trying to bring back a person who has dropped dead on the street, especially if there's no response from the heart and the brain is gone, commonly run between $5,000 and $10,000. I'm not suggesting directly that emergency physicians are reviving such patients for the sole purpose of gaining money for themselves or the emergency department, but that is the fact of the matter.

Another example comes from intensive-care units, which have become a major revenue center for many hospitals. I know of one hospital that in the late 1980s used ICUs for terminally ill AIDS patients. They kept the patients alive as long as they could because there was a huge profit margin in doing so. A physician asked me whether I thought that practice was all right, and I said, "Absolutely not. It's one of the worst things I ever heard of." Seeing doctors and hospitals profit from providing care for the dying only deepens patient distrust of the profession.

The right-to-life movement, buttressed by the trial bar, also plays a role. This movement was activated by the 1973 *Roe v. Wade* decision, which legalized abortions for women in the first two trimesters of pregnancy. *Roe v. Wade* crystallized the antiabortion movement in a much more formal way. When abortion was generally illegal, there was no need for antiabortion organizations. With legalization came concerted efforts to protect "innocent lives," a concept that quickly moved from the unborn fetus to the person at the other end of life—the dying patient.

Those in the medical community incidentally, especially obstetricians and gynecologists, have been strongly supportive of abortion on demand. Doctors were the ones who had to care for women suffering from botched abortions in back-alley clinics. They had to witness, all too often, the death of "guilty" women who had desperately tried to end an unwanted pregnancy. When I set out to publish position papers in *JAMA* on late-term pregnancy termination in 1998, I had a hard time finding any physician who would write about supporting federal legislation favoring a ban. That was partly because few, if any, physicians want to see the federal government regulating the practice of medicine, but it was also because most physicians think these decisions should be private matters resolved by patients and their doctors.

I took a neutral editorial position on the issue of abortion, but not on the issue of federal intervention in the practice of medicine. It was an astonishing departure for the AMA to support a federal ban on late-term abortion in 1997, inviting the federal government into the patient-physician relationship in this most difficult and intimate problem area. Physician licensing has always been a state issue, something the AMA had always supported until its ill-advised endorsement of that federal intervention into medical practice.

There were some who thought the AMA endorsement of the Republican-backed ban on late-term abortion was a quid pro quo for Republican support on Medicare spending for physician services. Faced with a congressional proposal to cut $115 billion over five years from projected Medicare spending, the AMA was involved in an intense lobbying effort to limit cuts for doctors. Doctors are now only one of a growing number of Medicare providers, which includes hospitals, nursing homes, home health services, managed care corporations, and medical device manufacturers.

By chance, the AMA letter to House Speaker Newt Gingrich outlining its proposal to limit the cuts was mailed on May 19, 1997, the very day the association announced its support for the late-term abortion ban; journalists had a field day. The *New York Times* columnist Frank Rich titled his story "Hypocritic Oath" and castigated the AMA for practicing "bad medicine."

It was later revealed that some interference by board members in the Washington lobbying effort had painted the AMA into a corner. But it was clearly understood in the Washington office that the AMA blessing of the abortion ban would enhance its relations with the congressional Republican majority. The AMA support of the ban added at least one vote in the Senate and brought it very close to a veto-proof number. Later that year the AMA did receive support for its Medicare position from the majority party. In early 2000 the Supreme Court refused to ban the late-term abortion procedure.

Protecting All Innocent Lives

The right-to-life movement quickly focused attention on the preservation of all "innocent lives," including those of terminal patients. Just as quickly, attorneys burst onto the scene with charges of neglect if physicians or hospitals did not do what could be done to prolong the "life" of a dying patient or a comatose patient in a vegetative state. One case after another—remember Karen Ann Quinlan and Nancy Cruzan?—made newspaper headlines. In the late 1970s and 1980s an imperative solidified to do almost anything possible to prolong a life.

A particularly grotesque case was that of a Massachusetts Alzheimer's patient in his eighties whose family wanted to stop hemodialysis treatments. Family members said that their father, had he been competent, would not have wished to continue living in his semivegetative state. They said he would have preferred a natural death, which would come quickly and painlessly if the life-prolonging treatments were stopped. During the lengthy legal battle the patient died despite continued treatment.

The imperative to keep patients alive at all costs seeped into the very culture of medicine. Soon physicians in training treated the prolongation of lives as a badge of professional competence. We published a piece in *JAMA* by Lynn A. Crosby called "Not on My Shift." In an ironic voice, Crosby described the extraordinary interventions he made all night long to keep a terminal patient alive so that she would not die on his shift: increasing the patient's fluids, transfusing blood, adding a dopamine drip, inserting a catheter and an arterial line, giving albumin, putting her on a ventilator, and so on. At the end of the shift Crosby warned the oncoming resident that the patient might die that day. "Not on my shift," came the reply, the same words Crosby had used when given the same warning at the start of his own shift.

Other physicians registered dismay over what was happening to aged patients who, ready and willing to die, were kept alive against their wishes. We published an article by Alvan R. Feinstein that began, "Her chief complaint is that she wants to die and that the doctors will not let her." He described the plight of a ninety-six-year-old woman who, until she was eighty-five, had lived a completely independent life in her own apartment. At that point she had tired of shopping and cooking for herself and moved into an apartment in a sheltered care facility. On her ninetieth birthday she articulated the desire to die in her sleep. Hospitalized that winter with pneumonia, she said her time had come and bid a loving farewell to her children, grandchildren, and great-grandchildren. Intravenous fluids and antibiotics restored her life, however, to her surprise and dismay.

In the succeeding years she grew increasingly frail. Each winter she was hospitalized for pneumonia, always prepared for death, always sicker than the year before, and each time she was pulled through by vigorous therapy. Finally she suffered a severely debilitating stroke and in lucid moments complained about becoming a burden, something she had always dreaded. Another stroke took her back to the hospital, and when she developed anorexia, fever, and pneumonia, her children pleaded with the house staff to let her alone. But the residents and the attending physicians said they could not "do nothing."

Before one of her sons, a physician at a medical school in a distant city, could arrive to dispute the doctors' plan, she was given intravenous antibiotics, fluids, and other vigorous support. She recovered and was transferred to a nursing home, her mind substantially destroyed. Her family members wondered why this was allowed to occur. Neither she nor her loved ones wanted her life to be prolonged in a vegetative state. Why wouldn't her doctors let her die in peace and serenity?

"I do not know the answers to these questions," Feinstein wrote. "But I, the physician son of this woman, weep for my mother and for what has happened to my profession."

Publishing articles on death and dying was not necessarily on my agenda when I became editor of *JAMA* in 1982. My goal was to publish material that would help doctors practice good medicine, based on solid science. I wanted to use *JAMA* to help doctors do a better job, with the most advanced information. James H. Sammons, the executive vice president of the AMA, inadvertently opened my eyes to the power of *JAMA* on other issues.

Shortly after I arrived, he asked me to his office to assure me that I had editorial independence and that I had the right to publish whatever I chose, particularly in the areas of science. But he warned me to treat three areas in particular with "sensitivity": tobacco, nuclear war, and abortion. So I thought that since those were particularly sensitive issues, those were the ones I should work on first. Part of a medical editor's job involves getting into hot water: honesty and disclosure are key elements of a learned profession.

The Shocking Death of Debbie

The pieces I published on dying reached that level of sensitivity with the 1988 article "It's Over, Debbie," the story of an apparently deliberate act of euthanasia. That essay, written by a practicing physician who requested anonymity, rocked the medical community, elicited a strong reaction from the public, and stirred public officials into action. New York Mayor Ed Koch wrote a letter to U.S. Attorney General Ed Meese demanding an investigation of *JAMA*, which, Koch alleged, was hiding a confessed murderer. Illinois State's Attorney Richard M. Daley issued a subpoena requesting the names of the author, the peer reviewer, and the whole file on the Debbie story. We declined and ultimately, months later, prevailed when a court ruled in our favor, quashing the subpoena and supporting the anonymity of the whole peer-review process as being in the best interest of the public good.

The AMA incidentally—starting with top administrative management and then the board of trustees—put its full support behind the editors of *JAMA*, although the association opposes euthanasia in any way, shape, or form. Many observers expressed the opinion that either my wife—Patricia Lorimer Lundberg, an English professor and dean at Indiana University Northwest with a particular interest in reader response theory—or I had authored the piece, but that simply wasn't so.

What was all the fuss about? Nothing less than an issue that is fundamental to all physicians from the time they enter medical school: death and the physician's role in aiding dying patients. The Debbie story electrified everyone because it was so stark, spare, and almost brutal in its depiction of an event.

The author, a gynecology resident, was called in the middle of the night to the bedside of a dying twenty-year-old patient named Debbie. She had ovarian cancer, weighed eighty pounds, and was hooked up to an intravenous alcohol drip and nasal oxygen. Even from the hallway the resident could hear her loud, labored breathing. "Her eyes were hollow, and she had suprasternal and intercostal retractions with her rapid inspirations," he wrote. She had not eaten or slept in two days and had been given supportive care only. Her only words to the resident were, "Let's get this over with."

The resident considered her plight and decided that, while he could not give her health, he could give her rest. He went to the nursing station, drew twenty milligrams of morphine sulfate into a syringe, and went back to the patient, saying that he had something that would give her rest. She "looked at the syringe, then laid her head on the pillow with her eyes open." The physician in training injected the morphine intravenously and waited. Within seconds her breathing slowed, her eyes closed, and her features softened. Within four minutes her breathing slowed even more, then became irregular, then ceased. The last lines of the essay were, "It's over, Debbie."

I invited the author to reveal his or her name for publication in this book, but the author declined, offering instead a follow-up essay that elaborated on the clinical hopelessness of the patient—the cancer had invaded her lungs, leaving no pulmonary reserve. The author also revealed that the dose had been limited to eight milligrams so as to provide rest but not kill her. That this low dose of morphine nonetheless initiated a cascade of biochemical events that led to death cannot be denied. The author, who had left the details in the original essay somewhat vague to allow room for different interpretations, was shocked to have been called a murderer, even by physicians, who apparently did not take into consideration Debbie's precarious condition. However, the purpose in writing was served, the author wrote later. The essay crystallized debate about end-of-life care and encouraged caregivers to pay more attention to patient and family wishes.

Certainly, my interest in publishing the essay at that time was to spur debate on the issue of how we die and to bring the profession back into the discussion. What surprised me was the wide gulf between the attitudes of patients and physicians about the issues raised. In the hundreds of letters that followed publication, physicians condemned the author-physician's actions by four to one and opposed the editor's decision to publish the account by three to one. "I am outraged by the action of the physician in this case who served as jury, judge, and executioner of this young patient," wrote one physician. The essay "constitutes a textbook example of medical arrogance, ignorance, and criminal conduct," wrote another. "That the resident could kill a patient, let alone one whom he did not know or with whom he had no relationship, represents a breach of any semblance of medical ethics and the rule of law. That *JAMA* could publish this cavalier description of homicide, however, bespeaks a social milieu that is tolerant to the killing of patients by physicians," wrote yet another physician.

The patient perspective was entirely different. The hundreds of letters from the public were generally highly supportive of the author-physician's actions and the decision to publish the account of how Debbie died. "I am fully aware that a physician's duty is to treat and heal, but when healing is clearly not possible, should not mercy killing be allowed?" wrote one. Describing the painful death of her own mother from lung cancer, a young woman wrote, "I feel very strongly that if such a patient wants to end her life by being injected with morphine or any other drug that will end her pain, then she should have that right. No one should have the right to make someone suffer." Another wrote, "I think it is important for the American Medical Association to consider the problems in caring for sick and dying patients, one of which is active euthanasia."

Looking back, I find it somewhat troubling that so many physicians made so many quick and negative comments on what was written. Certainly, we all feel bound by the Hippocratic oath, which enjoins physicians from giving any deadly medicine to anyone, if asked, but that doesn't go to the heart of the question posed, however vaguely, by the original Debbie essay. The fact is that her life had been prolonged far beyond its natural limit by various medical interventions, including the aggressive application of chemotherapy.

In the later commentary the anonymous author reported having considered telephoning Debbie's attending physician but deciding not to because of the likelihood that the physician would say one of two things: "Don't do anything," or, "Give her something to make her relax." The author considered neither response appropriate in view of the patient's acute, critical, and imminently terminal pain.

Professional Responsibility

It seems to me that the profession is out of sync on this issue, not only with the patients it serves but with its own professional goals. The Hippocratic oath also states, "I will follow that system of regimen which, according to my ability and judgment, I consider for the benefit of my patients." Death is not the enemy, as a physician and a theologian from the University of Chicago pointed out in a *JAMA* essay. The real enemies of medicine are premature death, disease, disability, pain, human suffering. Death is the final inexorable restraint and limitation, of which there are many, on human life, wrote Richard Landau and James Gustafson. They warned that a misguided physician fundamentalism now prevails: "The practical dogma is to preserve life as long as medically and technically possible."

It's somewhat difficult to understand why so many physicians lag behind their patients in confronting the new questions about death and dying posed by their high-tech medical interventions. Some studies suggest that physicians have a heightened fear of death and that they were attracted to medicine in the first place as a kind of coping mechanism. The theory is that gaining an understanding of biological processes and medical skills to conquer disease offers a powerful illusion that one can control life. By extension, when physicians fight to save a patient's life, they also are fighting to vindicate their expertise and save their own lives.

That's a theory. My own observation is that physicians are out of sync with patients because they don't know them as well as they did years ago. My parents' doctors could talk to me plainly about their terminal illnesses not only because I was a fellow physician but also because they knew me and my parents personally. Dr. Jordan watched me grow up in Silverhill. He had been taking care of my father for years and would never have wished to see him in pain. All too often today decisions about prolonging life through aggressive application of high technology are made by specialists who know their patients only as "cases." They move from one case to the next, making decisions after doing no more than reviewing chart material, asking some questions of house staff, and making cursory observations (in the opinion of too many patients) of the patients themselves.

These specialists have developed much more faith in their technologies and expertise than in any thoughts or opinions a patient might offer. Furthermore, they drive consensus decisions that almost always lead to intervention. The ethic is, "Don't just stand there, doctor. Do something." But there are times when the ethic should be: "Doctor, do nothing. Just stand there." Too many superspecialists are out of touch with the benefits of the latter ethic.

The spotlight was shown on the disconnect between doctors and patients in the state of Oregon in 1994, when voters approved the Death with Dignity Act, which allows physicians to assist patient suicide under strictly prescribed guidelines. The AMA opposed the bill, which was reaffirmed by 60 percent of Oregon voters in the 1997 general election. The law allows physicians to prescribe a fatal dose of drugs only for terminal patients within six months of death, as determined by two independent physicians, either one of whom can refer the patient for psychiatric evaluation. Other safeguards serve to prevent the thoughtless application of the law. The patient is allowed to self-administer the drug. I have no doubt that this legislation was spurred in part by the debate that followed publication of the Debbie essay.

Members of Congress subsequently passed legislation that would allow agents of the Drug Enforcement Administration (DEA) to scrutinize physician prescribing patterns in Oregon and make it a federal crime for physicians knowingly to prescribe drugs to assist a patient's death, punishable by up to twenty years in prison. Astonishingly, the AMA supported this legislation, once again not only inviting the federal government—as with the federal legislation banning late-term abortion—into the patient-physician relationship, but pleasing the Republican majority.

The federal government should not be a party in the physician-patient relationship. The AMA defended its position by pointing to language in the bill in support of better end-of-life care, which presumably includes controlling terminal illness pain more effectively by more aggressively prescribing narcotics. The language may be there, but with every doctor's license on the line, it's hard to believe that very many of them will engage in more aggressive use of "controlled substances."

There was an interesting response to the Oregon legislation. In the year following enactment only fifteen people chose to end their own lives—out of a total of 29,000 deaths in the state from all causes. But prescriptions for pain control medications rose substantially: more patients were receiving adequate doses of controlled substances to manage their pain. Why were doctors prescribing more freely? Because the threat of loss of license and practice was removed by the Death with Dignity Act. No longer was anyone likely to lose his or her livelihood for prescribing "too much" pain-relieving medication. The proposed legislation that has a DEA agent reviewing physician prescribing orders would have the disastrous effect of condemning thousands of patients to needless pain.

Doctors seem finally to be getting over their longtime difficulties with prescribing narcotics. When I worked as an orderly in a Mobile hospital before entering medical school, nurses were cautioned about providing too much narcotics because the patient might become addicted. The doctors ordered the narcotics but set a strict schedule for administration by the nurses. Even if patients complained of pain, they had to wait, sometimes for hours, until they could receive their next shot. Even as a youngster I thought it was crazy to worry about a dying patient becoming addicted. It didn't make sense. Patients were being denied pain relief because of policy, because of beliefs, because of law, and because of the fear of creating addiction.

My main purpose in entering academic medicine at the University of Southern California was to do serious studies on diseases caused by drugs. My interest in the subject began when I was a staff pathologist at Letterman Army Hospital in San Francisco in 1963. One night a patient who had overdosed on amphetamines entered the hospital. Because no one had ever seen such a condition before, no one knew what to do, and the patient died. The scientific literature on acute amphetamine poisoning in humans was virtually nonexistent at that time. Two internal medicine residents and I decided to look into it and developed a plan to conduct major research into the pathophysiology of acute amphetamine poisoning.

The plan resulted in months of experiments on dogs, overdosing them with amphetamine and studying its effects. We used very sophisticated physiologic and pathologic methods and ended up publishing six or seven research papers in highly regarded journals. Because there had been little or no research in the field, we more or less had it to ourselves just at the beginning of the "speed freak" era. My interest in drugs of abuse was largely created by that set of experiments, and I continued research in the area of drug-induced diseases when I became chief pathologist at the William Beaumont General Hospital in El Paso.

When I moved to USC in Los Angeles in 1967, I thought I would continue my research in the laboratory, perhaps with animals, perhaps with tissue cultures, or perhaps with electron microscopy. However, once in L.A., I quickly realized that all of southern California was a laboratory for studying diseases produced by drugs. People were giving them to themselves and to their friends en masse every day. At my hospital, the Los Angeles County–USC Medical Center, we began admitting thirty to fifty people a day who were sick from drugs of one kind or another. So I moved from laboratory experiments into a study of humans.

A tragic event focused the entire community on the problem of drugs. The daughter of Art Linkletter, the popular and warmly regarded broadcaster, either jumped, fell, or was pushed from a high-rise building in West Los Angeles. It was widely reported that she was under the influence of drugs, probably LSD. In response, we crafted a proposal to create a great toxicology laboratory that would help the doctors at our hospital take better care of the patients who came in sick from drugs. It was supported by the board of supervisors of Los Angeles County, and soon we had funded, built, hired staff for, and opened what we believed was the best clinical toxicology lab in the world. We could do it because we had the patients, we had the money, and we got the right people on board to support the project.

The laboratory was extremely helpful for attending physicians who were treating the patients because what the patients said they took and what they really took were not always the same. It helped determine what they had ingested, how much, and at what levels, and it guided treatment decisions. The work also led to my participation in founding the California Society for Treatment of Alcoholism and Other Drug Dependencies, now known as the California Society of Addiction Medicine. My involvement in that organization made me acutely aware of the dilemma of physicians who refused to take care of heroin addicts, or other addicts: they were afraid that the law would not let them handle treatment properly.

The Proper Use of Narcotics

Narcotics are defined one way legally and in an entirely different way medically. From the medical standpoint, narcotics are real or synthetic opiates. From the legal standpoint, narcotics are anything the government says they are, including all kinds of things that are not in fact narcotics. This open-endedness was frightening for physicians, even when they were treating dying patients in terrible pain. They were afraid either that they would addict the patient or that some district attorney would come in and say they were prescribing narcotics in doses that were too large and threaten them with loss of license.

In fact, physicians by and large don't addict patients with pain medication in hospitals when they treat pain, almost no matter how much they give them. That's not how addiction works. Theoretically addiction could result from stair-stepping the doses, but generally these patients do not become addicted. It is a false fear to a large extent. The real issue is the importance of keeping politicians and drug enforcement agents out of the doctor's office, and out of the patient-physician relationship. I can't think of anything worse than putting the DEA, after losing the "War on Drugs," in charge of pain management for terminal patients. It would be nothing less than an abomination.

But does that mean I'm in favor of physician-assisted suicide by means of prescribing drugs? Not necessarily. I have trouble with the types of physician-assisted suicide I've seen so far because generally the patient does the action, with chemicals provided by the physician. I know that once in a while those chemicals aren't going to do the job. Sometimes patients who thought they were going to die will wake up instead, sick because they aspirated.

What does the physician do then? I don't know the answer. If the physician and the patient intended for death to occur, however, the temptation will be overwhelming to assist in that death to a greater extent than planned when it was thought to be just a matter of the patient taking a handful of pills. The person standing by thinks, *This isn't working,* and may want to help by turning to suffocation with a plastic bag or a pillow. In that event, we're looking at an entirely different thing. If one person makes a deliberate attempt to take another person's life, a prosecutor might prosecute and a jury might convict.

This scenario is also quite different from that of a physician simply prescribing medication. If the patient takes an overdose of the medication and doesn't die, it's legally the patient's problem only. But that violates the patient-physician principle that they work together. The whole thing suddenly becomes a conundrum.

A while back the New York Academy of Medicine put a committee together to write guidelines for physician-assisted suicide. The committee members accepted the challenge, and after trying very hard to come up with guidelines, they declared the effort a failure.

They said, we can't do it. There are too many branch points with problems, and there are no ways to supersede the problems that make any ethical sense. They had to abandon the project.

So where does that leave us? In the hands of our patients. One of the mega-trends of the last decade of the twentieth century was the profound shift from physician paternalism to patient autonomy in the United States. The movement hasn't affected everyone, and some ethnic groups have stayed with physician paternalism to a greater extent than others. But in general the decade from the late 1980s to the late 1990s was a "take charge of your life" period for patients—including taking charge of their own deaths. Two more essays from *JAMA* suggest acceptable methods.

One, titled "When Jennie Took to Bed," was written by Roscoe E. Dean, a physician from a small town in South Dakota. Dean described the death of his Aunt Jennie, "a beautiful woman of quiet dignity" whose parents had emigrated from an area near Prague to the Dakota Territory and who lived with her brother, Uncle Bill, in their homestead farmhouse. At the age of eighty-two, she gradually started losing her strength to a silent carcinoma of the colon, and one day, Uncle Bill told Dean's mother, "Jennie took to bed."

Advised by her attending physician to go to the Mayo Clinic for treatment, Aunt Jennie said, "No, my family will look after me." And so they did, along with neighbors who brought food, words of comfort, and other expressions of love. The physician left medication for rest and pain. Near the end Jennie allowed her family to admit her to the town's small country hospital, where she soon died peacefully in her sleep. The total cost of her terminal care was a few hundred dollars, Dean noted.

By way of contrast, he described the plight of another elderly cancer patient. Bedridden with multiple tubes and surgical scars, she had lost her hair to chemotherapy and often cringed and cried aloud with pain at the slightest movement. The total medical bill of some $50,000 had bought her nothing to look forward to other than pain and institutional care. Dean had long known and respected the lady and very cautiously asked why she had consented to continued therapy. (She had returned to the country hospital after sessions at an academic center.) "The doctors at the university said there was a chance," she said.

A sophisticated hospital is the last place you want to be when terminally ill. Once you're in the hospital setting, you're trapped. The staff owns you, and they do all those terrible things they have been trained to do to prolong life, no matter how artificially or how hopelessly. Moreover, many nursing homes still send patients to hospitals to die because they do not want to take responsibility for end-of-life care. Ironically, the hospital medical staff often stabilizes the patient's condition and sends him or her back to the nursing home. This can occur several times before the fragile and exhausted patient dies.

Fortunately, the hospice movement has been gaining strength. Hospice personnel understand the nature of terminal disease. Their goal is not to prolong life unnecessarily but to make the life the patient has left as comfortable and as pleasant as possible. Hospice patients can talk freely to those they love about their impending death. All too often hospitalized patients talk only about the next round of interventions planned by their physicians. Today hospices are far more plentiful and far more frequently used, although methods of payment for these inexpensive services still lag. Greater funding recognition and support is clearly needed. Most hospice patients remain in their homes and are cared for by family members and visiting nurses. Ending a life this way is much less expensive and much more humane than high-tech hospital care.

The second *JAMA* essay, by David M. Eddy, a physician then from Jackson, Wyoming, may offer the definitive method for helping terminal patients die. In "A Conversation with My Mother," Eddy describes a series of medical events that overtook his mother in her eighties. Until then she had been an independent widow, taking her walks, reading her books and newspapers, working crossword puzzles, and watching the news and professional sports on TV. She enjoyed her life, was appalled by the medical complications that one by one were robbing her of her freedom, and dreaded the prospect of being confined to a nursing home, dependent on others for care as her body, mind, and ability to pursue her interests steadily declined. She didn't want to end her life with a blank stare.

She said to her son, "My decision is not about whether I'm going to die—we all will sooner or later. My decision is about when and how. I don't want to spoil the wonder of my life by dragging it out in years of decay. I want to go now, while the good memories are still fresh. . . . Help me find a way." Eddy says he discussed her request with his brother and sister as well as with his mother's nurses and physicians. All agreed that she satisfied the criteria of being well informed, stable, and not depressed, although some had negative feelings about her request.

Eddy considered helping her with pills and even found a physician friend willing to write the necessary prescription from a distance, since it was illegal to assist in a patient's suicide and there was always the danger that someone might discover the plan and report it. He and his mother discussed the various ways she might take the pills to ensure death, but before they could act she was admitted to the hospital with pneumonia. Both he and she thought this was the answer. She refused antibiotics and requested medication that would keep her comfortable, but against all odds, the pneumonia regressed.

"What else can I do?" she asked. "Can I stop eating?"

That would take a long time, Eddy told her. But if she stopped drinking, death would come within a matter of days. "Can they keep me comfortable?" she asked.

The attending physician reluctantly agreed that she was clear of mind and that her quality of life had sunk below what she was willing to bear. Furthermore, what she was asking of him was ethically acceptable. "He took out the IV and wrote orders that she should receive adequate medications to control discomfort," Eddy wrote, adding that, "over the next four days, my mother greeted her visitors with the first smiles she had shown for months."

She reminisced about times past. She slept between visits but awoke brightly whenever touched by a new visitor. By the fifth day she was too drowsy and weak to talk, and on the sixth day she could not be wakened. "Her face was relaxed in her natural smile, she was breathing unevenly, but peacefully. We held her hands for another two hours, until she died."

Eddy says it was not a sad death. Quite the contrary, it was a happy death. Death was not a tragedy in her view, but a natural part of life to be embraced at the proper time, and she had done it without pills, without making her son a criminal, without putting a bag over her head, and without huddling in a van with a carbon monoxide machine. (The reference is to the ghastly machines fashioned by Jack Kevorkian, the pathologist who supports physician-assisted suicide in a bizarre way. He has been the wrong person asking the right question at the right time, but his behavior and questionable selection of patients have put him beyond the pale of professional standards.)

"Of course we cried," Eddy said. "But although we will miss her greatly, her ability to achieve her death at her 'right time' and in her 'right way' transformed for us what could have been a desolate and crushing loss into a time for joy. Because she was happy, we were happy."

An Ethically Acceptable Method of Assistance

The action taken by Eddy and his mother was protected by ethical standards issued by the AMA's Council on Ethical and Judicial Affairs in 1986. The council said that it is acceptable for physicians to withhold life support, such as food, fluids, oxygen, and medications, from a hopelessly, terminally ill person after agreement by all concerned. It was an enlightened standard, substantially guided by the AMA's general counsel at the time, Kirk Johnson. A brilliant, young attorney, Johnson, working with Dr. Roy Schwarz, would later help create the progressive Institute of Ethics.

Interestingly, the announcement was made at a conference on medical ethics in New Orleans to which Lawrence Altman, a physician-journalist with the *New York Times,* had been invited as a participant. The *Times* maintains a policy that allows reporters to participate in outside conferences but prohibits them from reporting on the activities of such conferences, so as to protect the paper's integrity as an independent source of news. Altman was therefore stuck in a situation where a front-page story was unfolding before his eyes and he couldn't report it. The *Times* got the story, but not without a number of long-distance phone calls between New York and New Orleans.

These two end-of-life stories are instructive in many ways. Aunt Jennie decided she wanted to take control of her own departure from life, wisely resisted hospitalization at a high-tech medical center, and luckily was able to enter a small country hospital that allowed her comfort care until her natural death occurred a week or so after admittance. Had she entered another hospital, she might not have been treated so kindly. People sign living wills and grant durable powers of attorney that make their terminal wishes explicitly known, but there is reported proof that even when they do so, the hospitals, doctors, and nurses responsible for following their directives do not find out what they are. Furthermore, a study funded by the Robert Wood Johnson Foundation demonstrated conclusively that even in the "best" hospitals, physicians and nurses who know the explicit wishes of the dying patient, amazingly, often do not honor those wishes.

This is a fact that almost defies understanding, but obviously the cultural value to preserve life at any cost has permeated the profession of medicine much more deeply than the public it serves. We physicians are losing the trust of our patients partly because we are losing sight of our professional responsibilities. The state of the art, as Feinstein expressed it, makes one weep for what has happened to our profession. Of course we're supposed to be technically adept. Of course we're supposed to be knowledgeable and up-to-date on the state of the art and science of medicine. But we're also supposed to be humane caregivers, professionals willing to wait and listen, to answer questions and be honest with our patients and their family members. We cannot prolong life infinitely. We cannot make the old young again, although some of us try to at least make them look younger. We do not hold the keys to life and death, although we have learned a number of things that can brighten life's passage.

David Eddy's mother, for example, was the beneficiary of many high-tech interventions before she decided to refuse further treatments. As a younger person, she had been treated for diverticulitis and endometriosis. In her later years she was treated for a broken hip, a bout with depression, some hearing loss, and cataracts. She joked that, but for lens implants, hearing aids, hip surgery, and Elavil, she would have been blind, deaf, bedridden, and depressed. Those are interventions the profession can be proud of, and they occur in great numbers at high-tech medical centers.

So what are we to do? I'm not sure the profession can get out of this bind by itself, but physicians who care about the wishes of their terminal patients and want to assist them do have an ethically acceptable method at hand. They can follow the lead established by the mother of David Eddy. The conditions established by her and her family are a textbook guide. She was in full control of her faculties. She had been treated for depression and was clearly free of any sign of clinical depressive disease. She made it very clear that she wanted to die. The family understood and sympathized with her desire. Her attending physician was consulted and agreed with her plan, even if somewhat reluctantly. (A religious adviser might also have been consulted, as well as a second unrelated physician.)

If all agree that the time for death has come, then withholding all nutrition and fluids, orally and intravenously, is a very effective method of producing death. It is said to be reasonably painless, although it may involve discomfort from thirst and hunger. There's no reason, however, why the physician cannot provide narcotics to diminish discomfort.

My father's death probably resulted from dehydration. I know of a family that agreed with the elderly father, a multiple stroke patient, that they would allow him to die from dehydration. Everyone expected him to die within a day, and they all agreed not to have any kind of wake or funeral, just a memorial service later. He was given a very small amount of fluid, with morphine as needed, so there was no question of pain. He didn't die for a week, however, and during that week the family changed its mind about his obsequies. They decided to have a wake and a funeral after all. There was something about that week of waiting that changed their minds. Perhaps the extended time let them see the true nature of death, that it is not something to be shunned and set aside but the final event in the life of someone they loved whose memory they wanted to cherish and celebrate.

So it can be done. It may take a day, it may take a week, but death will come surely and peacefully. Physician-assisted suicide need not be done intravenously, or intramuscularly, or by prescriptions for pills. It can be accomplished simply by the agreement of everyone involved to withhold fluids and then to wait.

Will this method hold up in courts? It may be ethically acceptable, but will it be legally acceptable? I don't know. No court case seems to have tested it. The intent is for a death to happen. The process may be initiated by the patient, but it cannot succeed without the complicity of many others. There is shared intent, the progression of premeditated action, and the resulting death of an individual. I know of no one who has prosecuted a physician or family for doing it, but I expect that someone will—somebody, most likely, who sees the law in black-and-white terms or is politically motivated. How juries respond may depend on where the trial occurs and on the political winds of the moment. A Congress that wants to put DEA agents in charge (with the AMA's support) of medical practice associated with pain control might do anything. It's possible that someone who had assisted in such a death would be convicted of murder by a jury. But it isn't murder, and it probably shouldn't even be considered assisted suicide. It is the end of a natural life, an end sounded on a high note instead of a low one, and it offers a patient a death with dignity.

Furthermore, although it seems simple and unsophisticated, death by dehydration represents true high-quality care. Quality care is not necessarily expensive or high-tech; it is appropriate care offered in appropriate settings by attentive and humane caregivers. It is entirely possible that high-quality care is much less expensive than all of the interventions we now routinely prescribe and accept. Allowing David Eddy's mother to die peacefully may have saved society thousands of dollars. The financial angle, however, misses the point. She had received good care that restored her vision, hearing, mobility, and good spirits, but her death with dignity represented the highest quality of care she received in her entire life.

9

The Search for Quality

It All Begins on the Autopsy Table

M OST PEOPLE THINK THAT QUALITY of care is defined
by medical interventions, such as a hip replacement, lens
implant, or coronary bypass operation, but genuine quality of care
is defined by action based on good information. Physicians sometimes serve their patients best by standing by and doing nothing to
interfere, the scenario described by David Eddy in the terminal
care of his mother. That was appropriate action based on solid information.

Definitions of quality are often counterintuitive. Multiple lab
tests do not constitute quality medicine. Experimental new therapies do not define quality. More often than not the new treatments
or the comprehensive tests are driven by commercial rather than
quality concerns. Entrepreneurial physicians have a greater stake in
doing more than in doing good. Medicare, for example, provides
funding for autopsies of every hospitalized beneficiary, and good science suggests that at least 30 percent of deaths should be autopsied.
Very few are. The money goes instead for other hospital services.
This priority deviates from quality medicine and quality care.

In fact, lack of autopsy is the ultimate cover-up in medicine,
and the signature of poor-quality care. The whole issue of patient
safety is based on honesty, and the autopsy is central in a system
that finds truth, deals with it honestly, and tries to improve patient
care. High rates of autopsy have to be a key element in systemic

change aimed at curbing error in medicine and at promoting quality of care.

That was a theme I expressed in *JAMA* beginning in 1983, one year after taking over as editor. It was a theme that played a major role in my departure because by speaking honestly about problems in medicine I regularly embarrassed, insulted, and offended many doctors and their representatives in the House of Delegates and on the Board of Trustees.

Long before I was fired in January 1999, I knew that my forced departure from the AMA was inevitable; I simply did not know when or over what issue. I had irritated many doctors because I felt that my job as editor was to tell the truth and, as much as possible, the whole truth, no matter how embarrassing, insulting, or offensive. I tried to be sensible, diplomatic, and politic, to pick my spots and times—always appealing to the best sentiments expressed in AMA policy and ethics—but sometimes the truth was just too painful.

It wasn't my desire, but my duty, to be an irritant. When I was appointed editor in 1982, Sherman Mellinkoff, dean of the UCLA School of Medicine, gave me a call. "Congratulations, George. I'm glad you're getting the job," he said. Then he added a cautionary note: "But remember, the job of a medical journal editor is to shed light." I thanked him and said I was going to try my best to do just that, and I always did try. However, I learned soon after that conversation that another part of a medical editor's job is to take heat. That goes with the territory and is absolutely necessary. If there's no heat, there probably isn't much light being shed. It's all a part of handling the job.

But there was more. After taking heat for a while, my fellow editors and I decided that we had to give heat as well. Instead of waiting around for readers to complain, we decided to deliberately give them something to complain about. We would conduct preemptive strikes by publishing studies and running editorials that would make some practitioners squirm. A former editor of the

British Medical Journal got it right when he said, "A medical journal editor has got to be the conscience of the profession." In other words, an editor who is doing his or her job correctly is getting into trouble all the time.

And so I was. I knew that, sooner or later, something I said or ran would force my departure. Somewhere along the line enough pressure from enough people who had enough representatives in the right places at the right time inevitably would make that happen. Just when it might happen I never could guess, but even as I tried to straddle the line between truth and discretion, I counted my years at *JAMA* all the time I was there. Nevertheless, during my entire tenure I felt that I had the best job in the world.

Curiously enough, my countdown began with the centennial issue in 1983. As part of the celebration, I commissioned a paper about all the prior editors of *JAMA,* based on research developed by the AMA historian Frank Campion. There had been thirteen editors before me, and one, Truman Miller, had lasted a mere forty-eight days. I remember looking at his photograph and trying to figure out how he could have gotten into so much trouble in so little time. Nothing in his face seemed to tell the story. And nothing in the historical archives could enlighten me.

Of course, the first editor of *JAMA* in 1883 was the man who founded the AMA in 1846, Nathan Davis, a committed and forward-thinking man of medicine. An early great, but mostly forgotten, editor was George Simmons, who served from 1899 to 1924, a full quarter-century. Simmons was followed by Morris Fishbein, who lasted from 1924 to 1949, another twenty-five years. They served as models for me, since their longevity coincided with the *Journal*'s most vigorous years. I wanted to see how long I could last, and how well I could do. The comparison could never be quite fair, since Simmons and Fishbein also had been general secretaries of the association—the equivalent of executive vice president or chief executive officer—during substantial portions of their editorships. In effect, they ran the AMA as well as the *Journal* and had, from my perspective as an editor reporting to the EVP under other levels of management, undreamed-of power.

Nonetheless, I did fairly well. Year by year I watched my tenure pass that of eleven other editors, from forty-eight-day Miller on up. The longest editorship other than Simmons's and Fishbein's was about ten years, and I was well into my seventeenth year before my troubles became critical—ironically, because I repeated something I had written in a 1983 editorial: "*JAMA* is declaring war on the nonautopsy. Let us stop burying our mistakes. The goal is public trust." But those words were written when James Sammons was executive vice president. By 1998 a whole new regime was in power.

It all began in 1997, when I served as a moderator and speaker at the Indiana University School of Journalism, which was conducting a program for Midwest science reporters. At a dinner meeting that evening David Lansky, director of the Foundation for Accountability (FAACT) in Portland, Oregon, gave a speech on the quality of care in medicine today. At the end of the speech I stood up and expressed surprise that he had said nothing about the autopsy as a critical factor in quality of care. Had he thought about that? I asked. He was taken aback. "No one has ever asked that question before," he said. "I'll have to think about it."

After dinner the two of us discussed the role of the autopsy in quality care and the sorry state into which the autopsy had fallen. On average, fewer than 10 percent of deaths at hospitals across the country were autopsied. The percentage at some hospitals was less than five, and at others the percentage was zero. One hospital in Chicago, which had the largest number of deaths of any nonteaching hospital in the city in 1996, had not conducted a single autopsy. Lansky asked about the quality of care at that hospital: Was it any good? "I have no idea," I answered, "and no one at that hospital has any idea, because they don't look. They don't do autopsies, which means that they can't really care about quality."

Attending that meeting and hearing this information was Walt Bogdanich, a Pulitzer Prize–winning reporter, previously with the *Wall Street Journal,* who then worked for the CBS program *60 Minutes.* Sometime later he called the AMA and asked whether he could speak to me about the autopsy problem; *60 Minutes* might be interested in doing a segment on the issue. As the editor of *JAMA,* I often received queries from science reporters; these were fielded and approved by the AMA Science News Department. The upshot was a decision by *60 Minutes* in 1998 to do a program on the autopsy. Bogdanich asked whether I could come for on-camera interviews.

I had a long taping session with Mike Wallace about the autopsy situation in America. As more people at the AMA learned of a forthcoming program, fears were expressed. Colleagues were concerned about how a show produced by 60 Minutes might portray the medical profession.

As it turned out, I gave the official AMA position on the autopsy: autopsies are good, and more of them ought to be done. This was a long-standing AMA policy which had been elaborated upon and reaffirmed many times. I also discussed the AMA's role in the National Patient Safety Foundation, which was determined to curb error in medicine. None of that received airtime. What they ran were my comments about the sorry state of the autopsy in the United States, adding that people were going to their graves without physicians having any idea about what was truly wrong with them and there were hard data to prove it. When Wallace asked whether doctors were burying their mistakes, I agreed, a comment I had first published in *JAMA* in 1983.

The program aired in October 1998. It was effective and well done. While it didn't mention the AMA or the safety foundation, the information it did present was accurate. There is no question in my mind but that this program was important and in the best interest of the patients, the public, and the medical profession. *60 Minutes* ran the segment again in July 2000. The great majority of responses to me after both the 1998 and 2000 telecasts were favorable.

The Value of the Autopsy

About the same time that Galileo was mapping the stars in Padua, Italy, physicians working in another part of the same building were dissecting cadavers for one of the first times in Western medicine. Just as the great astronomer was attempting to understand the earth's place in the universe, the physicians were trying to understand the nature of disease and the causes of death. It was a remarkable juxtaposition as men of learning searched for galactic and tissue information about the human experience.

The autopsy has provided the basis for definition or clarification of almost any disease that can be named. Its purpose is to establish a cause of death, assist in determining the manner of death, compare premortem and postmortem findings, produce vital statistics, and monitor the public health. There is no better way to study the natural history of disease. But among the most important features of the autopsy is that it's the final and definitive method of monitoring the quality of care given to a seriously ill patient or provided by a medical system. Much can be learned about how a society lives by studying how its members die.

The most important reason for autopsy (as I wrote in *JAMA*) is that, when performed correctly, it provides the ultimate control over the assurance of quality in medicine. Think of it this way: Where would teaching be without testing students? Where would banking be without auditors? Where would law be without judges? Where would baseball be without umpires? Where would airline pilots be without air traffic controllers? That is where medicine would be without the autopsy. It is the one place where truth can be sought, found, and told without conflicts of interest.

I discovered the value of the autopsy and of pathology when I was a lab worker at the Druid City Hospital in Tuscaloosa, Alabama. Although I wouldn't enter medical school until 1953, a hospital pathologist named James Simon Peter Beck was sufficiently impressed with my interest in medicine to allow me to tag along and see what he did. He let me follow him down to the autopsy room, where I would see a pathologist examining a dead person, with clinical physicians in attendance.

Together they learned what happened to the person at or before death. Then they compared notes, trying to determine whether what was found after death was what they had expected to find before death. The clinicians often engaged in a good deal of soul-searching: Had they done the right thing, or had they messed up in some way? Had they hurt the patient or not? Would they have to change their methods of practice based on what they had learned?

Then I would follow Beck up to tissue committee meetings, at which one internist and one surgeon, along with the pathologist, considered all the tissue taken out in the operating rooms during the previous month. They looked at the patient charts, and then they looked at the tissue findings. Were the tissues showing what they were supposed to? How many were normal when they were thought to be diseased? How many uteruses were taken out, and of them, how many were normal? How many appendixes were removed? How many were normal? All of this was out in the open. There was no place to hide.

The committee then took the next step and reviewed individual surgeon records. Which doctors removed a large number of normal appendixes, and which doctors removed mostly diseased appendixes? Doctors in the first category were confronted with their records and urged to modify their practice. The autopsy and tissue committees worked hand in hand, uncovering crucial information that led to a better quality of care.

This was a stunning way to look at quality, I remember thinking, and the pathologists were in control. They were the ones who maintained the tissue committees, which were quality monitors of the surgeons' work. They were the ones who told the surgeons whether they had done what they were supposed to do.

By that time, even before medical school, I had pretty much decided to become a pathologist, as I told a Birmingham friend. "But what do they do?" my friend asked. I said, "It's as if a pathologist is sitting up there in the operating room, watching the surgeons do their work and telling them, 'Hey, don't do that. Do this.'"

My friend, who was in law school, said, "That's pretty dressy. I didn't know anybody did anything like that."

Pathologists were the main quality control people in the practice of medicine for much of my career. As a pathology resident, I attended and presented weekly mortality conferences in which every person who was autopsied was presented. The presentation findings were given to the physicians on service where the patient had been. There would be an active, open discussion about what they had found, what they had learned, what they didn't know, and what they could have done better. Mortality conferences were regular, routine events at every major hospital in the developed world and the United States during the 1950s and 1960s, when autopsy rates were in the range of 50 to 70 percent. I saw firsthand exactly how much physicians learned about medicine when they studied it from this perspective.

Then things began to change. A backlash against the autopsy began in the 1970s, when physicians started not liking what pathologists were finding. They didn't want the pathologist to see the outcome of their work, and they didn't want anyone else to see it either. So fewer and fewer clinicians asked for autopsies. They didn't want to face patients' families and suggest an autopsy. The attending physician who requested an autopsy was admitting a degree of failure because of the death, tarnishing the doctor-as-God image. It also opened the possibility that the diagnosis and treatment had been incorrect. Surprises could lead to an unhappy family and even litigation. Then the quality assurance committee of the medical staff might have to take action. None of these possible scenarios were attractive to physicians.

Family members also rarely expressed interest in autopsies. Generally ill informed as to the value of the autopsy, families often thought the procedure might cost them money. Many also felt that their relative had been through enough already and should not have to endure another ordeal, even though dead.

Hospital administrators did not want autopsies because they preferred not to dwell on the unfavorable results of hospitalization. They had to determine how to provide cost reimbursement, and autopsies never turned a profit. Furthermore, they believed the autopsy findings were unlikely to make their jobs easier and might even make them harder. Unschooled as to the value of the autopsy, administrators tend to comply with directives from higher authorities, and no licensing or accrediting agency was telling them they needed to do more autopsies.

Third-party payers, in and out of government, did not like autopsies because they cost money and were performed on dead people. Their bias was to direct resources toward the treatment of live sick people, and secondarily toward disease prevention. People who were already dead did not attract much fiscal attention.

Finally, pathologists began to lose interest in autopsies because they were unpleasant, time-consuming, unappreciated, and unremunerative. Autopsies took time away from tasks viewed as more important, such as running laboratories, which provided greater income within a much more pleasant environment.

The result? More or less disaster for quality care. By 1998 three major reports had validated that there is a discordance of approximately 40 percent between what the clinical physicians diagnose as serious diseases antemortem and what postmortem investigations reveal. For example, an attending physician might have been treating a patient for heart disease when the real problem was cancer, or vice versa. One study at the University of Pittsburgh not only showed discordance results of 44.9 percent but revealed that two-thirds of the undiagnosed conditions were considered treatable. Lives really could have been prolonged if better information had been available.

Another study, from the Medical Center of Louisiana in New Orleans, documented a 44 percent discordance between clinical and autopsy diagnoses, specifically of malignant neoplasms, between 1986 and 1995. Their findings compare with rates of 36 percent disagreement on cancer diagnosis in 1923 and 41 percent in 1965. Astonishingly, in the age of high-tech medicine, no improvement in diagnosis was recorded. In fact, doctors got it better in 1923.

The right answers in the sickest patients seem to come from more attentive care and low-tech autopsies rather than from high-tech medicine. The scramble to do more and more sophisticated things apparently misses the profession's traditional goal of doing the right thing. Some pathologists have told me that they are afraid to press for more autopsies—afraid they will be fired. Others have told me of pressures to change the actual findings at autopsy to protect the hospital from litigation, of being threatened with termination as a motivation to do so.

What is to be done? First of all, it is time for good pathologists to come out of their clinical labs and spend more time in the morgue. They can insist on doing autopsies for at least 30 percent of Medicare patients who die. The Health Care Financing Administration, which pays for Medicare claims, built the cost of autopsies into its diagnosis-related groups system of paying for care. Thus, the autopsy is prepaid for Medicare patients who die in the hospital, but it is rarely used because HCFA doesn't insist and allows hospitals to use autopsy money on other things. But in paying for more and more tests—which 44 percent of the time fail to lead to the correct diagnoses—we're misunderstanding what quality control is all about. HCFA could change this with a simple directive: hospitals that fail to autopsy 30 percent of Medicare patient deaths can no longer participate in the Medicare program. Since 75 percent of all deaths in this country affect Medicare beneficiaries, that mandate would result in a dramatic increase in autopsy rates overnight.

The Joint Commission on Accreditation of Healthcare Organizations also could support quality care through the autopsy by withholding accreditation of hospitals that do not meet standards. It simply could mandate an autopsy rate of 25 percent on hospital deaths as a condition of accreditation. In addition, the National Institutes of Health could require autopsies when death is one of the end points of NIH-approved clinical trials.

Something has to be done. It is unacceptable for physicians and the system to essentially continue to bury their mistakes.

The Measurement of Quality Care

Some years ago, when James Todd was executive vice president of the AMA, a *Washington Post* reporter asked him to define quality. After considering the question, Todd said, "Quality is a lot like pornography. It's difficult to define in words, but you know it when you see it."

Jarring though the analogy may be, it's more or less on target. The definition of quality depends, to a large extent, on who is looking at it. At the moment quality is being studied by a great number of people who are attempting to define it in a number of complicated ways. As an editor, I always preferred shorter definitions, and for that reason I always liked the definition offered by the American Society for Quality Control. The society defined quality as the "totality of features and characteristics of a product or service that bears on its ability to satisfy given needs."

Quality of care can be assessed by approaches of structure (anatomy), process (physiology), and outcomes. (Structure includes the buildings, the organization, the equipment and the like. Process or function refers to how it all works.) Currently, outcomes are given the highest priority in quality assessment, but all three approaches matter. Quality control is the operational technique and the activity that sustains a quality of product or service to satisfy given needs. Quality assurance resides in those planned or systematic actions necessary to provide confidence that a product or service will satisfy needs.

Many new measurement systems have been developed in recent years. They measure clinical performance, the satisfaction of the patient, the provider, the purchaser or payer, and the health status of the patient; these measurements can be financial or administrative in nature. In any event, quality should be the driver in powering change in any health care system, and quality measurements should do the following:

1. Be powerful enough to provide direction to the
2. Place patient opinion and preferences first.
3. Hold plans and practices accountable for outcomes.
4. Anticipate the behavioral changes that will be induced by the measures enacted.
5. Allow the health plans themselves to have minimal influence on the quality measures that are chosen.

My interest in quality control was shaped by my experiences in medical laboratories, starting in the early 1950s, when there was virtually no quality control being exercised. This began to change in the late 1950s and early 1960s, when all of the labs began doing quality checks. It began with simple checks. If a lab was going to do ten tests of a kind, such as blood sugars, a normal blood sugar would be added to see whether the test was performing correctly. When the normal sample, with a known result, was out of whack, then it was quickly apparent that something was wrong with the system.

Quality measurements became a science in laboratories long before clinical physicians even thought about the term "quality control." Pathologists were decades ahead in quality checks of analyses of blood and tissue specimens. It was natural for them to be in the middle of the quality issue, and it was natural for me as editor of *JAMA* to focus on the pathologist's role in influencing physician behavior.

It has been an uphill battle because the demand for lab tests, whether needed or not, escalated dramatically during my years in medicine. When I went to Los Angeles County–USC Medical

Center in 1967, less than 3 million lab tests were ordered per year. By 1975 that number had jumped to 14 million tests. Increases of this magnitude became a national phenomenon.

Why so many tests? Physicians are supposed to order them for diagnosis, monitoring, screening, prognosis, and confirmation of clinical opinion. In an ideal world a lab test would follow a history and physical examination by a doctor to ascertain or rule out a diagnosis. But that isn't the way it happens in the real world, where doctors' examinations are now almost superseded by batteries of tests. When we look at why physicians order tests, we discover a wide variety of reasons, but few of them have anything to do with science.

For example, physicians order tests because of pressure from the patient, family, or peers. They also order tests because of hospital or legal requirements. Curiosity and insecurity can play a role, and sometimes ordering tests is a delaying tactic. Profit for the hospital, managed care company, laboratory, or the physicians themselves may prompt more tests. Physicians may order tests to establish a baseline or complete a database; sometimes it's an act of frustration because there is nothing else they can do. Finally, tests are easy to perform, readily available, and routinely paid for without question by many patients and insurers. Ordering tests became a habit.

Why does it matter? Tests are expensive, and perhaps wasteful, and they may lead to more harm than benefit. Although we don't think of a lab test on a human being as an intervention, and it's certainly nothing like cardiac surgery, it is indeed an intervention. As such, it should be done at a reasonable cost, with reasonable risks. Researchers have pointed out that a cascade of interventions commonly follows screening or diagnostic tests. Researchers have demonstrated a tight relationship between rates of cardiac stress tests and rates of subsequent coronary angiography, which in turn often leads to coronary artery surgery or a coronary artery intervention of some kind. As noted, it seems that to inquire inevitably is to intervene. Whether all these tests are of genuine benefit to the patient or to public health is an unresolved question at the moment.

Yet the bias to test remains high, as do the financial rewards for testing. There are four ways in which charges for laboratory tests have been set:

1. The charge may be set at whatever the market will bear.

2. Pathologists may call around the community to see what the going rates are for a given test and then assign some fee value in the mainstream.

3. Pathologists may use time engineering and accounting techniques and then calculate all appropriate direct and indirect costs, add a specific profit factor, and arrive at an economically representative charge.

4. Administrators may determine what volume of revenue is needed by the institution and then set the ancillary charge at whatever level is necessary to produce that revenue, bearing in mind the highly variable reimbursement rules in our managed care environment.

All four methods have been used at various institutions. Usually some combination of the four methods is used, the most common being a combination of numbers two and four—going rates and revenue needs. Obviously, the method that should be used is the third, which attempts to apply some scientific discipline to pricing, but that approach has been overwhelmed by the creative accounting techniques used by most hospitals. To reach revenue targets, they simply increase charges for tests if there is a decrease in test ordering, creatively applying method four. Of course, diagnosis related groups (DRGs) for Medicare inpatients and fee schedules for outpatients, as well as managed care, have significantly changed the pricing of tests for some patients.

Some pathologists have challenged the routine use of laboratory services. E. B. Kaplan and his colleagues from San Francisco conducted a study that questioned the need for routine preoperative lab tests. They conducted a comprehensive, retrospective study of preop tests performed on patients admitted to their teaching hospital for elective surgery. They demonstrated that in those patients for whom there were no clinical indications for such tests, the likelihood of finding any abnormality that might influence perioperative management was extremely small. Furthermore, the few abnormalities uncovered were not even mentioned in the progress notes or discharge summaries. They had no effect on the management of the patient. It was a waste of time, money, and effort.

Another study published in *JAMA* looked at how clinicians order tests. Lab directors at one institution were concerned that physicians were inappropriately ordering a number of expensive tests, such as one for triiodothyronine (radioimmunoassay) and thyroid-stimulating hormone tests. They initiated an educational campaign, hoping to guide physicians to use the tests appropriately, but to no avail. Then they did something that reduced requests for the tests by two-thirds and one-third, respectively. How did they accomplish this stunning reversal? They changed the hospital lab test request form.

The lab test request slip looks very much like a restaurant menu. Just as most diners rarely order something that is not on the menu, so physicians rarely order tests not listed on the test request slip. So the simplest, easiest, cheapest, and most effective way to guide physicians to make appropriate decisions about lab tests is to design the request forms appropriately. Physicians who truly need a test not listed can and will write it in.

That's one way to change physician-ordering behavior. Some years ago John Eisenberg, now with HHS, suggested that there are six ways to change physician behavior: education, feedback, financial rewards, financial penalties, administrative changes, and physician participation. My experience in Los Angeles and Sacramento validated and extended those methods for changing behavior. Our lab changed its request forms and thereby eliminated improper but frequently used lab tests. By changing turnaround time, our lab promoted the use of good inexpensive tests. By training pathology residents to guide clinical residents about how to use complex tests properly, we guided the use of the toxicology and therapeutic drug testing laboratory, the blood bank and coagulation laboratory, and surgical pathology and cytopathology.

Data and experience support the following methods for changing physician test-ordering behavior (as I wrote in *JAMA*):

1. Know the literature, have the data, and be certain that you know the right thing to do.
2. Convene (preferably under the roles of the organized medical staff) a small committee of leading respected physicians in the health care setting—those who know the most about the subject at issue. These physicians usually will not be department heads but rather middle-level active clinicians.
3. Achieve agreement with this group about what should be done based on available scientific evidence and the best expert clinical opinion.
4. Implement the changes administratively, without seeking broader agreement in advance.
5. Add a large dose of education in writing and in conferences about what was done, why this is best for patients and the institution, and how to adjust to the changes.
6. Be open to communications, complaints, letters, visits, telephone calls, and even insurrection.
7. Ride out the actions and overreactions, carefully sorting all objections and responding with adjustments, usually minor, to valid complaints.
8. Enjoy the success of providing better, cheaper, faster, more effective diagnostic services in the best interest of patients, physicians, the public, the institution, and the payer.

The Push for Unproven Care

Ordering tests correctly is only one step toward providing evidence-based, scientifically validated quality care. The challenge is not merely to apply only proven therapies to patients, but also to avoid doing any harm. Despite these sensible restraints on the use of unvalidated care, we continue to experience a headlong rush to embrace it, propelled by every cultural bias Americans embrace.

Some patients may recognize that death is inevitable, but most Americans seem to think that something can be done about it. Physicians may know that experimental new therapies hold limited promise, but only American physicians seem to tell their patients about "hopeful" new options. Insurers who have historically refused to pay for "experimental" therapies, such as the bone marrow transplant for breast and ovarian cancer, quickly can be convinced—by courts and legislators—to accept them as standard, reimbursable care. The model for not testing many new therapies seems based on our experience with penicillin, whose results were so consistent and impressive that controlled, clinical trials were deemed unnecessary.

All these factors explain why expensive new technologies continue to be widely diffused in the United States without sensible clinical trials, as Louise Russell explained in her book *Technology in Hospitals,* published by the Brookings Institution two decades ago. She described the rapid acceptance of much more expensive intensive-care beds, which did not produce a corresponding increase in quality care. Similarly, proper management for patients with heart disease quickly fell under the spell of the coronary artery bypass graft, even though medical management for many types of patients can be less expensive, less invasive, and more appropriate.

The bias is to intervene, and to intervene expensively, even before any genuine benefits of expensive interventions are demonstrated scientifically. A famous example of premature acceptance of new technology, documented extensively by Gina Kolata and Kurt

Eichenwald in the *New York Times,* involved the bone marrow transplant procedure for breast and ovarian cancer. As noted previously, the use of this technology rushed far ahead of science until controlled trials proved that bone marrow transplant was no more effective than standard chemotherapy. At that point one of the largest insurance companies, Aetna/US Healthcare, announced that it would no longer reimburse the cost of the procedure.

Aetna was emboldened by five studies on the procedure, two from the United States, two from Europe, and a particularly troublesome study from South Africa. The last study was the only one to suggest that there could be beneficial results from bone marrow transplants, but the claim collapsed when outside researchers discovered that the South African data had been falsified. It was after that revelation that Aetna discontinued its coverage of the procedure.

It's not unusual for many controlled trials to come from countries outside of the United States. The important studies that recommended the use of mitoxantrone, a cancer chemotherapy drug, to control multiple sclerosis, for example, came from four European countries. Although American patients and physicians leap toward hope and unproven therapies, and work hard to get someone to pay for it, they are not as quick to support the laborious and lengthy work involved in proving the effectiveness of a new therapy beforehand.

Even when research suggests that a new treatment is ineffective, American patients and family members often insist that the science is wrong. This happened with the hormone secretin, which was used in the treatment of childhood autism. After a media and Internet news blitz spread the word that secretin might cure autism, controlled randomized trials were conducted at the Western Carolina Center and the University of North Carolina, and at the Thoms Rehabilitation Hospital. They concluded that secretin was no more helpful than saltwater in the treatment of autism. The results were immediately denounced by parents who had used the drug for their children at a cost of approximately $200 per injection.

Physicians who wish to conduct controlled trials find that few patients are willing to sign up. First of all, in a clinical trial the grim prognosis and limited evidence of cure from the new procedure are typically spelled out clearly in a consent form to be signed by the patient. Patients outside of trials, by way of contrast, are encouraged to believe that the intervention could save their lives. No wonder patients turn away from controlled trials.

Furthermore, physicians show a remarkable lack of interest in clinical trials. One health insurer, United Healthcare, worked out a program with major medical institutions to urge patients to enter clinical trials. The insurer agreed to pay for new treatments only if the patient agreed to enter a controlled trial. After one year United discovered little change. Few patients signed up, and those who did found out about the program on their own. Their doctors did not inform them of the trial option. Shockingly, the doctors seemed even less interested in scientific trials than did the general public.

Meanwhile, the media celebrate the stricken patient who refuses to enter a scientifically designed trial. One brain cancer patient in Baltimore told a reporter that she refused to enter any study in which she might be randomly assigned to a therapeutic approach other than the new, experimental approach under study. That might be acceptable for a new headache medication, the patient said, but not for a new treatment that might save her life.

An entirely different approach to experimental therapy was taken by Jesse Gelsinger, the eighteen-year-old suffering from OTC who signed up for a gene therapy experiment at the University of Pennsylvania that he hoped might benefit babies born with a fatal form of the disorder. There was a chance that the therapy might spare him continued diet restrictions and daily medication, but the point in his mind was to help medicine treat newborn infants with the disorder. Reportedly, his last words to a friend in Arizona before he left for Philadelphia were: "What's the worst that can happen to me? I die, and it's for the babies." Unfortunately, that was what happened to him on September 17, 1999. The deeper misfortune, as the story unfolded, was that business interests might have superseded science in the rush to find a genetic cure.

The treatment of Gelsinger involved infusion of corrective genes, encased in a weakened dose of adenovirus, a cold virus. This set off a chain of events that included jaundice, a blood-clotting disorder, kidney failure, lung failure, and brain death—multiple-organ-system failure, as his doctors reported. They speculated that the adenovirus caused an unanticipated and overwhelming inflammatory reaction. Later reports established that the Penn team already had seen monkeys treated in the same way succumb in a similar fashion. At the time Gelsinger was identified as the first person known to die as a result of gene therapy intervention. His very public death set off an intensive round of soul-searching by physicians, regulators, and members of Congress about the appropriateness of existing research protocols.

In January 2000 the Food and Drug Administration ordered that human gene therapy experiments at the University of Pennsylvania be halted temporarily. The FDA cited serious deficiencies, including a failure to report serious side effects that other patients had experienced. The debacle also exposed the loose regulatory structure governing gene therapy experiments. Unlike drugs, which are monitored by the FDA, gene therapy is monitored by the Recombinant DNA Advisory Committee (RAC) of the National Institutes of Health. Critics complained that the RAC was not sufficiently scrupulous in approving research protocols. Others added that the close connections between university researchers and the private bioengineering companies posed serious questions about the rush for gene-based cures.

Shortly after Gelsinger's death, it was learned that six other deaths had already occurred in gene therapy experiments. The fatalities happened in heart studies conducted by rival researchers, Ronald Crystal at New York Hospital–Cornell Medical Center and Jeffrey Isner at Tufts University. They reportedly were competing to be the first to develop a gene therapy alternative to coronary artery bypass surgery. Both claimed that they did not report the deaths to the NIH, as required, because their patients died from complications caused by underlying illness, not from the gene therapy experiment itself.

That became another part of the story, the all-too-familiar saga of the distorting role that money in medicine now plays. The principal investigator of the study that resulted in Gelsinger's death was James Wilson, who is director of the university's Institute for Human Gene Therapy and also the founder of Genovo, a biotechnology company in which he and the university held stock. Although Wilson contractually may not participate in studies funded by the company, the ties between the university and the for-profit company pose the same kind of ethical questions that arise with physician self-referral. Those questions simply should not exist when it comes to patient care. They tip the "rocking horse" of medicine so far toward the business side and away from the professional side that it's in danger of being overthrown.

These changes began some twenty years ago, when academic physicians studying genetics began filing for patents and opening their own bioengineering companies, financed by venture capitalists. Instead of dismissing the entrepreneurial physician-researchers, the academic centers joined them in business. Members of Congress liked this so much that they passed legislation in 1980 to speed the commercialization of academic findings, allowing researchers and universities to profit from work that was largely funded by taxpayers' dollars.

The new law offered incentives for universities to patent inventions and assign rights to private companies. As a result, universities gained income from licensing fees and royalties. They also gained prestige by being able to retain their "star" researchers, who were now part scientists and part businessmen. It was just such a Faustian bargain that has called into question the University of Pennsylvania's gene therapy program. Paul Gelsinger, Jesse's father, initially was very supportive of the attending physicians. He spoke of a "purity of intent"—which certainly characterized his son's approach to the experiment—but after learning of the apparent shortcuts taken by the physician-entrepreneurs to speed the experiment, Gelsinger retained an attorney.

Meanwhile, Wall Street seemed unfazed by the problems posed by "commercial" research involving biotech companies. The stock price of Cell Genesys went from eight dollars at the time of Gelsinger's death to more than thirty dollars in less than six months. During the same period Avigen stock went from eleven dollars to sixty-six dollars, and Targeted Genetics from less than two dollars to more than twenty. In fact, the Nasdaq biotechnology index more than doubled during that time, and investors considered it the next big thing after the Internet.

Researchers and patients seemed equally unfazed. A few months after Gelsinger's death, the Recombinant DNA Advisory Committee of the NIH received ten new research proposals at its quarterly meeting, well above its usual one or two. And patients reportedly continued to sign up for experimental treatments, perhaps driven by hope, fear, or inertia. The early promise of gene therapy so far has not materialized. It could provide new and powerful ways to treat illness, but at the moment the entire enterprise lives under a cloud of financial self-interest and inadequate regulation.

Building an Evidence-Based System

Of all the specialties, pediatrics seems most wedded to science-based medicine, perhaps because resources for child care are uniquely constrained and must therefore be deployed judiciously. That is one of the ironies of American culture. Great lip service is given to the needs of children, the next generation of leaders and citizens, but scant funding supports these windy words. School-teachers are near the bottom of America's income ladder, and pediatricians are near the bottom of medicine's income ladder.

Their status notwithstanding, pediatricians have developed a number of excellent, science-based programs. Among the most successful is their immunization schedule for babies. By age two, all children should have received four doses of diphtheria-tetanus-pertussis (DPT) vaccine, three doses of polio vaccine, and one each of the measles, mumps, and rubella (MMR) and H influenzae type B vaccines. Their research informed them, however, that only 67 percent of children had received DPT, 76 percent polio, 90 percent MMR, and 71 percent H influenzae type B. Further research revealed a number of barriers to immunization, including insufficient education as to its benefits, a fragmented health care system, lack of insurance coverage for preventive medicine, and various financial barriers. In response, the American Academy of Pediatrics (AAP) developed a thirteen-point program aimed at removing these barriers and realizing the goal of 100 percent immunization.

The pediatricians provide a model of self-governance and self-regulation. People don't go into pediatrics for big bucks or great prestige. They seem drawn to the practice because they want to care for children. Pediatricians have a low percentage of membership in the AMA, but a high percentage of membership in the academy. When I once asked a group of pediatricians why this was so, I was told, "The AMA is for doctors, but the AAP is for kids." One result of their commitment is their tendency to burn out. A great number of doctors in administrative posts turn out to be pediatricians who were exhausted by practice.

Pediatric oncologists provide another model for professionalism. Several years ago they organized themselves into two major consortia in order to enroll essentially every child struck by cancer into controlled clinical trials. The consortia vowed not to pursue every new departure as soon as it made itself known and agreed to conduct only credible studies with genuine prospects for advancing knowledge in the field. Then they lobbied health insurers to cover the costs of their clinical trials and succeeded in gaining coverage for experimental therapies, which, as noted earlier, insurers historically have not covered. The companies also agreed to refuse to cover experimental procedures outside of the trials. The result is that more than 60 percent of children with cancer in this country enroll in clinical trials, compared with about 1 percent of adult cancer patients. A further result is that effective therapies reach patients much more quickly than before.

Other factors helped define and contain the program of treating childhood cancers. Happily, very few children get cancer. Neuroblastoma, a cancer affecting the nervous system, strikes only about 500 children per year. It is a devastating disease for two- to four-year-olds, since it spreads to the bones and causes excruciating pain before death. The bone marrow procedure was recognized as a possible therapy for neuroblastoma in the early 1990s, and randomized trials were promptly initiated, with some receiving the transplant treatment and others standard chemotherapy. By the time the program reached its enrollment goal of some 500 patients within less than five years, it was apparent that bone marrow transplants did improve survival rates.

Oncologists and surgeons who care for adult cancer patients also are beginning innovative programs of patient care, but it appears that they are being pushed into it by their patients. They discovered that many patients in their seventies were not following their treatment recommendations. Older breast cancer patients, for example, were refusing lumpectomies and opting for mastectomies instead. At first, analysts at the National Cancer Institute thought that doctors were talking patients out of lumpectomies, on the theory that older women cared less about retaining breast tissue. In fact, the women themselves refused the procedure because they didn't want to undergo the six-week follow-up radiation therapy, which commonly follows the lumpectomy procedure. Women who lived in rural areas were particularly resistant because they would have had to drive many miles for treatment. They didn't want the bother and discomfort of going back and forth to radiation treatment centers.

The observation prompted NCI researchers to rethink therapeutic protocols for older cancer patients. People in their forties or fifties usually want and can tolerate aggressive medical treatments, which might prolong their lives twenty-five or thirty-five years. Older people with a life expectancy of ten additional years or less often do not want aggressive treatment and typically are less toler-ant of it. The researchers asked: Do patients in their seventies really need radiation therapy after a lumpectomy? Perhaps all that is needed is hormonal therapy with tamoxifen. Accordingly, a clinical trial study is under way.

A related study also is under way for older lung cancer pa-tients. Instead of offering older patients the same debilitating and powerful chemotherapeutic agents that are offered to younger pa-tients, researchers are offering them the drug Taxol, which is milder, easy to take, and nontoxic. Quality of life improves with milder therapies, and it is possible that cancers in older people can be held at bay until other illnesses associated with age eventually end their lives. This approach holds the promise of returning a hu-man face to the physicians offering care. Physicians could discuss a wide range of options for older cancer patients, many of whom need and would prefer to receive more palliative care and to leave the heroics to younger patients, who generally have greater stamina and a stronger desire to prolong their lives.

Another promising development is a change in attitude by in-surance companies toward the funding of experimental proce-dures. Many have decided to cover patients who agree to enter federally sanctioned clinical trials of new treatment programs, but not new treatments for patients who refuse to enter sanctioned tri-als. Some of the largest insurers, including Cigna HealthCare and Aetna/US Healthcare, recently announced an agreement to cover cancer clinical trials in New Jersey on a test basis. The insurers fur-ther agreed to work with government officials, physicians, and pa-tients' groups to inform patients about the new availability of ex-perimental treatments in clinical trials.

Other insurers, such as Coventry Health Care and United Healthcare, announced pilot programs for similar trials in the Mid-west, South, and mid-Atlantic region. This could provide a giant step forward for evidence-based medicine. As with everything in medicine, the approach could be challenged in court by patients seeking access to experimental therapies, but they could be met by the convincing argument that clinical trials serve a societal interest. Under the new program, promising therapies could quickly be tested and generally applied if found to be effective. That would be a major advance for quality care in medicine.

The insurance companies also ruefully acknowledge that funding experimental trials probably would not cost any more than the current methods. Built into their premium structure is an allowance for unproven new technologies, coverage for which often is imposed on them. In fact, everyone might discover that a scientific system provides built-in economy, greater compassion, and enhanced quality of care. Science-based quality care is the key to health system reform. The quickest way to change the system so that it provides good care for all is to reassert true, professional values in medical care. Disclosure, honesty, truth, and trust will flow from a practice of medicine based on the profession's code of ethics. That kind of medicine might even be remarkably affordable.

10

The Way to Reform

Thinking About a Better System

STRANGELY ENOUGH, ALTHOUGH QUALITY CARE is at the core of the reformation of the health care system, no one talks about it. Instead, everyone is mired in discussions of the financing of health care. We need to break out of the rut. We need to stop talking about *how much* care will be covered and start talking about *what* care will be covered. Professional standards, woefully lacking today, must be reasserted.

In my dream scenario, the government would pay for all scientifically proven preventive medical services, and insurers, whoever they are, would cover all scientifically established catastrophic, expensive care. In between those poles would be the private practice of medicine, in which routine care would be a matter between patients and physicians, with no third-party intrusion.

The probable scenario is that a government program, similar to Medicare, will be established for all U.S. residents within a decade or two. The push will come not from liberal legislators but either from the flame-out of insurance companies or from employer support for such a national system. Unless insurance companies miraculously exercise self-discipline, they will cherry-pick themselves out of business.

Alternatively, the Internet may allow us to directly set up 280,000,000 individually brokered health plans between patients and groups of providers who would share risks along with a broad-based backup reinsurance system to take care of the outliers; the traditional health insurance companies would be eliminated as su-perfluous. Unless the cost and coverage problems mysteriously re-solve themselves, employers will want to get rid of their health benefits programs: better to pay an employment payroll tax than to continue with the headache of managing employee health bene-fits. *If people get mad,* the typical employer may think, *let them blame the government, not me.*

Once a formidable power broker, the AMA may be only an ineffectual bystander during the reform debate. Sadly, the associa-tion has lost much of its political credibility. Even though it still maintains its professional responsibilities toward medical educa-tion, physician training, and publication of scientific information, it is perceived as an income maintenance organization that faithfully serves a dwindling number of member physicians.

The Clinton proposal exposed the central problem in system reform. No health system reform will ever get off the ground if people believe they have to surrender something to make it hap-pen. We won't manage even a half-step forward if anyone perceives a loss. Without that overwhelming hurdle, the health care system could be corrected quickly. Certainly, there's enough money al-ready on the table to make it happen.

During 1998, the most recently reported year, Americans spent $1.25 trillion on health care. With a population of about 276 mil-lion people, that works out to approximately $4,500 per person, or $375 per month. Surely that's enough money to take care of every-one's current needs.

In fact, the number of people covered by health insurance is significantly less than the total population. The 229 million Ameri-cans with insurance spend about $5,360 per year on average, or $446 per month per person. Of course, part of what everyone pays for health insurance is used to cover emergency care for those who do not have insurance.

So goes the all-American shell game called health insurance, which, as I pointed out earlier, is really sickness insurance. We take a little from here, patch together something from there, shake the quilt, and spread it as best we can over the entire population. It's a question of perception, and so far everyone who has "health insurance" is reasonably satisfied. Their only concern, justified by recent history, is that the coverage they have is under attack. Right now most people are less concerned about providing a big umbrella for everyone than they are about retaining whatever protection they already have against the elements. Time and again management and union negotiations have stalled or become inflamed over the issue of health benefits. Most workers now are concerned about the erosion of their benefits.

So how are we to do this? How can we fix our system and close ranks with every other developed country in the world by offering universal access to care for all U.S. residents? The sum of $4,500 per person per year ought to be enough. Obviously, millions of healthy young people won't account for even $500 per year. Equally obvious is the fact that some people will expend up to ten times the national average for care when catastrophe strikes. Many of these are older people who contract illnesses associated with advanced age, such as cancer, stroke, or heart disease. If our health insurance system were totally and strictly risk-related, young people would pay premiums of less than $1,000 per year and older people would pay premiums of more than $15,000.

In fact, if we follow the risk selection system to its logical conclusion, all of the people who are truly in need would have no place to turn for financial assistance. Think of what would happen if the health insurance industry gained access to genetic information about insurance applicants. Too bad about the diabetes you will contract in your forties. We can't accept the risk, so you're on your own. Breast cancer at fifty? Good-bye. Lung cancer at forty-five? So sorry. Over time insurance premiums would moderate or decline because the low-risk people covered would remain healthy until retirement and Medicare. No sickness, no costs—nirvana.

But what about those left out? Anyone who supposes they would not be heard from is tone-deaf to American cultural values. The excluded would petition their members of Congress. They would appear at presidential rallies to present their cases. Inevitably, legislation would move forward to cover the uninsurable, perhaps even disease by disease, as with kidney failure, and the rule of rescue would be enforced by disease entity. There would be a program, similarly attached to Medicare, for diabetic patients, then breast cancer patients, lung cancer patients, and so on, step by step. In time private insurance would be a marginal business, managing minimal payment transfers within a pool of healthy beneficiaries.

The industry has begun to notice. The Health Insurance Association of America went so far as to revive its "Harry and Louise" television commercial campaign. In 1994 Harry and Louise had become famous for their criticism of the complexities of the Clinton health care proposal; their tag line was: "There's got to be a better way." In commercials produced six years later they comment on the fact that more than 44 million Americans have no health coverage.

"That's huge," Harry says. "An epidemic. We can't leave working families and kids without insurance." Then Louise points out that HIAA has a plan: tax relief for workers and small businesses, and special help for the working poor. Charles N. Kahn III, president of the association, said that, with new subsidies and tax credits, the plan would cost government $40 billion to $50 billion a year. Most of that money would be passed on to doctors, hospitals, and other providers, he pointed out. But of course, some of it, perhaps as much as a substantial 15 to 20 percent or more, would be retained by insurance companies for administrative costs.

Everyone wants to make money from the current system. That is why it will be difficult to reform. No better example exists than the reform effort aimed at providing adequate coverage for prescription drugs. The Medicare program is managed by the Health Care Financing Administration, which sets the prices paid to hospitals through its prospective payment system (PPS) and the fees paid to physicians through the resource-based relative value system (RBRVS). Since drug benefits were not included in Medicare, drug prices have been free to rise to whatever level the market will bear.

At first that made little difference. The costs of drugs as a percentage of total costs were in the 5 to 6 percent range. That began to change in 1990. In that year the Veterans Administration, for example, paid $11 billion for health and 6 percent of the total went for drugs. Nine years later it spent $17 billion and drugs accounted for 11 percent of the total.

Throughout much of that period two-thirds of Medicare beneficiaries were partially protected from the drug cost escalation through Medigap insurance or through HMOs, which paid varying percentages of the total costs. As the costs increased, so did pressures on the HMO premiums, and many managed care insurers pulled out of regions, dumping their Medicare policyholders back into the traditional program without drug coverage. With prices going up and new medications coming onto the market, more and more Social Security recipients were facing drastic choices between purchasing prescribed medications and covering household expenses, including food.

In June 1999 President Clinton addressed the problem with a drug proposal that formed the centerpiece of his plan to overhaul Medicare. For an initial premium of $24 per month, or $288 per year, beneficiaries could gain drug coverage that would include a 50 percent government co-payment on drugs up to $2,000. The premiums would rise gradually over time, but so would the benefit, up to $5,000 for the 50 percent share. Projected government cost over ten years would be $118 billion. An alternative proposal, based on a deductible and co-payments up to a specified dollar limit, was proposed by Democratic senators some months later. Although no budget figure was attached to the latter proposal, it too would cost billions of government dollars, and federal expenditure on that scale carries the threat of government price controls.

The Pharmaceutical Research and Manufacturers of America (PhRMA), the trade association for pharmaceutical manufacturers, immediately struck back, mounting an advertising program that featured an elderly woman urging everyone to keep government out of the family medicine chest. Clinton counterattacked, ordering a study of the pharmaceutical industry's tax breaks and profitability.

Results released in December 1999 showed that pharmaceutical companies enjoy significant tax advantages. On average, all industries have a tax rate of 27 percent. Tax rates for manufacturing companies are 23 percent on average, and 31 percent for wholesale and retail trade and financial services, including insurance. Pharmaceuticals pay only 16 percent. After-tax profits for all industries are 5 percent of sales, while pharmaceuticals profit to the tune of 17 percent of sales.

Among the tax credits that pharmaceutical companies enjoy are those offered to companies with manufacturing plants in Puerto Rico, general tax credits for research, foreign tax credits, and credits for research and development of orphan drugs (those for patients with rare diseases). Other studies show wide variations in pricing by drug companies, with Americans paying outrageously high prices compared with other countries. In a recent year the psychiatric drug clozapine, for example, sold in Spain for $51.94 for ninety 100-milligram tablets. The same drug in the same formulation sold for $88.15 in Germany, $271.08 in Canada, and $317.03 in the United States.

Release of this kind of information had a stunning impact on PhRMA. In February 2000 it invited Robert Pear of the *New York Times,* an influential reporter who had been covering the story, to interview two of its leaders, Raymond V. Gilmartin, chairman of Merck, and Gordon M. Binder, chairman of Amgen and also chairman of PhRMA. They told Pear that they wanted to work with the White House to establish Medicare coverage for drugs, and said they would support legislation that would provide all seniors with access to pharmaceutical insurance policies.

It just so happened that there was a bill in the hopper to that end. In August 1999 Republican Senator Olympia J. Snowe from Maine and Democratic Senator Ron Wyden from Oregon introduced legislation aimed at encouraging a competitive market for drug insurance, with 25 percent of the premiums to be paid by government. Theoretically, that would make insurance accessible, affordable, and free of government regulation.

There was only one problem, said Kahn of the Health Insurance Association of America: no insurer would sell it. Why? Because such a voluntary system would be destroyed by adverse risk selection—the only people who would buy the insurance would be those with big drug bills. Furthermore, Kahn expressed a perfectly logical fear that prices would rise more quickly than premiums, and that legislators would resist premium increases but not drug price increases.

Kahn's point was well taken. Two of the ten standard Medigap policies charge people over seventy-five an additional $1,200 per year in premiums for drug coverage but limit drug benefits to $1,250. For an additional $1,200 premium a policyholder can have a net benefit of $50. That is not a highly salable insurance package, since it literally defines adverse risk selection, and an official of AARP, the association that represents senior citizens, concluded that the private sector would not be able to provide a drug benefit.

Missing from this debate was any discussion of which drugs should be covered and which should not. As with most discussions about the health care system in general, the focus is on financing methods rather than on methods of care and efficacy of care. Everyone wants to figure out only how we are to pay for drugs, or for care, and as long as the debate retains that focus, significant numbers of Americans will be left without insurance coverage.

Financing mechanisms will not solve America's health care problem, but both Republicans and Democrats almost single-mindedly talk about them. Republicans generally favor tax schemes that encourage people to purchase health insurance. A key Republican proposal is the medical savings account (MSA) plan. With MSAs, individuals and families could establish accounts up to a set dollar figure per year with tax-free money, similar to income retirement accounts (IRAs). As needed, accounts could be drawn on to meet medical expenses. Unneeded funds could be rolled over and added to over the years, building an account large enough to handle large expenditures in the future. Catastrophic events would be covered by high-deductible insurance. The theory holds that health care costs are thus held down because people who pay for their own medical care are more prudent purchasers. Low-income families would be offered vouchers to purchase their insurance.

Republicans also favor "defined contribution" insurance coverage for Medicare beneficiaries as well as for those who are privately insured, who already have such coverage to a large extent. Instead of defining the benefits of an insurance package, defined contributions spell out a dollar level of support. Individuals would shop around for an affordable insurance policy; some would buy less expensive policies, presumably with fewer benefits, and others would buy more expensive policies, presumably with greater benefits.

Critics contend that both approaches favor the well-off at the expense of middle- and lower-income families. Only the wealthy would choose MSAs, they say, constraining the market for comprehensive insurance and thereby boosting premiums for the ordinary policyholders left behind. Defined contributions would herd middle- and lower-income families into cheaper insurance plans with fewer benefits, greater hassles, and inadequate coverage.

Democrats generally favor approaches that build on or extend accepted federal programs. Clinton proposed allowing a Medicare buy-in for people fifty-five to sixty-four years old. Such a plan would cover many early retirees who are stuck with extremely expensive health insurance plans or with no plans at all as a result of price constraints. At the other end of the age spectrum, Democrats have urged expanding the Children's Health Insurance Plan (CHIP) so as to allow more children to gain insurance coverage from Medicaid. Congress created CHIP in 1997, hoping to enroll five million children up to age nineteen. Enrollments lagged largely because they were overseen by state agencies, which showed little enthusiasm for expanding Medicaid and thereby increasing state costs. Federal, state, and local governments share Medicaid costs. Three years after enactment only one-fifth of those eligible had signed on.

Clinton made another coverage-by-disease proposal during his last year in office. He suggested that low-income women be afforded full Medicaid coverage for state-of-the-art treatment for breast cancer. If adopted, that could pave the way to other disease-specific conditions, but if administered by Medicaid, coverage could lag as it has under CHIP.

Critics contend that the Democratic approach is high on taxes and government interventions, including price controls. They say that Democrats have demonstrated a heavy hand in their approach to management of Medicare, imposing multiple rules, regulations, and directives on hospitals and physicians and creating confusing red tape and frustration for patients and providers.

Sense over Dollars in System Design

No matter what the plan, both Republicans and Democrats assign dollar projections to its implementation. For the power brokers in our country, health care is no more than a matter of dollars and cents. What we need is common sense. What we also need is direction by the profession and patients. We need a system that delivers demonstrably beneficial care for patients who wish it. Once again, information rather than financing provides the key.

Consider the problem of childhood vaccinations. The American Academy of Pediatrics has reported far less than 100 percent compliance with its schedule of immunizations for children. Some of the barriers are understandable, such as insufficient education about the benefits of immunization. This is a diverse country, with many newly arrived residents and different languages and cultural backgrounds. Many residents do not understand the social benefits of immunizations and do not trust government or medical bureaucrats.

Other barriers to 100 percent immunization are just plain unacceptable, however, such as the fragmented health care system and, especially, health insurance that excludes coverage for preventive medicine. The state you happen to live in, or your employer, determines whether scientifically proven preventive medical interventions are covered by your insurance. That is not reasonable or sensible.

In another example, the commonwealth of Massachusetts requires mass spectrometry tests for every newborn infant. A drop of blood is taken from the baby's heel and tested for nearly thirty inherited diseases. A handful of other states have begun similar programs, but many have not, including the state of Texas, where babies are tested for less than half a dozen inherited disorders. Thus, a baby in Massachusetts born with a rare metabolic disease was identified and treated, avoiding the coma, brain damage, and even death associated with the disease. Another baby in Texas was not screened, was not identified as a patient with a metabolic disorder, and subsequently experienced massive seizures, fell into a coma, and suffered brain damage that left him unable to walk or talk.

Think of the money that could have been saved if the Texas baby had been tested. He would not have been hospitalized; he would not have required neurological attention; and he would not need continuing rehabilitative therapy. Appropriate testing makes not only human sense but fiscal sense.

These and other examples make the case for national standards based on scientific knowledge and expertise. Lotteries for dollar payouts on a state-by-state basis might be acceptable, but lotteries for health are not. Medicine and insurance traditionally have been governed at the state level. States license doctors to practice, and states oversee insurance coverage and practices, but perhaps it is time to reconsider either this way of governing the profession or, at the very least, the development of standards of practice.

If that were to occur, a national entity would need to be designated for the job. I would nominate the Institute of Medicine of the National Academy of Sciences. A strengthened IOM could do much to improve health in the United States, including:

- Assisting in making optimal technological choices in public policy

- Addressing problems through collegial efforts with other organizations
- Providing information on complicated issues to the press and public
- Restoring self-respect in the profession and public trust in medicine
- Conveying information between the public and the profession
- Explaining the needs of medical education and research to legislators
- Recognizing the human, scientific, and theistic breadth of medicine

All this could be accomplished by a medical organization that is beholden to no one and represents all aspects of medicine, with unquestioned integrity and courage.

At the moment some medical clout resides in membership organizations, such as the AMA, the American College of Physicians/ ASIM, the American College of Surgeons, and scores of others. These groups do many wonderful things in the public interest, but in the final analysis they must be what they are—membership organizations—and they must respond first to the needs of their members. Placing more authority in the IOM holds great promise, as its recommendations on limiting error in medicine demonstrated.

Particularly distressing for me, as a long-standing member of professional medical societies, has been the devolution of the AMA to a nuts-and-bolts trade association. The association has too much money and too little purpose. In fact, its main purpose now seems to be shoring up income to maintain its senior staff and entertaining a group of voluntary officers. The perquisites of office are outrageous, with inflated per diems and multiple junkets. Almost 70 percent of practicing physicians have no illusions about the AMA and have refused to join.

Desperately needed is a decisionmaking authority that is not dependent on government or a membership organization for funding. Bad things can happen in political environments. For example, after the Agency for Healthcare Research and Quality of the Department of Health and Human Services released a study that posed a question about the effectiveness of surgery for lower back pain, the American Academy of Orthopedic Surgeons lobbied members of Congress to do something about the agency. At first there was talk of eliminating AHRQ entirely, but Congress finally settled the matter by cutting back its budget. Congress had much greater success in shutting down its own Office of Technology Assessment (OTA), which had produced helpful analyses of new medical technologies but was deemed a wasteful bureaucracy.

The independent IOM could review matters dispassionately and offer recommendations. Desperately needed are protocols for all preventive measures, followed by the will to make them mandatory for all insurance carriers. This might require a neutral federal agency, such as the Federal Reserve Board or the Securities and Exchange Commission (SEC). Such an agency could set the rules for insurance coverage for proven preventive interventions.

It also could tackle the complicated task of identifying and certifying beneficial treatment protocols, based on randomized controlled clinical trials that are, whenever possible, double-blinded. That is, patients are randomly assigned to different treatment protocols and neither the patient nor the physician is aware of which group is receiving the experimental treatment and which the placebo or standard treatment.

The search for a way to handle respiratory distress syndrome is one example. Pneumonia, trauma, or major surgery can cause the lungs to partially fill with fluid, necessitating artificial respiration. Some fifty thousand people die from the disorder per year, and scientists have been searching for a way to lower that number. The National Heart, Lung, and Blood Institute (NHLBI) of the NIH sponsored a study involving 861 patients randomly assigned to one of two treatments. In the first, patients received large volumes of air at high pressure to gain maximal oxygenation. In the second, patients received less oxygen; this made them more "air-hungry," and sometimes sedation was required to manage their distress. The results were startling: 40 percent of the patients in the first group died, while 31 percent in the second died. This suggested that overall death rates could be cut by almost 25 percent. Although contraindicated intuitively, less air under less pressure was the better protocol. The results were so convincing that the study was stopped nine months short of its scheduled termination so that everyone could receive the preferred treatment.

The results of a Rand Corporation study suggest that new protocols for a number of commonly used treatments may be needed. The study found that 16 percent of hysterectomies were performed for "inappropriate reasons," while the outcomes of another 25 percent indicated "uncertain clinical benefit." Four percent of coronary angiography procedures were deemed inappropriate, and 20 percent were "equivocal." In addition, 14 percent of bypass operations were deemed inappropriate and 30 percent equivocal. The number of patients in the study was relatively small—1,300 patients in the angiography study and 380 in the bypass review—but the results could be indicative. Sharper protocols could result in much better use of the technology available and in much less stress for patients.

In offering its study results, Rand commented on the "surprisingly small amount of systematic knowledge on the quality of health care delivered in the United States." From the limited amount of information available, Rand researchers nonetheless concluded that "whether care is preventive, acute, or chronic, it frequently does not meet professional standards."

This is where the profession should reassert itself. As stated earlier, we need more autopsies, and we also need more rigorous practice standards committees, as well as evaluation of other major clinical activities. If physicians confront one another on questions of quality and demonstrate that what they are doing is scientifically appropriate, they can trump the confrontations offered by insurance company administrators and government bureaucrats. No doubt there are situations in which the need for a hysterectomy is equivocal and it is wiser to err on the side of intervention rather than on the side of cautious observation and waiting. But if the tissue findings from one surgeon's cases are consistently inappropriate, that surgeon must be confronted by his or her peers. Good intentions are no substitute for science.

It is clear that insurance companies are expressing new interest in science. After years of resisting coverage for investigative new therapies, several have announced their willingness to pay for investigations, but only if they are conducted in clinical trials. This requirement could short-circuit the rush to accept experimental and unproven therapies as standard care, as with the ill-fated bone marrow transplant procedure for stage 4 breast cancer patients. The approach could lead to science-based instead of merely hope-based medicine.

Another useful initiative was announced last year by my friend of long standing, Donald Lindberg, director of the National Library of Medicine. All clinical trials for serious illnesses would be listed on an open database via the Internet. Included would be basic explanations of how the experiments work, along with suggested questions that a patient could ask before enrolling to make sure he or she has a clear understanding of the risks involved.

At the time of the announcement 4,000 studies at 47,000 sites nationwide were listed. Most were sponsored by government agencies or academic medical centers. It was anticipated that many more studies, including drug company trials, would be added to the list. Lindberg advised patients to discuss participation in trials with their physicians, cautioning that patients often are extremely vulnerable to information that sounds too hopeful.

To recapture the profession, physicians also must play a much tougher role in rationalizing the diffusion of new technologies. This is especially important now, with so many expensive new technologies in the pipeline. It would involve some risk and great difficulties. Physicians would have to oppose the proliferation of some technologies, such as the liver transplant program, that dilute the efficiency and effectiveness of regional centers. The breakaway units should not be covered by insurers until full due process has allowed the medical scientific community to make its case. It's well known that doctors do not like to make a fuss about what other doctors do, despite the "Code of Ethics," but in some situations it is a professional requirement. Again, the IOM and a federal medical board would be involved in the certification process.

Of real concern is the question of whether innovation would be stifled. No one wants to see the development of a rigid system in which only tried-and-true treatments are available. Identified academic centers should be encouraged to explore new therapies, and perhaps all limits should be relaxed in the face of an unexpected health crisis.

For example, what should be done when a new epidemic emerges? Can we afford to wait for evidence-based interventions while a new infectious agent threatens public health? When the AIDS epidemic emerged, researchers set aside the old rules as they rushed to find new treatments that might work. From that intense activity came new drug protocols that have extended many lives and transformed HIV infection for some patients from a lethal disease into a chronic disorder. The profession has to be similarly alert and sensitive to new health threats.

My Proposal for Reform

So how do we shape a system that makes scientifically proven preventive services and treatment therapies available to all Americans without creating a giant cookie-cutter that stamps out standardized products for standardized people?

If I were starting an American health care system from scratch, this is what I would do. All residents would choose their own primary care physician, who would provide comprehensive continuing care and refer them to specialists as appropriate. I would emphasize prevention and early detection of disease through proven interventions such as immunizations, Pap smears, blood pressure tests, and mammography after age fifty. Proven preventive services would be free to patients and paid for by government tax revenues.

Specialty and subspecialty physician care would be available by referral, although individuals could use their own money to jump the primary care queue if they chose to. Ambulatory care provided by physicians and other health care professionals or organizations would be paid by patients out of their own pockets up to a fair annual legal maximum—a reasonably high deductible adjusted by income. Patients would be expected to pay their bills, and physicians and other members of the health care system would be expected to provide a reasonable amount of free care or to offer reduced charges for medications, diagnostic tests, and therapeutic procedures, when a patient's economic circumstances so indicated, with sliding scales determined by law.

Sickness insurance would be available for purchase by individuals, employers, and government. Everyone would be required to carry hospital and catastrophic, or high-deductible, insurance. Primary care physicians would not have admitting privileges at hospitals, to decrease the temptation to overhospitalize. They could not be in groups with specialty physicians or receive kickbacks, split fees, or other inducements for referrals.

In nonemergency care situations, all mentally competent patients and all physicians would be informed of the cost of care (ambulatory or hospital) in advance of receiving or providing services, regardless of the source of payment. This would be called the economic informed consent. Only after receiving information about costs could the patient be expected to make a fully informed consent to the proposed treatment, no matter who pays the bill.

Physician fees and other charges for ambulatory care would be set by the providers of that care. The government would establish charges for services rendered in the hospital, taking into consideration length of stay and intensity of services so that there would be no imbalance of payment for procedure-oriented care.

A "free marketplace" would decide the number of physicians and their fields of endeavor. Medical education would be handled as a public trust: there would be very low or no tuition or fees for training in the health professions. The fiscal resources of applicants would not enter into decisions as to who would be trained to be a physician, and no substantial educational debt would be incurred by the medical student. Basic and applied medical research would be encouraged, sponsored by private industry, foundations, and government.

Competence, communication, trust, and caring in medical practice would be so strong that excess malpractice problems would diminish dramatically. This approach would provide incentives on several levels: patients would be motivated to take steps to preserve their own health, providers to control costs, and institutions to ensure quality care.

Think of what would happen to the relationship between the patient and the primary care physician. Since only preventive measures would be covered by insurance, physicians would have an incentive to schedule such tests and procedures, but patients, free to choose, would not want to sign up with doctors who had little time for anything other than tests. To win patients, primary care physicians would have to be good, sympathetic caregivers. They also would have to be independent-minded professionals focused on ambulatory patients, since they would not have hospital admitting privileges. Their time would be devoted to people and knowledge—to caring for patients and keeping up with developments in primary care medicine.

I can think of a number of young and midcareer doctors who would welcome the luxury of practicing medicine this way, substantially free from third-party-payer red tape. Quite a few medical professionals feel they were trained to help people, not to be accountants or businesspeople. This system would support them. Specialists such as dermatologists, obstetrician-gynecologists, and ophthalmologists could gain support as well from this system of direct payment from patients.

I also can think of a number of patients who would respond favorably. In fact, one friend decided he would accept his employer's high-end option for insurance coverage because he wanted to be able to choose his physicians freely. Instead of joining an

HMO or PPO, my friend took traditional insurance with a high deductible—$2,000. He also enrolled in a "flex" plan, which allowed him to recover out-of-pocket medical expenses up to a certain amount—the deductible figure, in his case.

In my plan, many of the specialists to whom primary care physicians refer patients would be hospital-based. Many would be engaged in the more dramatic interventions, but the performance of all specialists would be subjected to peer review. They would enhance their skills through information gained from continuing education in all forms, especially autopsies and interactive medical committees. They would be assured that they were doing the right things for their patients, and they would gain the satisfaction that comes from successful application of sophisticated therapeutic treatments. In addition, they would enjoy the respect and recognition of their peers for work well done. All physicians, inpatients, and outpatients could benefit greatly by full utilization of electronic medical records to decrease error, increase communication, enhance privacy and confidentiality, and eliminate coding problems and administrative paper waste.

The system would address one of the most awkward—or usually nonexistent—interchanges between patients and doctors: the discussion of costs and fees. More resentment than physicians can imagine results from undiscussed charges. Patients pay ruefully, even when they merely oversee third-party payment, suspecting that they have been ripped off by their remote, high-earning doctors. No explanations are provided, no discussion is encouraged, and no recourse from the final bill is offered. Requiring full disclosure, whether for ambulatory or hospital care, would remove a great deal of patient distrust and resentment, which, as we have seen, is a chronic source of malpractice allegations. Many patients see their care as, in effect, an insurance "blank check."

Removing the economic barriers to medical school education would free physicians from an overwhelming concern about money and debt. They wouldn't have to begin practicing medicine already $150,000 or $200,000 in the hole. Money would also be less of a concern for those choosing a medical specialty; physicians in train-ing could gravitate toward the modes of practice most congenial to them. Those who like patient care and patient interactions would move toward the primary care specialties. Those more intrigued with sophisticated medical and surgical interventions would move to the referral specialties. Those drawn to basic and applied medical research would move in that direction.

While the marketplace as well as personal preference would determine the mix of specialties, some thought should be given to workforce needs. Just as therapies should be subjected to outcomes research, so should the total number of physicians needed be sub-jected to well-designed research.

High-deductible insurance policies would be community rated, and everyone would have to sign up, just as everyone has to be licensed to drive. No country has achieved universal health in-surance voluntarily. It must be mandatory. High deductibility would tend to moderate premium charges. Many young people would never reach the deductible limit, but they would be assured of coverage in the event of medical catastrophe. With better de-fined coverage responsibilities, insurance companies would com-pete on the basis of service rather than on the basis of benefit ex-clusions. This could restore a human face, and heart, to the health insurance industry.

The system would be dominated by disclosure, honesty, and earned trust. Obviously there would be warts and wrinkles, but the direction and goals of the enterprise would be clear and well un-derstood by all involved.

My plan could work, but reform of our health care system is not likely to happen this way. Health care is full of too many other distracting and conflicting developments—some of which have nothing to do with policy, systems, or reform—that probably will have to run their course. Some of these developments are re-sponses to the market. Ophthalmologists, for example, are doing more laser eye surgery and fewer cataract procedures. Dermatolo-gists are prescribing more injections for wrinkles than acne med-ications. Plastic surgeons are doing five times more liposuction procedures than they did four years before. And obstetrician-gynecologists are offering their patients laser hair removal.

Many of these physicians concentrating on cosmetic procedures maintain comfortable, well-appointed offices and cater to their patients, who don't wait three weeks for an appointment and who expect to see the doctor on time. The office support staff is polite and the doctor deferential.

Some offices are located in buildings with support facilities that include massage, facials, nutritional therapy, and Eastern medicine. What's going on? The patients are paying out of pocket for cosmetic procedures not covered by insurance. The doctors are receiving fees, as much as $5,000 for laser eye surgery, up front and without having to deal with the rejected bills, excessive paperwork, discounts, and delay generated by insurance companies.

In addition, some primary care physicians, especially in California, are opting out of insurance programs; they are taking their names off preferred provider lists and seeing only those patients who will pay out of pocket. Indeed, the patient can submit the bill to an insurance company, but the patient is reimbursed directly, as was done historically. What these physicians offer is better service. They attend to the patient and not to the clock, and many are building substantial practices, especially those in urban areas with intense managed care insurance penetration.

Timothy J. Murphy is the head of QVS Technology Group, a health care consulting firm in Des Plaines, Illinois, that assists in the establishment of alternative medical practices. Murphy told the *New York Times* that these changes are related to significant declines in insurance reimbursement fees for physicians. "And when doctors lost that, like any red-blooded American, they thought to themselves, 'What am I going to do here?'"

Commenting on the new emphasis on cosmetic treatments, David Friend, a physician-consultant with Watson Wyatt Worldwide in Boston, told the *Times,* "What you will find is that the supply of low-profit services will decline. The result is a tiering effect, where the best doctors are doing the private stuff and doctors unable to succeed in those things will provide the public service care. We have created an incentive for everyone who can to get out of low-margin businesses, and that could have enormous policy implications."

Patients are willing to pay out of pocket for services they value. Patients and their families even will pay for assistance with death and dying, as the *Wall Street Journal* reported last year. Entirely new organizations have popped up in California and other states to help people deal with death. With names like Home Funeral Ministry, Zen Hospice, the Chalice of Repose Project, and the Natural Death Care Project, the organizations are helping people manage death by taking it out of the hospital and allowing it to take place in homes and hospices, where the dying person can be surrounded by family and friends. People are searching for a "good death," and they're not finding it in hospitals or nursing homes, where more than 70 percent of deaths now occur. Even private commuter autopsy services are popping up.

Doctors should help those patients who are seeking a better way. They should recapture the responsibility they have held from time immemorial. Indeed, many medical schools and hospitals now are beginning to train physicians in the nonclinical aspects of death. If the profession is to restore itself and reassert its humanistic roots, helping patients and families deal with death is essential. But the real point is that patients and families want to restore themselves. They sometimes may even reject suggested therapies, such as lumpectomy followed by radiation. They sometime request less aggressive chemotherapy, and sometimes, when it is clear that further intervention is useless, they want a timely, peaceful death. A fundamentally positive change in our health care system could be orchestrated by physicians who listen carefully to their patients and attend to their wishes as well as their needs.

What Will Happen to Health Care

Nothing much will happen quickly, but everything is in place for a gradual move toward federal standards and more professional care.

The patients' bill of rights movement clearly is one that would provide federal standards. The right-to-sue issue could boomerang for trial lawyers. Legislators might include language that would set either federal limits on noneconomic damage awards or limits on contingency fee percentages. Concern about research protocols and disclosures will strengthen federal oversight of experimentation in academic centers and large teaching hospitals. Discrepancies in insurance premiums, especially with respect to coverage for people with preexisting conditions, will lead to further federal oversight of the insurance business.

The Democratic strategy of incremental reform probably will prevail. The public generally trusts Democrats on the health care issue, and Medicare, the brainchild of Democratic politicians, remains extremely popular in the United States. It's quite possible that Medicare, in some form, will be made available to people as young as fifty-five who for one reason or another are not fully employed and desperately need affordable insurance coverage. It's also possible that coverage of children will be moved into Medicare, since the CHIP program run by states has failed to cover all eligible recipients with Medicaid insurance. At some point states may wish to get rid of Medicaid altogether. In past discussions the quid pro quo proposed has been state assumption of elderly care. No doubt, it will be discussed again in the future.

That would confine the private insurance industry to the fully employed population of twenty- to fifty-four-year-olds. The industry would have two alternatives. One would be to suck out as much money as possible before the entire private structure collapses. The other would be to try to shore up its business through imaginative programs aimed at including as many adults as possible and at reforming its marketing processes. If the insurers don't stop cherry-picking, they will pick themselves to death.

Employers may well tire of the system. It initially gave them great power to skim the cream of the workforce and was a useful recruitment device. Like pension plans, it has become much less useful. Lifetime employment is a thing of the past. Neither workers nor employers desire it, and portable 401K plans have replaced company pensions. If an insurance program that includes genuine portability could be devised, the private insurance system might be maintained. Lacking that, employers might wish to get out of the benefits business. By contributing a payroll tax to a national system, they could dispense with the headache of administering health benefits. Certainly contract workers, most of whom do not have health benefits, would welcome a payroll-supported national system. Or they might move to defined contribution only.

Finally, I see a great opportunity for physicians to take back their profession. Each doctor could start by making sure that a portion of his or her time is devoted to charitable care. In doing so, doctors would unite themselves with a tradition reaching back to Hippocrates. Physicians also could insist that their hospitals conduct more autopsies. This has to be done. Autopsies are crucial to science-based, professional medicine. So are quality-of-care committees and other quality controls. Physicians cannot ignore outliers who undermine the credibility of the entire profession. Wasteful tests, inappropriate procedures, kickbacks, and self-referrals simply cannot be tolerated. If physicians don't discipline themselves, someone else must and will.

But the most important key to taking back the profession is learning to be more attentive to patients. If doctors don't listen to patients, they have lost their essential reason for being. The Internet might help. Actually, the Internet provides the tool for patients and health care providers to contract directly with each other without any insurance company intermediary. That will probably happen. Patients and physicians can be co-workers in the search for correct and useful information. Doctors also might explore imaginative methods for resisting insurance company pressures to limit time spent with patients. That could be risky, individually and/or collectively, but it goes to the heart of what medicine is all about, which is caring for and attending to patients.

Another entirely unexpected phenomenon could emerge: people may become disenthralled with medicine. For fifty years or more we have seen almost magical powers in the practice of medicine. It has seemed that medicine could really "save" patients' lives. At the very least, it could make people live longer, feel better, and look younger. Unfortunately, this attitude encouraged medicine to become self-centered: both patients and physicians began to think exclusively about their own well-being and to ignore the general health of the community. It's a dangerously narrow-minded view. Everyone knows that an infected individual can quickly infect an entire community. We all have a stake in good public health; it's the essence of enlightened self-interest.

No doubt there always will be people willing to pay for "elixirs" of any kind that promise to make them feel better, look younger, and live longer. In an open and free society such as ours, that should be permitted. Expensive care, however, is not necessarily quality care. Let people buy what they like—as long as everyone is entitled to solid preventive medicine and quality catastrophic care.

11
Patient–Focused Control

Fixing Our Broken Health System

IN ORDER TO FIX OUR BROKEN SYSTEM of American health care, we must put the people who matter most, and for whom this is all about, back into the driver's seat: the patients themselves (as health care consumers) and the physicians and other caregivers. For a wide range of reasons described in the previous chapters, these key constituencies have become disenfranchised, and their disenfranchisement is the principal reason the system got so out of whack in the first place. We call upon the public and the profession to rise up and take medicine back from the business interests and the bureaucrats and to reestablish the patient–physician relationship as the core of the service profession of medicine.

Americans are a diverse people. And politics is the art of the possible within diversity. Any sweeping changes in our health care system, if they are to succeed, must be ethical and moral, as well as broad-based, appealing to ideologues of the right, the left, and the center. A key goal of meaningful health reform is to create a system that does not have to be changed with every inevitable shift in the political power base. The ideal U.S. Congress to deal with change in such a complex health care system would be one that is balanced politically. The ideal president would be a problem solver and a public servant who has the capacity to look beyond narrow

This chapter was written by George D. Lundberg, M.D., James Stacey, M.A., Teresa Waters, Ph.D., and Patricia Lorimer Lundberg, Ph.D., in September 2001, especially for this paperback edition.

ideologies to the short- and long-term best interests of the populace, and who can negotiate ethical and principled compromises that endure. Finally, if our broken health care system is to be fixed, a large majority of Americans must believe that it needs fixing. They must also support any changes that are fair and in the public interest, regardless of how much governmental involvement is required.

The American health care system is an economic juggernaut. In 2002, it will use up 13.9 percent of our GDP—$1.54 trillion— according to National Health Care Expenditure Projections of the Office of the Actuary at the Centers for Medicare and Medicaid Services (CMS), formerly the Health Care Financing Administration (HCFA). Any challenges to the current system must bear up under the weight of the huge general and special interest forces that come along with such a giant price tag.

Given the rapid deterioration of the American health care system between the time the first edition of *Severed Trust* was written in 1999–2000 and its publication in March 2001, we have been compelled to go beyond the brief solutions offered in Chapter 10. Toward this end, and fully aware that money is a monumental factor in any reform, we secured the collaboration of a professor of health economics from the University of Tennessee Health Science Center, Teresa Waters. We are also grateful to Patricia Lorimer Lundberg, an associate vice chancellor at Indiana University Northwest, who contributed to the content and editing of this new chapter.

Learning from Failed Efforts

The American health care system has undergone periodic and painful attempts at reform. But such attempts need an evaluation mechanism. In the issue of *JAMA* dated May 13, 1992, we proposed eleven key factors for assessing the strength of any health system reform proposal: Provides Access for All, Controls Cost, Ensures Quality, Reduces Administrative Hassle, Promotes Prevention, Encourages Primary Care, Considers Long-term Care, Promotes Patient Autonomy, Provides Physician Autonomy, Limits Professional Liability, and Possesses Staying Power. Two years later, the May 17, 1994, issue graded those serious proposals then available for consideration. On a scale where 9 denoted the high ideal for each factor and 99 represented the best possible system of reform, the best score was 72—for the Stark markup of the Clinton plan. The health care system in place during 1994 scored 55. Other proposals ranged from 38 to 70. According to our most recent analysis, the health care system of 2001 scored a disappointing 43.

The most significant element of change between 1994 and 2001 has of course been managed care. Given that annual percentage increases for employer-paid health insurance premiums exceeded 25 percent by 1990, change simply had to happen. When the government-led Clinton plan failed to get off the ground, nongovernment "market forces" began to take over.

Managed care may actually have begun thousands of years ago in Babylon, which featured a system of universal coverage and outcome measurements with accountability for results. Slaves received only basic coverage, however, and physicians may well have lost a hand for poor surgical results. The for-profit managed care heyday in this country began about 1990. There was so much inefficiency in American health care that this system was able to roar in and capture much (later most) of the market by drastically cutting costs—as well as insurance premiums—while still making big profits. The curve of plummeting annual premium increases bottomed out in 1995 at near 0 percent inflation. But the slope of the upward movement that followed was practically a mirror image of the downward one (see Figure 11.1).

The principal social reason underlying for-profit managed care was cost control, but the companies involved have been unable to control costs over time: Although investors and leaders of the health insurance industry pulled in abundant profits through for-

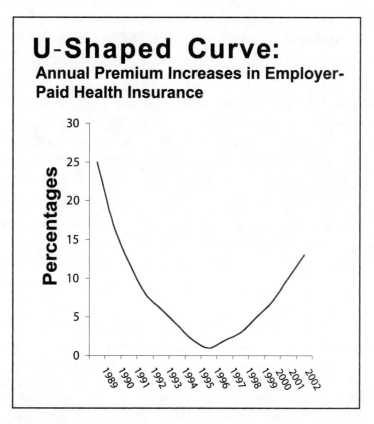

FIGURE 11.1   U-Shaped Curve: Annual Premium Increases in Employer-Paid
Health Insurance

Source: Composite of data provided by William M. Mercer, Health Care Financing Admistration,
Congressional Budget Office, KMPG Inc. (Klynveld, Peat, Marwick, Goerdeler), and California
Public Employees' Retirement System (CalPERS)

profit care in the 1990s, those days are now gone. Incomes for
top executives and administrative costs remain hefty, however.

The beneficiaries of for-profit managed care never did become enamored of the new system, although they did like the
lower premiums, the inclusion of preventive services, and low to
zero deductibles for such items as prescription drugs. But, unfortu-

nately, for-profit managed care concerned itself too much with managed costs and too little with improved health care (with the exception of highly successful disease management programs, notably for diabetes and asthma). It was doomed to fail. In 2001 Harris Interactive polls showed approval ratings for managed care companies to be a mere 28 percent—tied with the tobacco companies for last place.

The era of for-profit managed care in America is now over. The doctors hate it, the patients hate it, it no longer holds down cost escalation, and it no longer makes big bucks for stockholders. Do we need these for-profit managed care companies? We don't. The problem is what to do with them (and their 150 million or so "covered lives") while we replace them with something else.

Don't Mess with Medicare

Without question, Medicare is one of the great American achievements of the twentieth century. But also without question, this singularly popular medical program faces severe fiscal constraints as we begin the twenty-first century.

Medicare needs more money. An expanding elderly population and ever-advancing medical technology will absorb fund surpluses during this decade. How will additional funds be generated? Should they come from higher taxes, private incomes, or greater efficiencies? Each of these options is unattractive, but each has a political constituency. Democrats favor greater government spending. Republicans favor adding more private dollars. And the American Association of Retired Persons (AARP), which represents senior citizens, historically has favored greater efficiency.

The only real solution, it seems, is to apply all of the above, but specifically in a way that makes sense to Medicare beneficiaries. The Medicare program itself needs to be tinkered with, touched up, and modernized. There is no panacea. Getting rid of the HCFA, as former House Speaker Newt Gingrich once proposed, and herding beneficiaries into private managed care plans is not the answer. Indeed, managed care plans have recently dumped more than 1.6 million enrollees as it is.

Equally ineffective is the idea of defining the federal contribution, as President George W. Bush proposed in 2001. Under that scenario, the government would offer a fixed dollar benefit to each beneficiary, who could then choose a plan such as CMS or a private insurer or a managed care plan. If the plan ended up costing more than the defined contribution, the individual would pay the difference, putting more private money into the program but at a cost to lower-income individuals. Over time, CMS would have to charge more than the federal contribution would pay, and cut-rate plans would meet the defined level by limiting or constraining services.

The Democrats' idea that the government should meet all the costs of the program is equally flawed. It simply cannot be done—at least not without increasing taxes. And as for enhanced efficiencies, which usually means holding the line on health care costs, we've gone about as far as we can go.

What America really needs is to go back to the defined benefits provided by Medicare and figure out a sensible way to revise them. One of the good features of Medicare as administered by CMS is that benefits are spelled out. For example, under Part A, beneficiaries pay $776 for a hospital stay up to sixty days, and under Part B, beneficiaries face a $100 deductible as well as a 20 percent co-payment for covered services, including physician services (though not routine physical exams).

These terms haven't changed for decades, except for the addition of certain preventive services, which essentially amount to routine medical exams. Now included, for example, are bone mass measurements, with payment applying after the deductible and a 20 percent co-payment, and periodic colorectal cancer screening, with full payment coverage (i.e., without a deductible or co-payment charge). Diabetes monitoring, Pap smear and pelvic examinations, prostate cancer screening, and certain vaccinations have also been added, with varying methods for payment. These additions have been made on a condition-by-condition basis as a result of pressure applied by patient groups. No doubt the list will continue to expand, whereas the concept of excluding routine physical exams will fade.

Instead, why not make a deliberate decision to fully cover all scientifically valid preventive health services at absolutely no cost to patients? In return, the deductible could be doubled to $200 for routine medical care; it could also be indexed to inflation.

A similar approach could be used in behalf of prescription drug coverage, with a deductible set at $250 and an absolutely unregulated market applied up to that limit. Drug manufacturers could charge whatever they wished, but once the threshold was passed, prescriptions would be filled only according to a federal formulary, which in turn would include appropriate generic drugs. Price controls, similar to those imposed on hospitals and physicians, would then come into play.

Pharmaceutical manufacturers have resisted Medicare drug coverage for precisely this reason, claiming that they need to charge high prices in order to cover the costs of research; but, in fact, they spend twice as much on sales and marketing as on research. Bear in mind that, since 1998, the amount Americans spend on drugs has increased 40 percent per year, much of it driven by advertising.

What the pharmaceutical manufacturers really fear is being subjected to the same kind of scrutiny that hospitals and physicians undergo. But there is simply no reason why these companies should be spared, and no reason why prescription medications shouldn't be integrated into the Medicare program. Furthermore, it has become abundantly clear that Medicare cannot cover drugs unless price constraints are part of the package. Market-based approaches, which would allow drug makers to charge what they please, are unaffordable for many Medicare recipients. Let them charge what they want up to $250, then apply price discipline. Additional funding could come from patient premiums, which would have to cost between $10 and $15 per month to attract enrollees.

A controversial approach to putting more private dollars into Medicare services is private contracting, a practice that would allow patients and physicians to step outside the program on a case-by-case basis. Medicare law now prohibits such contracts. If a physician wants to contract privately, she must opt out of the system completely, accepting no Medicare patients; in addition, her patients are not allowed by CMS to pay more than Medicare pays for services. Who would want to contract privately? Wealthy patients who want to support a physician's medical program. Some already do so by making private donations to their physician's hospital or surgical department. In this way, private contracts would allow the physician to attend to more Medicare beneficiaries needing expensive services not adequately reimbursed by Medicare fees.

Critics warn that physicians could abuse private contracting by misinforming patients that particular services are available only on a private basis. But in a world where patients often change health plans just to save $10 per month, that is an unlikely scenario. Even well-to-do seniors show a keen interest in making sure that Medicare pays for all covered services. A doctor bent on abusing private contracting would probably find few patients who'd go along. Still, in recognition of its controversial nature, private contracting could be given a trial run before a final decision is made about implementing it.

In short, Medicare should permit some escape from price controls. People should be able to buy out of the system. This point may sound undemocratic or elitist, but it resonates with the American psyche. If a rich person wants to pay top dollar for "boutique" care, or even wants to "jump a queue," as some Canadians now do by coming to the United States for certain services, that person should be allowed to throw money at the system.

As for price controls themselves, physicians may grumble but most now find Medicare to be their favored third-party payer. Private insurers and managed care plans are accompanied by too many forms, regulations, and price constraints. Furthermore, many years have been required to develop, implement, and refine the resource-based relative-value scale system for reimbursement. The system may seem cumbersome, but its aim is to ensure equity—not to maximize profits for insurers.

Mandating Universal Health Insurance

Despite this country's per capita income, which is one of the highest in the world, more than 39 million Americans—a full 14 percent—have no health insurance at all. And as demonstrated by study after study, no health insurance translates into poor health.

Are all Americans entitled to health care? Although most of us would agree that this is not a right envisioned by our founding fathers, as a compassionate nation we find it difficult to *deny* anyone access to beneficial medical care. But the expense of providing health care to the uninsured often seems too much to bear. How can we afford to purchase health care for these 39 million people? Economists estimate that doing so would cost $30–$40 billion per year. Of course, we are already paying—but in hopelessly inefficient ways that waste money and result in needless pain and suffering. Every time an uninsured patient is admitted to the hospital for diabetic complications because she couldn't get good outpatient care, those costs are passed on to other people. Every time an uninsured patient is diagnosed with late-stage cancer because he failed to heed early warning signs, our nation loses one of its citizens. We can't afford *not* to have basic universal coverage.

But how do we achieve it? If we are truly committed, we must mandate that everyone receives an essential level of basic health care coverage, just as many states require auto insurance. Drivers can choose where to buy their insurance and, to a large extent, what kind they want, but everyone behind the wheel must get coverage. A mandate can work for health insurance as well, if we think carefully about what constitutes an acceptable level of coverage for all citizens.

Of course, we can't afford to mandate the Mercedes Benz of health insurance for all Americans. Nor should everyone be restricted to a basic level of coverage. We have a free market. People should be able to buy what they want. They should be able to purchase coverage above the basic level, right up to "boutique" levels. Universal coverage does not have to mean that everyone has the same type of coverage—only that everyone has sufficient coverage.

Even a basic level of coverage, however, may be unrealistic if we can't figure out a way to control health care costs. In contrast to moderate premium increases in the mid-1990s, costs have risen dramatically in recent years. Average premium increases for 2002 may exceed 15 percent. And national health expenditures, which totaled $1.2 trillion in 1999, are expected to more than double by 2009, amounting to $7,173 in personal health care expenditures (excluding things like research and construction) for every man, woman, and child in the United States. A mandate could become untenable if the cost of health care becomes too high relative to the cost of other necessities such as food, housing, clothing, and transportation. Any reasonable proposal must address cost control.

Our current untenable situation is the result of several major financial distortions, including (1) insular insurance coverage, which involves having insurance for every possible health expense, anticipated or not; and (2) the tax treatment of health insurance. Both of these practices prevent health care consumers from making well-informed purchasing decisions. As a result, health care markets are unable to function properly, and costs are out of control.

Health insurance was originally created to protect against unexpected, catastrophic events, such as prolonged hospitalization for a serious illness. But such catastrophes are rare. During 2000, in fact, 60 percent of Americans spent a *total* of less than $700 on their health care, and 80 percent spent less than $2,000. (These figures include not only what they paid but also what their insurance companies paid on their behalf.) Over the years, however, health insurance has grown to the point where it covers every type of health care service, including the two or three visits to the doctor that we all make each year. The problem with this type of coverage is that it insulates patients from the market realities of their health care purchases and puts patients in the passenger rather than driver's seat, causing patients to become insensitive to medical care costs and less in control of the care they receive. We're not suggesting that a patient facing open-heart surgery should have to worry about whether she can afford to have the procedure; rather, our point is that patients should be exposed to the economic implications of everyday decisions such as choosing a physician or selecting a generic versus brand-name prescription.

Today, comprehensive coverage almost always implies managed care coverage. And that in turn generally means that someone who has never seen the patient and has little, if any, clinical information about the patient's current or past medical history makes decisions about that person's care. These decisions are based primarily on the best interests of the managed care organization. Why do we subject ourselves to this kind of treatment? Only because we think we have to—in order to control costs.

As noted above, another financial distortion in the health care market is the current tax treatment of health insurance. Consumers are not only unaware of the true cost of medical care because of overly comprehensive health insurance; they are also less sensitive to health care premiums because of generous tax treatment. For Americans who have employer-based health insurance, the employee's portion of the health insurance premium is paid with pre-tax dollars, so the federal government is essentially subsidizing their health insurance. Because of this subsidy, which is directly related to the value of the coverage and the tax bracket of the employee, health insurance is cheaper for that individual—who, naturally, then wants more insurance coverage. More health insurance, more medical price insensitivity.

How can we overcome these financial distortions? Many thought the answer lay in placing financial incentives on managed care organizations and providers to control costs. It didn't work.

Instead, we need to put fiscal responsibility and control directly in the hands of the health consumer. Basic insurance coverage should involve reasonably high deductibles—$1,000 to $3,000. With deductibles this high, most Americans won't have to worry about insurance clerks making decisions concerning their health care. They will make the decisions themselves, and so will be sure to be well informed. High deductibles also result in very modest premiums. High-deductible plans in the individual market currently cost about $600 to $1,000 per year.

These deductibles should be adjusted based on income to avoid heavy financial burdens on people with lower incomes. One possibility is to set deductibles as a percentage of the previous year's declared income, up to the maximum deductible amount. The cost of implementing this sliding scale would be borne by federal and/or state authorities.

Once individuals meet their annual deductible, they would not be responsible for co-payments or co-insurance. They would also not be subject to lifetime maximums. Although co-payments, co-insurance, and caps provide supplemental cost controls, we believe that they expose the consumer to undue financial risk. If existing insurance mechanisms continue, some methods of (insurer-based) cost controls will remain in place. Such controls, of course, introduce unwanted decision makers to the mix; but we believe that in the tradeoff between risk bearing and cost control, this solution is the lesser of the two evils. In order to help consumers make informed decisions, providers would be required not only to obtain economic informed consent before providing services but also to outline the costs of services and the costs of any available alternatives, including watchful waiting.

In addition, health care consumers should assume financial responsibility for his or her level of insurance coverage. The current tax system not only provides large subsidies but disproportionately subsidizes the wealthiest Americans. In 2000, the average value of this tax treatment of health benefits was $1,155 per family. These benefits, however, were worth $2,638 to families with an annual household income of $100,000 or more, and only $79 to a family earning less than $15,000. Families earning less than $15,000 essentially do not pay income taxes and therefore do not benefit from protecting their health care premiums from taxes, whereas families earning $100,000 face some of the highest tax rates and thus benefit the most. Under our plan, by contrast, basic insurance coverage would be mandated. The federal government would subsidize the purchase of that insurance coverage—and nothing else. Those able to purchase coverage above the basic level would face the true price of that insurance.

Two major inequities could also be addressed in a reformed health care system. First, those who cannot purchase health insurance through an employer currently face much higher premiums in the individual market. At least 10 million people under age sixty-five buy coverage in this costly way. They are doubly penalized in that they cannot deduct the premiums from their taxable income unless their medical expenses exceed 7.5 percent of their income, and they are prevented from enjoying most of the benefits of tax-exempt health insurance premiums inasmuch as tax deductions only serve to lower taxable income. As an answer to both of these problems, we propose to institute refundable tax credits (not deductions) for all premiums (not just employer-based ones) paid to purchase basic health insurance coverage.

A second inequity is the cost of health insurance for higher-risk individuals. In our current system, some of these people get their health care through large employers. Others seek coverage through the private market, often facing "preexisting condition" waiting periods, exclusions, and high premiums. For those who cannot obtain coverage in the individual market, many states have implemented "high-risk pools." Premiums have typically been extremely high and levels of participation low.

Two related proposals could address this inequity: community rating of premiums or pooled purchasing power. Community rating would set all premiums for a given community at the same level, not discriminating based on health or employment situation.

This approach builds on the basic principle of insurance that risk must be spread among those at high and low risk. The low-risk person contributes based on the possibility of becoming a high-risk/high-cost person tomorrow.

A pooled purchasing power proposal uses the purchasing power of each state to set reasonable premiums. Each state government is a significant purchaser of health care; it purchases health care for all its Medicaid and State Children's Health Insurance Plan (S-CHIP) enrollees, as well as all state employees. States could use this power to obtain reasonable premiums and require that the same premiums be offered to any employers or individuals who desire to purchase the same policy.

One final issue that any major health proposal must address is *trust*. Throughout this book we have talked about the central role of trust in the physician-patient relationship and the ways that trust has been broken down, sometimes inadvertently, by financial and political interests. Restoring trust must be a central goal of the system changes we propose and remain the yardstick by which we measure significant progress.

We can restore trust between physicians and patients by removing or restricting the presence of "nonessential personnel." One of the main reasons patients may not trust doctors is that so many other parties have been inserted into the patient-physician relationship. Hospital utilization review managers tell physicians when to discharge patients from the hospital; managed care organization clerks tell patients they can't get a prescription filled until a week from Tuesday; faceless insurance administrators review patient therapy progress notes to determine whether the company is getting its money's worth. Although the Health Insurance Portability and Accessibility Act (HIPAA) may address some of the information flow issues, it does not address who makes the decisions. Sooner or later, Americans need to decide who they want to make these decisions. We would argue that the only appropriate decision makers are the patient and the physician.

Why were these nonessential personnel inserted into the equation in the first place? They're keeping track of the money. A major part of the solution we propose for extracting them from the relationship is to change the flow of money. Replace insular insurance coverage with larger deductibles. Place consumers squarely in charge of their health care. Require economic informed consent from providers. And let consumers own their electronic medical records, storing them at a secure Web site. Consumers could give their password to health care providers with whom they wish to share information, establishing informed consent, and they could change passwords when they no longer want to allow access.

In order to minimize disruptions, the changes we propose build on existing insurance and health care delivery structures. Most Americans (86 percent in 2000) have health insurance. Many, if not most, do not want to see a major revolution in the American health care system. They may dislike managed care, but that doesn't mean they're ready to throw the baby out with the bath water. Also keep in mind that major disruptions—no matter how well intentioned the ultimate goal—can lead to serious problems with access and delivery of care. Our proposal would allow health care consumers to purchase insurance from existing companies (or new ones) and get their care from their current providers.

Our proposal largely maintains a free market system in health care. Setting up a system that will automatically do what you want it to is much better than setting up a bureaucracy. The free market system is a fundamental premise of our American economy, and we should not be willing to give up on that tenet in health care. Despite some obvious market failures (communication problems, lack of price sensitivity), these issues can be addressed without scrapping the entire market-based system. In fact, many of our health system's failings are probably more strongly related to political issues than to problems with the market.

Will our plan flat-line health care cost inflation? Unfortunately not. As with any proposal for reform, we have to balance many factors: cost control, access, exposure to financial risk, consumer control, quality, and political reality. But our plan does offer real hope for cost control. Why? Because it addresses the root causes behind exploding health care costs: financial distortions in the price of medical care and health insurance.

Ensuring Quality of Medical Care

In 2000 the Institute of Medicine (IOM) issued a report titled "Crossing the Quality Chasm: A New Health System for the Twenty-first Century." It defines six specific areas in which significant improvements need to be made: (1) Care should be safe; (2) care should be effective; (3) care should be patient-centered; (4) care should be timely; (5) care should be efficient; and (6) care should be equitable.

The IOM report also includes ten rules to guide patient-clinician relationships in an improved health system: (1) Care should be based on continuous healing relationships; (2) care should be customized based on patient needs and values; (3) decision-making control should reside with the patient; (4) knowledge and information should be shared with the patient; (5) clinical decisions should be evidence-based; (6) the care system should be safe; (7) the health system should be more transparent, allowing patients and families to make informed decisions; (8) the health system should anticipate needs rather than simply reacting to events; (9) the health system should not waste resources or patient time; and (10) there should be more cooperation among clinicians to ensure an appropriate exchange of information and coordination of care.

To implement these improvements and guidelines, the IOM proposes, among other strategies, that Congress establish a health care–quality innovation fund and provide $1 billion over a three- to five-year period to communicate the need for rapid change.

This is not enough. The health care field also needs and deserves a Federal Medical Board, presided over by a chairman who would be relatively free from political pressure. The model would be the Federal Reserve Board, whose chairman is a virtual czar over monetary policy. It seems ironic that members of Congress would cede fiscal policy, but not medical policy, to a quasi-independent board. Surely congressional constituents are as concerned about their medical care as they are about their economic livelihood. The answer must lie elsewhere—specifically, with the special interests in finance and medicine. Commercial banks across the country support the Federal Reserve Board more or less uniformly, but the special interests in medicine are often arrayed against one another, pleading their interests individually with members of Congress.

In 1995, for example, the Agency for Healthcare Research and Quality (AHRQ) released a set of policy guidelines that discouraged surgery in the management of lower back pain. A number of politically active surgeons took offense at these guidelines and aggressively lobbied members of Congress, demanding that the agency back away from the design of strict practice protocols and urging Congress to threaten the agency's funding if no changes were made. While the surgeons lobbied vigorously, the American Medical Association stepped back, not wanting to interfere. As a result, Congress nearly eliminated the agency and slashed its budget. The AHRQ abandoned many of its protocols.

Decision makers must be insulated from this kind of pressure. Someone will need to make difficult calls about quality of care, evidence-based procedures, and control of medical errors. We can no longer allow American citizens to be whipsawed by special interests. Just as it took the collapse of the banking system in 1933 to get bankers to back a strong Federal Reserve Board, it may take the collapse of the medical system to impose a strong Federal Medical Board. This collapse could happen within ten years if costs continue to spiral out of control. But it's entirely possible that such a board could prevent a collapse altogether.

Consider the six specific areas for improvement identified by the IOM. At first glance, all seem simple enough to implement, but a more in-depth look uncovers problems:

(1) Of course care should be safe; patients should not be harmed by the care intended to help them. But this idea suggests a degree of caution not always associated with medical intervention, especially in lifesaving scenarios. (2) Similarly, care should be effective, based on sound scientific knowledge; it should also be (3) patient-centered, (4) timely, (5) efficient, and (6) equitable. But cost implications have an impact on all of these areas, as do criticisms of current practices. Physicians are not used to thinking about being respectful of and responsive to individual preferences. They are accustomed to being the final authorities on what is best for patients—an approach some patients find comforting and therapeutic.

Timely delivery of care may increase costs through early interventions, thus undercutting not only the managed care strategy of holding down costs by delaying intervention but also the tendency of physicians to overrely on diagnostic procedures and medications. Equitable delivery of care strikes at the heart of documented inequities based on ethnicity and geographic location.

Improvement in these six areas, then, will depend on strong central authority. Neither patients nor physicians are inclined to break bad habits simply because they ought to know better. Good intentions are not enough.

The IOM's ten rules to guide patient-clinician relationships also require regulation when being implemented. (1) The rule that care should be based on continuous healing relationships is one that strikes at the employer practice of changing health care coverage plans at will, often severing connections between patients and their primary care physicians. (2) Customized care that meets the most common needs but also responds to individual patient choices and preferences strikes at managed care strategies aimed at increasing a physician's patient load. (3) The rule that patients should control decision making flies in the face of medicine as it is currently practiced. More often than not, patients today are told what they should do, whereas it takes time and effort to explain medical care options. (4) The rule regarding shared information (specifically, through unfettered patient access to one's own medical files) would provide another break with tradition. Most difficult of all might be rule (5), which states that clinical decisions should be evidence-based; that is, patients should receive care based on the best scientific evidence of efficacy. Someone has to make that call, and it has to be definitive. Those desiring treatment outside evidence-based medicine would have to reach inside their own pockets to pay for it. Meanwhile, practitioners operating outside evidence-based medicine would soon marginalize themselves. According to rules (6) and (7), the health care system should be safe and transparent, thereby reducing the chances of injury and allowing patients to make informed decisions in the selection of health plans, hospitals, and practitioners. These measures, too, would require firm enforcement. Rule (8) states that the system should anticipate rather than simply react to patient needs. Of the fifteen to twenty-five medical conditions that call for the majority of health care services, nearly all are chronic, including diabetes, asthma, and heart disease. Anticipating such needs will require focused development and dissemination of evidence-based therapies—a task that the IOM suggests should be undertaken by the Agency for Healthcare Research and Quality, the same agency that was undermined by congressional lobbying. Finally, rules (9) and (10) hold that the health system should not waste resources or patient time, and that clinicians should be more cooperative in coordinating patient care. These rules, like the ones before them, are laudable but difficult to enforce.

The six areas for improvement and the ten rules to guide patient-clinician relationships would enhance patient care almost beyond measure. But they cannot be implemented without a powerful, centralized authority to back them up. Such an authority can come only from the establishment of a new Federal Medical Board with the power to mandate high-quality strategies while also preventing costly medical errors.

Preventing Medical Errors

In its 1999 report "To Err Is Human," the Institute of Medicine offers several recommendations aimed at lowering the alarming number of deaths that result from medical errors. Between 44,000 and 98,000 Americans die each year as a consequence of such errors—more than from auto accidents (43,458), breast cancer (42,297), or AIDS (16,516)—and the IOM adds that a significant number of these deaths are preventable. Accidents may happen, but their rate can be curtailed. The risk of unintentional death in an airplane declined from 1 person in 2 million during the 1970s to 1 person in 8 million during the 1990s as a result of programs for setting and enforcing standards established by the Federal Aviation Administration.

The IOM thus recommends above all that Congress create a Center for Patient Safety within the Agency for Healthcare Research and Quality. This center should set national goals for patient safety, track progress in meeting goals, and present an annual report to the president and Congress. In addition, it should develop a research agenda, fund Centers of Excellence, evaluate methods for identifying and preventing errors, and fund dissemination and communication activities to improve patient safety.

These measures would require a fiscal commitment by Congress, which so far has shown much greater interest in funding clinical research than quality assessment or safety assurance. There's a reason for that. The special interest research community is extremely receptive to funding support, whereas the special interest health care delivery community has deep reservations about quality and safety programs, which contain the seeds of potential embarrassment and greater exposure to legal liability. In our increasingly litigious society, hospital officials and practitioners have been reluctant to publicly admit that medical errors are frequent and often serious. Many are now involved in changing this culture of blame seeking and error suppression to one of openness, disclosure, and systematic error prevention.

Recognizing institutional resistance, the IOM recommends that a nationwide mandatory reporting system be established to collect standardized information by state governments concerning adverse events that result in death or serious harm. Initially, only hospitals would be required to comply, but eventually other institutional and ambulatory care delivery settings would be included.

This task would be handled by a Forum for Health Care Quality Measurement and Reporting, to be created by Congress as a unit of the Health and Human Services Department (HHS). The forum would promulgate and maintain reporting standards to be used by states, require all health care organizations to report information on a defined list of adverse events, and provide funds for state governments to adapt their current systems to meet national standardized reporting criteria. If a state chooses not to implement the mandatory system, HHS would assume the responsibility for measurement and reporting of health care quality.

Another recommendation gets closer to the real problem. The IOM advises that Congress should pass legislation to extend peer-review protections to patient safety improvement data that are collected and analyzed for internal use or are shared with others solely to improve safety and quality of care. Dealing with medical errors is a sticky business, involving not only blame assessment but also legal liability. The only way out of this difficulty is to bring such errors into the light, remembering that no one wants to make them but everyone wants to prevent them. Information is essential.

So is clout. The IOM suggests that regulators and accreditors should require health organizations to implement safety programs; that professional and licensing boards should implement periodic reexaminations for recertification and relicensing of physicians, nurses, and others based on both competence and knowledge of safety practices; and that the boards themselves should develop better methods to identify unsafe providers and take action.

The reach of the Food and Drug Administration should be extended, the IOM further proposes. It should develop and enforce standards for the design of drug packaging and labeling to maximize user safety. It should require companies to test proposed drug names to eliminate sound-alike and look-alike confusion with existing drugs. And it should work with physicians, pharmacists, and patients to respond quickly to postmarketing surveillance that identifies safety problems.

Virtually all of these recommendations depend on a strong central authority. Decisions concerning safety and quality cannot be left in the hands of local jurisdictions but, instead, must be defined, overseen, and enforced by a national agency. The intellectual case in support of this proposition is compelling. The political case is much shakier. Issues involving local control are as old as the republic itself, but the banking system offers instructive guidance.

Paper money was essentially worthless when the first Congress assembled under the Washington administration and Treasury Secretary Alexander Hamilton won support for a United States Bank, a joint-stock concern that ensured uniform value to the dollar. By the 1830s, farmers in the South and Midwest were clamoring for "cheaper" money—that is, for an abundance of paper bills. President Jackson vetoed legislation to recharter the United States Bank, and it disappeared. In its place, banks chartered under state laws proliferated and issued tons of paper money, which fluctuated in coin value from one hundred cents on the dollar to ten cents or even less.

To finance the Civil War, the federal government required sound money and once again established a national banking system in which the Treasury Department controlled dollar values. President Wilson extended the controls by creating the Federal Reserve System, which gave central government greater authority over banking administration. In the midst of the banking crisis of 1933, President Roosevelt completed government control by abandoning the gold standard and substituting a currency issued and managed by the federal government. He also increased federal regulation of banks and safeguarded deposits through federal insurance.

The only banking decision based on ideology rather than necessity was that of President Wilson. The press of politics and catastrophe guided all other banking decisions until the chaos of bank closings and failures in 1933 forced the creation of a federal system that has flourished ever since.

The question for medicine is twofold: Do we wait for a catastrophe before establishing a Federal Medical Board to regulate and safeguard the system, or do we establish such a board proactively to avoid catastrophe? The goal is to implement national standards that are sensitive to local needs, but the imperative is the national standards themselves.

In addition, as readers of earlier chapters will recall, neither patient safety nor the quality initiative has any chance of success unless we reestablish consistent and reliable methods of measuring the quality and safety of care given to the sickest patients, the ones who die. Ascertaining quality and safety of care can be accomplished only through a high rate of autopsies. Without this measure of care, no one ever really knows for sure what happened to the patient who died.

Preventing Disease in Behalf of the Public's Health

The notion that it is in the best interests of society to sustain a healthy population and promote individual health dates from antiquity. The traditional practice of medicine is oriented toward the single patient, and the Hippocratic oath speaks to the manner in which such practice should be performed by individual physicians. Centuries ago, organized efforts to combat the Black Plague used quarantine techniques intended to stop the spread of the dread disease across populations. And, indeed, the Bible enjoins us to "love one's neighbor as oneself," to care for our neighbor, just as one of the best definitions of love includes a fervent wish that the loved one be healthy and happy.

In 1798, President John Adams signed into law a bill that formed the basis for establishing the revered U.S. Public Health Service (PHS), which currently consists of eight key agencies, including the National Institutes of Health, the Food and Drug Administration, the Centers for Disease Control and Prevention (CDC), and the Office of the Surgeon General (of the PHS). Even the U.S. Army Medical Corps has as its mission to "preserve the fighting strength," which amounts to a population-based health mission (albeit with a special purpose).

Some would say that London's Dr. John Snow was the father of modern public health; certainly he was the father of epidemiology. In his epic work on the epidemiologic basis for the spread of cholera in London during the 1850s, he observed that people who drew water from the Broad Street pump had a greater likelihood of becoming afflicted with cholera than did other Londoners. This observation led him to remove the handle of the pump, thereby halting the cholera epidemic among those water users. This was one of the most important scientific public health interventions of all time.

Internationally, public health is embodied in the World Health Organization in Geneva, Switzerland; founded in 1948, it takes top honors for all its wonderful work in behalf of the health of humankind. But other successes also abound, including international efforts to rid the world of smallpox and to eradicate polio from the Western Hemisphere and soon, perhaps, the Eastern Hemisphere as well. In the United States, malaria has been halted, owing to recognition of the causes and mechanisms underlying its spread. And HIV prevention has been more effective here than in many other countries of the world, thanks to risk-factor behavior modification—although we can certainly do more. Other campaigns include those against tobacco addiction, violence, and obesity, all spearheaded by the organized public health community, especially the CDC and the Surgeon General of the United States.

Who among us, of any political persuasion, would argue against the use of public money in behalf of public health in such scientifically proven areas as sewage disposal, prevention of tobacco addiction in children, and avoidance of the spread of HIV among all age groups? It is a small conceptual step to move from these accepted public health initiatives to interventions that are just as scientifically proven to counteract the killer diseases currently affecting a large number of our people.

Our modern civilization can do much better at preventing these terrible killer diseases. We should study and act against them just as our forebears studied and acted against cholera, plague, pellagra, scurvy, yellow fever, malaria, tuberculosis, hookworm, and, yes, smallpox and polio. It is in our national interest to have a strong, vibrant, healthy, and productive population, well into advanced age. As examples of common preventable (or curable by early detection) diseases producing premature death in adults we list coronary artery heart disease, cervical cancer, and stroke caused by untreated hypertension, among others. Interventions against these common killers—interventions whose efficacy is supported by solid scientific evidence—should now be recognized as a matter of public health, in the nation's best interests, and thus paid for by federal or state government.

How might a country go about implementing a prevention program such as this? The first step is to agree on a national priority to rid our populace of preventable heart disease, stroke, and cancer—and to spend our collective money to do so. Then we can build on the splendid ongoing work of the U.S. Preventive Services Task Force in identifying the common diseases most amenable to interventions, the interventions proven most effective, and the cost and benefit implications of both. Then, as we argued in Chapter 10, a nongovernmental, nonorganized medicine group insulated from political interference and commercial conflicts of interest should determine what interventions are appropriate for public funding and effort. The IOM would be the most suitable group to make these determinations.

The actual expenditure of funds would probably best be administered by the federal Centers for Medicare and Medicaid Services since the CMS is highly organized for just such an effort of payment, once the determination of eligibility is made based on science and the public interest. How much would such an effort cost? It would depend on the size and scope of the intervention, but the amount could be large if, for example, prevention of a disease such as stroke by treating hypertension were considered an appropriate application of this principle.

How would such an approach differ from the way things are now? (1) Medicare by statute does not pay for prevention for people sixty-five and over, except in the case of specific conditions. Under our proposal, by contrast, beneficiaries of prevention services could be any age. (2) Medicare now pays for nearly anything the medical system provides (including many procedures that have not passed the "scientifically proven" test); under our proposal, payment would be made only for scientifically proven interventions for those under sixty-five. (At this time, we do not recommend diminishing fundamental benefits through Medicare for those over sixty-five.) (3) As of this writing, Medicare is not allowed to cover prescription costs; under our proposal, prescription drug coverage would be provided for proven, approved prevention. In addition, all such prevention services would be covered without deductibles or co-payments, since this activity is deemed to be in the nation's best interest as well as in the interest of individual health.

Some readers might describe these changes as drastic. But we believe they are no more so than the mass government-provided serologic testing for syphilis in the late 1940s, when we finally had a good treatment for syphilis (penicillin), and no more so than the mass governmental distribution of polio vaccine in the 1950s.

Other readers may deem our proposal to be at high variance from the thesis of this chapter, which places economic responsibility on the patient for much of the cost of treatment following an economic informed consent. But such individual responsibility would begin only after this "first-dollar" coverage for preventing serious, life-threatening diseases subject to scientifically proven prevention. Americans have been prone to delaying, deferring, or refusing to pay their own money for prevention when they feel healthy. Standard indemnity insurance traditionally has resisted paying for prevention. For a brief time, it appeared that managed care would also manage prevention as a public good and as a way for the for-profit managed care companies to increase profits by keeping enrollees well. Unfortunately, like much of the promise of managed care, that effort is over.

Our proposal puts the collective health of the populace first, recognizing that prevention *is* public health.

Internet Medicine

Rarely has physicians' use of any technology they have not been paid to adopt taken off as rapidly as their acceptance of the Internet. The medical Internet came into use around 1994. In 1995, only 3 percent of doctors in the United States were routinely accessing the Internet for any purpose. By 1996, physician usage had increased to 15 percent; four years later, in 2000, it had climbed to about 90 percent. The number of physicians accessing the medical Internet for medical and health information on an almost daily basis is now about 60 percent. Many of us who have been in the field of computers and medicine from the early days (as early as 1963) have lamented the slowness with which physicians as a group included computers in their daily practices prior to their use of the Internet. But once they understood that the technology would truly help them get their daily work done better, faster, and cheaper, they embraced it.

Medicine is both an art and a science within which individual doctors specialize. Some are known primarily for their ability to cut; they are called surgeons. Others shoot ray guns at patients; they are called radiologists. Still others are known primarily for their ability to give patients doses of poisons; these are oncologists and other internists. But much of the practice of medicine can be divided into two major categories. The first involves the "high-touch" activity of caring, which includes intense interpersonal relational feelings. The second involves information: the seeking, observing, gathering, assimilating, interpreting, dispensing, feeding back, and monitoring of information.

In what ways, then, might the Internet be applicable to transmitting high-quality medical information? The answers are many: It can be used as a medical library; it can replace functions served by the telephone or fax machine; it can replace hand-delivered notes, letters, brochures, or certificates; it can be used to place orders for diagnostic tests or for medications, to report laboratory or X-ray results, and to record verbal communications; and it can be used whenever distance separates people and copies are needed quickly. In short, the Internet provides virtual stat service. In 2000, through sampling techniques, Cyberdialogue learned that 34 million Americans wished to communicate with their physicians electronically but only 3 million had actually done so. This is a terrific opportunity gap for physicians to fill. Also in 2000, Harris Interactive polls reported that 84 percent of U.S. consumers wanted electronic alerts from physicians; 83 percent wanted lab results online; 80 percent wanted personalized medical information; 69 percent desired online charts to monitor their chronic conditions; and 43 percent said that they would select a physician based at least in part on the availability of Internet services.

Why hasn't a greater number of physicians responded to these patient requests and market demands? Many doctors feel that they are already overly busy and that e-mail will tie up their time even more. So far there are few ways for them to get paid for e-mail medicine (a problem that also applies to telephone consultations). Some doctors believe that the Internet will cause them to lose close contact with their patients; they prefer to maintain the "high-touch" factor essential to the art and practice of medicine. Others fear the misuse of specific documentation that e-mail establishes, preferring telephone interaction because it poses a lower potential liability.

One counterargument is that physicians and patients will save rather than lose time by using e-mail, since the wasted minutes playing "telephone tag" can be eliminated. But our proposal recognizes that, like all professionals, physicians need to be compensated fairly for their time. Experimental methods of payment for e-mail use are now under way. In the new world of out-of-pocket pay for ambulatory treatment that we espouse, the physician, given the economic informed consent of the patient, can charge directly for e-mail interaction without bothering with an insurance carrier. An electronic communication between two people who know each other can be meaningful, clear, and succinct—in many instances, an even better outcome for both patient and physician than "high-touch" care. We also urge physicians to experiment with the use of an e-mail triage nurse or physician's assistant in cases where time worries persist. And as a final argument, we suggest that the clear permanent record of an e-mail interaction provides excellent documentation of exactly what transpired between physician and patient, with little room for misinterpretation in cases where something does go amiss and there is a need to investigate. So the Internet, far from posing a threat, has the potential to become a positive opportunity for better medical practice. (Conventional wisdom wisely holds, of course, that e-mail medicine should not be used for the initial or sole interaction when "high-touch" care is essential.)

As we emphasized in Chapter 5, the Internet not only provides physicians with new tools to improve patient care; it also gives patients an unprecedented opportunity to take charge of their health care with the best medical information. More than 100 million computer users in the United States have accessed the Internet for health information so far—especially information regarding specific diseases, diagnoses, and treatments. Online health users are more typically women than men; they also tend to be older, Caucasian, married, and college-educated. These are the people who arrive at the doctor's office with a printout of options and too often leave with a lower opinion of a practitioner who seems less informed than they. Unfortunately, data show that only 15 percent of U.S. physicians recommend any specific medical Internet site to their patients. But we suggest that *all* physicians should encourage patients to become Internet-savvy—specifically, by recommending two or three general health information Web sites with demonstrated high standards of quality and two or three condition-specific sites on which they can rely for whatever ails them. In this way, patients can be armed with information that the physicians themselves trust, and they can study this information on their own time, away from the stopwatches of the managed care bean counters.

Electronic medical records provide a useful tool both for achieving high-quality efficient medical care and for preventing medical errors. To a greater degree than almost any other force, consumer activism in medical care—including careful Internet searches for reliable medical information—can drive doctors and hospitals to use electronic tools more rapidly. We call upon you, as informed patients, to protect yourselves by insisting that your doctor and your hospital automate their information handling for your benefit and safety and freely share access to your medical records with you. Of course, insurance claims should also be electronic.

Understand that changing physician behavior, like any human behavior, can be very difficult. Methods for change include education, feedback, administrative changes, and financial rewards and penalties. According to Forrester Research, a doctor is more likely to use an electronic or Internet tool if it saves time, works as advertised, has a trusted quality stamp, strengthens the doctor's power position, helps meet a mandate or requirement, and is free of charge. In a related vein, Healthtech 2001 has reported that physicians consider the following to be "essential" Internet applications: clinical diagnostic reporting, medical records, administrative claims processing, eligibility and referral authorizations, and information technology systems support.

In theory, the Internet could virtually eliminate the health insurance industry in America. What do health insurance companies do? They take as much money as they can from as healthy a group of people as possible; they keep as much as they can; and they pay out as little as they can. With Internet technology, people—individually or collectively—can negotiate directly with physician groups or other providers for their care. They would have to assume some risk, of course, but the banding together of patients or of providers can spread out that risk. In addition, secondary insurers may be able to cover procedures with huge price tags, such as organ transplants. But the money that could be saved by eliminating or greatly downsizing the health insurance industry (which has only marginally higher public approval ratings than the for-profit managed care companies) could be as much as $200 billion per year in administrative overhead and profit. This newfound money could help cover the uninsured and fund preventive medicine/public health initiatives.

Where Do We Go from Here?

The future of American medicine really centers on money: How much does it cost, who will it benefit and how, is it worth it, and who will pay whom how much for what? In an ideal world, economics would not drive decisions such as these. But in the real world, actual costs for much of what medicine and health care represent matter hugely.

We take the position that medicine is essentially a moral enterprise, grounded in a covenant of trust; it is also a service profession, though historically composed in part by business elements. In addition, despite the absence of any constitutional or other legal guarantee to this effect, we believe that universal access to basic medical care is an American right rather than a privilege or a commercial good to be purchased like a product in the marketplace.

To move forward into a future offering truly cost-effective, basic medical care of acceptable quality for all people, the United State would seem to have three important but fundamentally different options.

The first is *government-funded basic health care for all.* Since almost 50 percent of our medical expenses are now paid by some government entity, it is time to join the rest of the economically developed world and guarantee basic health care for everyone— with government money, but without nationalizing the medical establishment. We're not referring to socialized medicine here. This would not be a "single-payer" system because Americans would still be allowed to jump the queue, using their own money for diagnostic and therapeutic interventions that are not scarce or dangerous. We could simply decree by federal law "Medicare for All," shift the massive sums of money expended in private forums into taxes that would cover all citizens, and thereby control costs through government decision on all matters. Because of Medicare's efficiencies and the elimination of any profit motive, this could be accomplished economically and still leave money over. Furthermore, any problems with the resulting system could be worked out at the ballot box in subsequent elections. Some Americans, and many people from other countries, see this as an obvious solution that should have come about already; but we do not anticipate its enactment into law any time soon.

The second is *an entirely not-for-profit managed care complex.* The problem is not managed care but for-profit managed costs. Its benevolent counterpart, not-for-profit managed care, is ethically as well as economically alive and well in many states, especially California, Massachusetts, and Washington. It is true that in order to remain solvent, not-for-profit managed care groups have had to behave more like their for-profit competitors than they or we might have liked; but they have retained their distinct identities and kept patients, whether individuals or entire populations, at the forefront. Indeed, they have done about as good a job of maintaining quality and controlling costs as could be done and stand poised to take on a far greater role in the future. Why not a Kaiser America? Or a Harvard Pilgrim America? How about one for each state or region, with all Americans included? Frankly, this solution is a difficult one to argue against.

The third is *public-private collaboration*—a measure for which we have laid the groundwork throughout this book. Following is a summary of our specific proposals in this and the preceding chapters:

- Don't mess with Medicare. It is a great success and should remain largely as it is, except for the addition of an affordable prescription drug benefit. Those who wish to dramatically change Medicare fail to recognize that it works far better than most of the rest of our medical system.
- Recognize that the economics of our health system will never work right until *all* Americans have health insurance. Such an achievement can come about only through federal law. We believe that the "individual mandate" could have enough ideological resonance with the right, left, and center to propel it into law. Of course, such an effort would require a bipartisan group of congressional champions—along with a president who understands the wisdom of these reforms and wishes to go down in history as the first Health Care President. Under this proposal, people would obtain their health insurance from Medicare or Medicaid, from their employers or those of their spouses or domestic partners, or individually, perhaps with tax-credit help in some instances.
- Reinstitute a true market in the purchase of medical care. Encourage the vast majority of Americans to pay for their ambulatory medical care in a free market, unfettered by third-party interference. Let the market demand that physicians and other providers compete ethically based on price, quality, patient satisfaction, convenience, availability, and medical need. Require that physicians and other providers (in nonemergency situations) obtain an economic informed consent from payer-patients by explaining what each action will cost and deciding together whether or not it is worth the patients' own money. This changed situation can be achieved through the purchase of high-deductible insurance that is means-based. Once the annual deductible has been

met (likely only for a small minority of Americans), all expenses would be paid by the insurance in effect, with the insurance carrier responsible for controlling costs.

- Define scientifically proven preventive medicine as a public health goal, and recognize that it is in the nation's best interest to have a healthy population. Government payment should cover such preventive care.
- Follow the lead of the Institute of Medicine of the National Academy of Sciences, which has become a major source of medical knowledge and ethical objectivity in only twenty-eight years. Our concerns about quality and safety in the American health care system can be met largely by adopting the recommendations of the institute's committees in the 1999 and 2001 IOM reports and by accomplishing the hard work such adoption entails.

As we begin this new century, we stand at the leading edge of the implementation phase for two great scientific achievements: the human genome project and the medical Internet. The opportunity to add these two powerful knowledge and technology bases to an already extraordinary medical armamentarium, and to do so in the best interests of people individually and collectively, presents a scintillating challenge—one to which we can rise if we deal forthrightly with the problems of our mighty but flawed system, working together in mutual trust to effect the best solutions for American health care.

Epilogue

International Health Care Reform

NUCLEAR WEAPONS ARE THE SINGLE greatest health care threat to residents of the entire world. Nuclear war would be the final epidemic of humankind. Thus, the elimination of nuclear arsenals is the ultimate preventive medical strategy of international physicians.

On August 5, 1983, *JAMA* published its first annual issue commemorating the bombing of Hiroshima on August 6, 1945, and pointing out that there is no adequate plan in place for responding to a nuclear holocaust. In that issue, Toshie Maruki, the immediate past president of the Japan Medical Association, offered a personal account of his diagnosis of the atomic bomb at Hiroshima and his involvement in the ending of the war in the Pacific. In addition, researchers provided a study on the mortality and cancer frequency among military nuclear test participants, while other reports detailed a long-delayed case of leukemia in a Hiroshima survivor and a case of testicular cancer in adult twins whose father had been exposed to atomic radiation nine months before their conception.

The AMA had taken a position on nuclear war only eighteen months before in response to a House of Delegates request to "prepare appropriate informational materials to educate the physician population and the public on the medical consequences of nuclear war." The AMA response, expressed in a board of trustee report, was that "available data reveal that there is no adequate medical response to a nuclear holocaust." Led by James Sammons, the executive vice president who was at the height of his power in organized medicine, the board was acting on the highest medical ethical standards.

It should be added that while the AMA did the right thing by taking this position, Sammons did not want to make a big fuss about it. Nuclear war, after all, had been at the top of his list of sensitive subjects I should treat with care as editor of *JAMA*.

The position stemmed from the association's first code of medical ethics, adopted in May 1846, at the time of its founding. "As good citizens, it is the duty of physicians to be ever vigilant for the welfare of the community, and to bear their part in sustaining its institutions and burdens," the code stated. Although code wording changed over the years, the commitment to a physician's social responsibility did not. The preamble to the most recent code states, "As a member of this profession, a physician must recognize responsibility not only to patients, but also to society, to other health professionals, and to self."

From 1983 through 1998, *JAMA* under my tenure presented a theme issue in the first week of August dedicated to the prevention of nuclear war. Over the years we added studies on other horrors associated with war, such as chemical and biological warfare, state-sponsored torture and rape, and information on refugees from war-torn countries.

International physicians joined our cause. One of the advantages I enjoyed as editor of *JAMA* was regular contact with international medical editors. The AMA since 1919 had been involved, with varying levels of success, with publication of *JAMA* information in international editions. The first was the *Edición en Español* published for physicians in Central and South America. That edition lasted only until 1928. Twenty years later the first Japanese-language edition was published. That edition lasted until 1958.

Other ventures were tried, but it wasn't until the early 1980s that the AMA made international editions of *JAMA* a high priority. Soon there were *JAMA* editions in German, Flemish, Chinese, Japanese, French, Italian, Russian, and Spanish. There were Southeast Asian editions, Korean, Middle Eastern, Turkish, Indian, and

Pakistani editions. By the mid-1990s the international circulation of *JAMA* was greater than that of the U.S. *JAMA*—388,000 versus 360,000.

From these international connections came support and even progress in the struggle to control nuclear arms. In the early 1980s, for example, there was widespread discussion of the viability of limited nuclear war. American physicians petitioned President Reagan to argue that there is no such thing as "limited nuclear war," a position echoed by Russian physicians in their petitions to Premier Gorbachev. Arnold Relman, then editor of the *New England Journal of Medicine,* made the point that burn treatment facilities would not be adequate to care for the victims of even a limited nuclear war. The arguments were persuasive, and talk of limited nuclear war soon vanished.

In 1998, following the nuclear tests by Pakistan and India, I published an editorial in the form of an open letter to the prime ministers of India and Pakistan, demanding that they not attack each other, pointing out that a nuclear attack on either country was an attack on the whole world. The authors included a recipient of the Nobel Peace Prize and the presidents of the medical associations of India and Pakistan. The physicians of the world recognize the clear need for containing the nuclear threat. But how do we effect it?

The use of force as an extension of diplomacy to achieve national ends is unlikely to cease. Nuclear power would seem to be here to stay, and the threat of using nuclear weapons as agents of war apparently will not go away. Therefore, any solution to prevent nuclear war must be sweeping, bold, idealistic, visionary, and solidly based on the fundamentals of human behavior. The predominant method used throughout the cold war was the deterrent power of matching killer weapons among the superpowers, and it was based on Maslow's key need—personal security and safety.

That method was successful in preventing nuclear war for more than forty years, even though it led to a massive arms race that was extremely expensive to all and extremely dangerous to the survival of humankind. Now the world is concerned with nuclear threats from "rogue" states, and a new round of discussions aimed at building a "fail-safe" antinuclear missile system is under way. In the long run systems that depend on massive stockpiles of nuclear arms cannot succeed. We need new ways of thinking.

We have not had nuclear war since 1945, for whatever reasons. If nuclear war were to occur, however, it is hard for the public to believe that physicians and the medical establishment, with its excellent emergency capabilities, wouldn't somehow be there to swoop down and care for them. Physicians know that it can't be done, that there is indeed no adequate medical response to nuclear war. What is abundantly clear to physicians, however, does not automatically resonate with politicians and the general public.

Physicians have made various proposals. Susan Hollan, medical editor with *Haematologia* in Hungary, has proposed that all medical journals, general and specialty, participate in large public health issues, such as nuclear war. Ian Munro of *Lancet* suggested that physicians run for elective office to work toward the prevention of nuclear war. Dimitri Venediktove, director of the Health Information Institute in Moscow, proposed that physicians, as proponents of health and the preservation of life, must cooperate in preventing the destruction of life on earth by nuclear war.

E. Grey Dimond has suggested that the presence of 10,000 or more Chinese scholars in American universities serves as a potential guarantor of peace with China because people are unlikely to bomb their own children. That is an intriguing idea, and it argues forcefully for an open world, one in which international travel is widely encouraged. The growing global economy could make a contribution by dispersing people and economic interests around the planet. Intermarriage across national borders might help, as would extensive scientific and cultural exchange programs. Although it is true that people might be less likely to take steps that would destroy their own families and progeny living abroad, the even more important point is that to live in health, we must learn to live in peace.

Acknowledgments

SHORTLY AFTER MY ABRUPT AND well-documented departure from the *Journal of the American Medical Association* on January 15, 1999, a gratifying number of diverse career opportunities came available for me. I sought counsel from the published precedent of the extraordinary former *JAMA* editor Morris Fishbein. He also had been terminated—in 1949, after twenty-five years of service. As the story goes, he was offered three full-time jobs and he took all three, continuing his productive career for decades after the AMA. Thus, when fourteen work possibilities arrived in two weeks, I was open and prepared, carefully accepting the best five that I believed could interdigitate compatibly.

An early caller was Herb Katz, the illustrious New York literary agent, who, with his spouse and partner, Nancy Katz, convinced me to write this book and found a respected publisher, Basic Books, which matched me with the experienced, critical and helpful editor Joann Miller and project editor Richard Miller (no relation). The other four jobs I chose were part-time teaching appointments at the Harvard School of Public Health with Barry Bloom and Karen Donelan and at Northwestern University with Peter Budetti, speaking engagements arranged by superagent Harry Sandler of the American Program Bureau in Newton, Massachusetts, and what has become a consuming passion as well as a more than full-time job at Medscape with Bill Silberg and Christina Myers (and many others).

By trying to follow Fishbein's energetic lead, I quickly learned that in order to meet proper timelines at Basic, I would need a writing collaborator. My wife, Professor Patricia Lorimer Lundberg of Indiana University Northwest, who can do pretty much anything she sets out to do, and do it well, was the obvious first choice. But, alas, she was fully occupied as a dean in Gary, Indiana, so I had to look further. By pure good luck, about that time an old and close colleague from the AMA, Jim Stacey, chose to retire. Jim had also been an English professor in an earlier life, plus a longtime successful journalist and writer. For the past eleven years, Jim had been the media interface for the AMA's Washington office, where he had dealt with the underbelly of organized medicine every day, trying to make it seem less tawdry to the public through the media. He agreed to work with me. Without Jim, this book would not be.

This book is not a health policy wonk book, although health policy issues loom on every page, and I must here acknowledge and thank many wonks.

This book is also not an exposé about the AMA, but I must acknowledge and thank many of my former colleagues and members of the AMA for extraordinary experiences and insights.

Nor is this book a memoir, but I must acknowledge and thank a huge number of teachers, students and co-workers without whose work and teachings all would be different.

Perhaps this book is a "medical memoir" with explanations about how we got into this amazing medical mess and suggestions about how we can get out of it sensibly. It is a product of experiences and observations during my fifty years in American medicine, from the vantage points of the lowliest (operating room floor mopper) job to the highest (top medical editor).

I here acknowledge and thank the unnamed thousands of people, big and small, who were instrumental in so many ways in inspiring and informing these tumultuous medical times. My job as author has been to experience, observe, evaluate, remember, capture, focus, criticize, reflect and filter these often stupendous and often troubled times, and to try to collect all the really big stuff into one readable package for the public at large interested in the health and medical care of themselves, their families and friends, and their fellow citizens.

To whatever extent I have succeeded in this effort, I credit the innumerable aforementioned. If we have missed the mark, I take full responsibility.

Index

About the Authors

GEORGE D. LUNDBERG, M.D., is editor in chief of Medscape, the leading provider of medical information on the Internet. He was for seventeen years the editor of *JAMA: The Journal of the American Medical Association*. A resident of Chicago, New York City, and Los Gatos, California, he is on the faculties of Northwestern University and the School of Public Health at Harvard. He has published widely in scientific journals and the popular press and has appeared regularly on national television.

JAMES STACEY was until his retirement in 1999 the director of media and information services for the Washington office of the American Medical Association. He is the author of *Inside the New Temple: The High Cost of Mistaking Medicine for Religion* (1993). He lives in Baltimore, Maryland.